Quality Control in Fraud and Corruption Investigations

**Tom Willems, Carsten Stahn,
Darren Frey and Antonio Angotti (editors)**

**2025
Torkel Opsahl Academic EPublisher
Brussels**

Editors of this volume:

Tom Willems is co-ordinator for inter-institutional relations at the European Anti-Fraud Office (OLAF). Dr. **Carsten Stahn** is Professor of International Criminal Law and Global Justice at Leiden University and Queen's University Belfast. Dr. **Darren Frey** is Lecturer in Behavioral Economics and Cognitive Sciences (Sciences Po). **Antonio Angotti** is a Fellow of the Centre for International Law Research and Policy (CILRAP) and an attorney at the Bar Association of Florence.

Front cover: *Books in TOAEP's series on quality control in criminal justice feature eminent artisans at work on the front cover, as symbols of the skill, effort and meticulousness that quality requires. Maestro d'Arte Orafa Paolo Penko is one of Italy's most outstanding goldsmiths, whose works are displayed in the Bargello National Museum and the Silver Museum in Palazzo Pitti in Florence. He is one of the founders and a teacher at the Sacred Art School of Florence. Photograph: CILRAP.*

Back cover: *On the back cover of books in TOAEP's Publication Series you find a picture of public ground, a tangible commons accessible to all. The present photograph shows an ancient floor in the Natural History Museum of the University of Pisa (opened in 1596, one of the world's oldest museums), located within the Carthusian convent (1366) in the Monte Pisano hillside of Calci. Human wear and tear enhance the beauty of handmade terracotta tiles and Pietra Serena. Photograph: CILRAP.*

ISBNs: 978-82-8348-281-2 (print) and 978-82-8348-282-9 (e-book).

PREFACE BY THE CO-EDITORS

Fraud and corruption are critical global issues that necessitate a robust and effective response. A key element of this response is the implementation of thorough and equitable investigations, which can be quite challenging. It is widely recognized that tackling white-collar crime presents some of the most formidable obstacles in investigative work, largely due to the inherent complexity of the domain (such as intricate procurement regulations) and the characteristics of the offenders, who are often intelligent, confident, and financially well-off. Even when evidence is available, these individuals frequently assert their innocence, denying any intention to commit wrongdoing,[1] and out-of-court financial settlements sometimes seem the best justice can deliver.[2]

While numerous claims have been made about improving efforts to combat fraud and corruption, resulting in a proliferation of initiatives, codifications and conferences, there remains a notable lack of transparency regarding the quality of investigative practices. Research focused on police practices is limited, and when evidence-based methodologies are proposed, they predominantly address common crime rather than the complexities of fraud and corruption investigations.[3]

This anthology seeks to enrich the discourse surrounding the quality of so-called 'PIF'[4] investigations by drawing comparisons with more conventional – yet equally significant – types of investigations. By examining the unique aspects of PIF investigations alongside the investigative practices utilized by the International Criminal Court ('ICC')[5] and relevant scientific literature on

---

1 See, for example, Gresham M. Sykes and David Matza, "Techniques of Neutralization: A Theory of Delinquency", in *American Sociological Review*, 1957, vol. 22, no. 6, pp. 664–670.

2 See, for example, Mari Sognnæs Andresen and Mark Button, "The Profile and Detection of Bribery in Norway and England & Wales: A Comparative Study", in *European Journal of Criminology*, 2018, vol. 16, no. 1, pp. 18–40.

3 Nadine Deslauriers-Varin and Francis Fortin, "Improving Efficiency and Understanding of Criminal Investigations: Toward an Evidence-Based Approach", in *Journal of Police and Criminal Psychology*, 2021, vol. 36, no. 2, p. 1.

4 'PIF' stands for '*Protection des Intérêts Financiers*', or 'Protection of the Financial Interest of the European Union' ('EU'), a crucial concept for the definition of criminal offences like fraud and corruption detrimental to the EU budget and the scope of activity of instances created to protect this budget.

5 Between 2012 and 2020, the Centre for International Law Research and Policy's ('CILRAP') Quality Control Project investigated international criminal justice's key work-

common crimes, this dialogue among experts aims to provide deeper insights into the field and foster meaningful discussions.

While this book delves into the intricate investigation of PIF offences, it claims relevance not only to PIF cases, but also to a range of other financial and economic investigations or audits relating to corruption and fraud. It upholds the distinction between criminal and administrative investigations while acknowledging their shared foundation in fact-finding, making for similar practical challenges and cognitive hurdles.

The primary emphasis of the chapters is on the concept of 'investigative thinking', which is essential for guiding successful investigations, but is increasingly challenged by the rapid advancement of new technologies and the overwhelming influx of information.

In collaboration with both academic scholars and practitioners in the field of fraud and corruption investigations,[6] the chapters featured in this book are inspired by and strive to uphold the esteemed standards established by CILRAP's pioneering Quality Control Project. A conference held in December 2022, focusing on judgment and decision-making in PIF investigations, reinforced the significance and timeliness of the Quality Control publications for all attendees, underscoring the need for rigorous discourse in this vital area.[7]

---

processes in fact-finding, preliminary examination and investigation. More than producing a mere catalogue of proposals for reform, the project aimed to have a longer-term impact on thinking about the appropriate mindset and culture of different jurisdictions. It enjoyed support from several individuals and institutions, including the Office of the Prosecutor of the ICC, to which proceedings a number of project-contributions are relevant. The excellent books on, respectively, *Quality Control in Fact-Finding* (Morten Bergsmo (ed.), Torkel Opsahl Academic EPublisher ('TOAEP'), Florence, 2013 (https://www.toaep.org/ps-pdf/19-bergsmo/), and the Second Edition, Morten Bergsmo and Carsten Stahn (eds.), TOAEP, Brussels, 2019 (https://www.toaep.org/ps-pdf/19-bergsmo-stahn-second/), *Quality Control in Preliminary Examination* (Morten Bergsmo and Carsten Stahn (eds.), TOAEP, Brussels, 2018 (*Volume I*: https://www.toaep.org/ps-pdf/32-bergsmo-stahn/; *Volume 2*: https://www.toaep.org/ps-pdf/33-bergsmo-stahn/)), and *Quality Control in Criminal Investigation* (Xabier Agirre, Morten Bergsmo, Simon De Smet and Carsten Stahn (eds.), TOAEP, Brussels, 2020 (https://www.toaep.org/ps-pdf/38-qcci/) can be found in the Quality Control Project's online thematic library (https://www.cilrap.org/quality-control/). As the research on ICC investigations and, generally, on international crimes case-work typically relates to fact-rich cases, these studies are particularly relevant also for PIF investigations. They are a major source of inspiration for this work.

6 All authors and editors contribute in their personal capacities. The positions taken neither reflect the practice nor commit the employers of the authors or editors.

7 On 7 and 8 December 2022, the OLAF organized a conference on "Judgement and Decision-Making in Investigations". Many of the authors of this book offered a presentation at the conference.

Consistent with the earlier publications in this series, this anthology features a collection of chapters that propose a framework for understanding and encourage dialogue about the quality of PIF investigations.

Tom Willems, Carsten Stahn, Darren Frey and Antonio Angotti
Co-Editors

FOREWORD BY SUSAN E. BRANDON

I am honoured to write a foreword for this anthology. When the invitation first came to me, I thought I would have very little to contribute about financial crimes or the investigatory processes of the European Anti-Fraud Office (OLAF) and the European Public Prosecutor's Office (EPPO). However, the invitation gave me an opportunity to read the chapters, which describe the many decision points inherent to conducting fraud and corruption investigations, including what is particular and general to the investigation of 'PIF' offences:[1] understanding implicit and explicit cognitive processes and how these affect decision-making; how to understand and deal with various kinds of 'noise' and biases; the standards and uncertainties of instigating an investigation; setting up a plan that is team-based, defensible, coherent and efficient; when and how to use evidence; models of rational proof, and proving intent.

My background is in intelligence interviews. I set up and managed two research programmes in interview strategies, techniques and tactics for the United States ('US') government, first for the US Department of Defense and then for what is now known as the High-Value Detainee Interrogation Group ('HIG').[2] The HIG (a multi-agency entity under the auspices of the Central Intelligence Agency, the Federal Bureau of Investigation, and the Defense Intelligence Agency) was established via an Executive Order of the Obama Administration in 2009.[3] It had two missions. One was (and is) an operational mission to deploy interrogation teams (interviewers, analysts, subject-matter experts, and interpreters) to talk with individuals either in the US or abroad who were determined to have significant information about threats against the US or our allies. The second was (and is) to study the effectiveness and propriety of existing interview practices, techniques and strategies and develop new ones that meet the requirements of US domestic law and obligations under international law.

---

1 That is, relevant to the protection of the European Union's financial interests.

2 On the HIG, see also Susan E. Brandon and Christian A. Meissner, "From Research to Practice: The High-Value Detainee Interrogation Group", in Gavin E. Oxburgh, Trond Myklebust, Mark Fallon and Maria Hartwig (eds.), *Interviewing and Interrogation: A Review of Research and Practice Since World War II*, Torkel Opsahl Academic EPublisher, Brussels, 2023 (https://www.toaep.org/ps-pdf/42-interrogation/).

3 US, Executive Order No. 13491: Ensuring Lawful Interrogations, 27 January 2009, 74 Fed. Reg. 16 (https://www.legal-tools.org/doc/5axj6m/).

Analyses of US interrogation programmes set up after the 2001 terrorist attacks on the US were fairly consistent in claiming that these programmes not only failed to collect operationally useful intelligence, but also failed to meet those same domestic and international obligations to treat those whom we interview with humanity and respect. Those same analyses pointed out that interrogation "training manuals, materials, and anecdotes contain information about common and recommended interrogation practices [...] but virtually none of those documents cites or relies upon any original research, and no scientific research substantiates the effectiveness of these approaches".[4] This gap was, in some sense, hard to understand: psychologists had been studying topics related to interpersonal communication for decades (topics such as memory, motivation, persuasion, resistance, deception, and communication): why had interrogation programmes in agencies with intelligence-gathering missions so failed to take advantage of this knowledge?

There are no doubt multiple reasons for this failure. My experience suggests that some intelligence professionals have a tendency to regard their field as deeply unique, to such a degree that behavioural and social science studies conducted in unclassified settings, with people from outside the secret world of intelligence gathering, are *presumed* to be unable to inform how best to interview, for example, an al Qaeda commander captured in the mountains of Pakistan, or even an intelligence source operating within the US. And yet, as the HIG identified areas of research pertinent to intelligence collection and 'translated' that research into a training programme for the interview teams, the relevance of those decades of research was apparent.

Interestingly, some chapters of this book contain similar claims that the investigation of PIF offences is "a complex endeavour [and] PIF investigations differ from most other investigations because of their complexity".[5] Far from challenging these claims, I could not but observe the parallels with intelligence operations in that both fields deal with complex judgments and decisions like: should there be an interest in a person who (i) may or (ii) may not have information (iii) relevant or (iv) irrelevant concerning a (v) potential threat and, if so, how many (vi) resources should we mobilize, (vii) which are the partners we should inform before (viii) conducting operations and with what powers? Or, in a PIF context: should there be an interest in an allegation that (i) may or (ii) may not indicate (iii) in a credible or (iv) non-credible way that (v) an intentional criminal offence has been committed and, if so, how many (vi) resources should

4 Robert A. Fein, Paul Lehner and Bryan Vossekuil, *Educing Information. Interrogation: Science and Art, Foundations for the Future*, National Defense Intelligence College Washington, DC, 2006.

5 See, for example, Section 1.5.1. of Chapter 1.

we mobilize, (vii) and what partners should be informed before (viii) executing what investigative powers?

What the chapters in this book do so well is to apply what has been discovered, researched and field-tested about human decision-making, to the complex operations of PIF. As the chapters unfold, we are offered detailed descriptions of how to prepare and carry out an investigation in ways that help avoid the errors of reasoning and judgement to which PIF investigations – and intelligence operations – are vulnerable. And, as noted by the authors, these same processes can assist in criminal investigations more generally.

During my tenure within the US intelligence community, I was privy to stories of intelligence operations gone awry. In one particular instance, a person was taken into custody and held in a country outside the US, to be interviewed by US intelligence. However, despite great efforts, the interviews yielded no results in critical information or intelligence. Upon reflection, it became apparent that this was not the person we had assumed him to be. Despite being willing to share whatever he knew, no useful information was obtained. The human cost was high, as the person could neither return to his home country, nor stay in the country to which he had been taken for interview, nor come to the US. I never learned what happened to him, and this story remains with me as a stark and tragic instance of what happens when those with the authorities of state and law fail to take into account our human vulnerabilities to errors of cognition, reason and motivation.

This book contributes to avoiding such errors, by providing *an invaluable resource to guide strategic decision-making and thinking, addressing human vulnerabilities and mitigating errors of cognition, reason and motivation in investigative practice*. When I can, I will recommend this book to intelligence analysts and agents because they also need to have the tools described here.

Susan E. Brandon, Ph.D.
High-Value Detainee Interrogation Group (ret.)
Consultant, New York

TABLE OF CONTENTS

Evidence-Based Approaches to Investigative Thinking

Tom Willems, Carsten Stahn, Darren Frey and Antonio Angotti*

1. The Meaning and Implementation of Quality in Investigations

The term 'quality' is inherently elusive; descriptors such as 'good' or 'excellent' must encompass sometimes conflicting perspectives on efficiency and ethical considerations.[1]

Empirical research that could substantiate specific views on the quality of investigations is notably scarce, likely due to confidentiality constraints[2] and a lack of interest from practitioners in collaborating with the scientific community, and vice versa.[3] Additionally, the variations across different areas of criminal law, as well as diverse procedural and legal traditions, present significant challenges for those seeking to formulate universal recommendations for policies and procedures in criminal investigations.

When, however, quality is defined as "an activity conducted according to certain agreed standards",[4] it follows that quality in investigations can be

---

* **Tom Willems** is co-ordinator for inter-institutional relations at the European Anti-Fraud Office ('OLAF'). Dr. **Carsten Stahn** is Professor of International Criminal Law and Global Justice at Leiden University and Queen's University Belfast. Dr. **Darren Frey** is Lecturer in Behavioral Economics and Cognitive Sciences (Sciences Po). **Antonio Angotti** is a Fellow of the Centre for International Law Research and Policy ('CILRAP') and an attorney at the Bar Association of Florence. This chapter is authored in the contributors' personal capacity and does not necessarily reflect the views of EPPO, OLAF, CILRAP or other institutions mentioned therein.

1 This debate would require a presentation and comparison of the specificities of inquisitorial versus accusatory-adversarial legal systems, which is outside the scope of this work.

2 As suggested in Ivar Fahsing, "The Making of an Expert Detective: Thinking and Deciding in Criminal Investigations", Ph.D. Thesis, Gothenburg University, 2016, p. 6.

3 As suggested in Richard Reyes, "Tactical Criminal Investigations: Understanding the Dynamics to Obtain the Best Results Without Compromising the Investigation", in *Journal of Forensic Science and Criminal Investigation*, 2017, vol. 2, no. 2.

4 Tor-Geir Myhrer, "Kvalitet i etterforskningen: Særlig om påtaleansvarliges rolle og betydning" [Quality in the Investigation: The Role and Responsibilities of the Police Prosecutor], Politihøgskolen (Norwegian Police University College), Oslo, 2015, p. 9.

understood as managing cases in line with reasonable expectations. These expectations include:[5]

- accurate fact-finding: ensuring that all relevant facts are thoroughly and correctly identified;
- lawful procedures: adhering to established legal standards, particularly with respect for the rights and interests of both suspects and victims;
- consistent progress: maintaining steady advancement throughout the investigation, culminating in a (prosecutorial and adjudicatory) decision within a reasonable timeframe;
- transparency and oversight: ensuring that the investigative process is transparent and subject to appropriate supervision.

Conversely, failed or deficient investigations can stem from several issues, including:[6]

- poor planning: complex and fact-rich investigations, such as those involving the protection of the financial interests of the European Union ('PIF'), require detailed planning that defines objectives, timelines and resource allocation;
- insufficient evidence collection: it is crucial to identify relevant evidence and ensure that its collection complies with legal and procedural standards;
- loss of information oversight: a failure to maintain a clear overview can lead to missing evidence gaps or becoming overwhelmed by an excess of information;
- inadequate evidence analysis: perhaps the most significant risk, this often results from a lack of specialization and co-ordination within the investigative team;
- uneven evidence-review: difficulties faced by investigators or review teams in aligning findings with legal qualifications can hinder the investigation's effectiveness;

---

[5] Runar Torgersen, "The Concern for Quality Control and Norwegian Preliminary Examination Practice", in Morten Bergsmo and Carsten Stahn (eds.), *Quality Control in Preliminary Examination*: *Volume 1*, Torkel Opsahl Academic EPublisher ('TOAEP'), Brussels, 2018, p. 69 (https://www.toaep.org/ps-pdf/32-bergsmo-stahn/).

[6] See the concept of 'bottlenecks' in Xabier Agirre Aranburu and Morten Bergsmo, "Investigative Bottlenecks and the Mindset of Quality Control", and Carsten Stahn, "From Preliminary Examination to Investigation: Rethinking the Connection", in Xabier Agirre, Morten Bergsmo, Simon De Smet and Carsten Stahn (eds.), *Quality Control in Criminal Investigation*, TOAEP, Brussels, 2020, p. 44 (https://www.toaep.org/ps-pdf/38-qcci/); see also Rod Gehl and Darryl Plecas, *Introduction to Criminal Investigation: Processes, Practices and Thinking*, Justice Institute of British Columbia, New Westminster, 2017, p. 60.

- unsubstantiated attribution of responsibility: this occurs when responsibility is assigned without sufficient evidence;
- tunnel vision: a narrow focus on certain aspects of the investigation may result in overlooking other critical elements.

This book explores quality standards for investigations from a dual perspective. First and foremost, it emphasizes the crucial role of the human factor, arguing that the expertise[7] of investigators is often pivotal in generating high-quality investigations. Research indicates that many investigation shortcomings arise from the actions of individual investigators rather than organizational factors, such as the commonly cited lack of resources.[8] Many of these issues can be traced back to cognitive errors, which is why they are a primary focus of this work.

Conversely, the book also asserts that established procedures and processes should be designed to mitigate the limitations inherent in human cognition. However, there is a risk that procedural compliance and stringent reporting requirements may become so burdensome that they hinder addressing other vital quality concerns, such as ensuring that investigators possess in-depth knowledge and can strategically manage their cases. To counteract such paralyzing effects, it is essential to implement proportionality requirements that balance procedural demands with the need for effective investigative practices.

Finally, this book advocates for the establishment and promotion of a "culture of quality control"[9] within investigative practices. Key aspects of this concept include:

---

7 This book conceptualizes and upholds the concept of expertise, whereby, rather than finding the correct, particular answer to a case example, it aims to extract by analogical reasoning, the underlying, more abstract insight(s), to be used when facing similar situations later. See Anthony J. Pinizzotto, Edward F. Davis and Charles E. Miller III, "Intuitive Policing; Emotional/Rational Decision Making in Law Enforcement", in *FBI Law Enforcement Bulletin*, 2004, vol. 73, no. 2, pp. 1–6.

8 See, for example, Kim Rossmo and Joycelyn Pollock, "Confirmation Bias and Other Systemic Causes of Wrongful Convictions: A Sentinel Events Perspective", in *Northeastern University Law Review*, 2019, vol. 11, no. 2, pp. 790–835. This study looked at 50 criminal investigations in the United States, Canada and Europe (6 per cent) for murder, rape and aggression, to find that around 60 per cent of the shortcomings could be attributed to individual mistakes or failures. This study would seem less relevant for PIF investigations, but reminds of the crucial role of the individual investigator.

9 Morten Bergsmo and Carsten Stahn, "Preface to the Second Edition by the Co-Editors", in *id.* (eds.), *Quality Control in Fact-Finding*, Second Edition, TOAEP, Brussels, 2020, p. ii (https://www.toaep.org/ps-pdf/19-bergsmo-stahn-second/).

- encouraging critical self-reflection: quality control should primarily aim to inspire critical self-reflection, prompting investigators to reconsider and rethink current practices;[10]
- fostering analytical rigour: this process necessitates a thorough analysis of established practices, questioning existing assumptions, and fostering an open dialogue to develop recommendations that can address and resolve prevalent challenges;[11]
- focusing on underlying work processes: rather than merely reforming procedural rules or evidence standards, the emphasis should be placed on the less visible, everyday work processes that shape the reality of investigations. By honing in on these foundational elements, a more substantial impact on the quality of investigative work can be achieved.

2. Outline of the Book

This book is structured into two main sections, featuring ten interconnected chapters that stand alone while also complementing each other. Cross-references among the chapters are designed to facilitate a gradual introduction to and elaboration of key concepts, ultimately creating a coherent narrative that highlights effective practices.

The first part includes four foundational chapters that establish the groundwork for the subsequent six practice-oriented ones. The latter contributions delve into the essential and sequential stages of a typical investigation, addressing the thinking challenges identified in the first part and suggesting strategies for their mitigation. Through this structure, readers are equipped with not only theoretical insights but also practical guidance on improving investigative quality.

In Chapter 1, "Investigating Allegations of Fraud and Corruption Affecting the European Union's Budget: A Classic Investigative Process?", Ivar Fahsing, Andon Tashukov and Anton Penneman introduce essential concepts and define critical terms related to the investigative process. They then shift their focus to the specific nuances involved in investigating PIF offences[12] by OLAF and

---

[10] Stahn, 2020, p. 37, see *supra* note 6.

[11] *Ibid.*

[12] Whereas 'offences' typically refers to criminal acts, we take the word to refer here as well to PIF 'irregularities', that is, administrative shortcomings consisting of a violation of a rule with financial implications: see Article 1(2) of Council Regulation (EC, EURATOM) No. 2988/95 of 18 December 1995 on the protection of the European Communities financial interests (https://www.legal-tools.org/doc/95p8lazw/):

> 'Irregularity' shall mean any infringement of a provision of Community law resulting from an act or omission by an economic operator, which has, or would have, the effect of prejudicing the general budget of the Communities or budgets managed by them, either

EPPO. The authors outline the potential objectives of an investigation, underscoring the vital interaction between individual cognitive processes and the procedural safeguards designed to mitigate inevitable shortcomings and errors. To support this discussion, they present several practical tools: the '6WH' framework, the 'ABC' of investigations, and the '6 Cs' model, all aimed at enhancing investigative thinking and methodologies. Furthermore, they advocate for a hypothesis-testing and falsification-based approach, emphasizing its applicability to PIF investigations. The second part of the chapter emphasizes the roles of the two primary European institutions involved, OLAF and EPPO. The authors detail the mandates and operations of both organizations, delineating the various stages in their investigative processes while highlighting the specific challenges they encounter. This comprehensive analysis sets the stage for understanding the complexities of PIF investigations within the European context.

In Chapter 2, titled "The Investigative Mindset", Tom Willems, Milanka Jug and Marian-Vladut Cozma explore the essential conditions for effective investigative thinking. They address the uncertainties that are inherent to the investigative process and advocate for an approach characterized by open-mindedness, critical analysis, and strategic thought, collectively referred to as the 'investigative mindset'. The authors argue that such a mindset should ideally be grounded in evidence and rationality; however, they also discuss the various challenges investigators face in striving to achieve this ideal. Drawing on their background as practitioners, they point at the continued impact of intuitive decision-making in investigations, while emphasizing that such intuition must be tempered by specific conditions to ensure sound judgment. A key take-away from their analysis is the assertion that effective investigative decision-making can be cultivated and continuously refined through practice and reflection. Nevertheless, like the first chapter's authors, they acknowledge that human cognition is inherently flawed, necessitating the implementation of standardized processes and procedures to ensure fairness and consistency in treatment across investigations. This recognition underscores the importance of structure in complementing the individual investigator's capabilities and enhancing overall quality.

The challenges and shortcomings of human thinking, highlighted in the first two chapters, take the centre stage in the subsequent two contributions. These chapters represent the most theoretical segment of the book, and provide critical insights into how individuals, particularly investigators, make judgments and decisions. By delving into the cognitive processes that underpin decision-making, the authors explore the intricacies of human perception, bias and

by reducing or losing revenue accruing from own resources collected directly on behalf of the Communities, or by an unjustified item of expenditure.

reasoning. They articulate how these factors can affect investigative outcomes, offering a nuanced understanding of the psychological landscape that informs the work of investigators. Through a blend of theoretical frameworks and practical implications, these chapters aim to illuminate the complexities inherent in the investigative process, encouraging readers to consider how cognitive biases can be mitigated and overcome in pursuit of more effective investigations. This theoretical discourse sets the stage for deeper understanding and better practices in the field.

In their Chapter 3 on the topic of "'Noise' in Investigations", Darren Frey, Charidimos Chaloftis and Tom Willems introduce the concept of 'noise' as the unwanted variability that affects judgment and decision-making. They argue that complete objectivity is impossible, even in the realms of legal decision-making and investigations. The authors illustrate how seemingly competent and dedicated investigators can arrive at markedly different conclusions due to systematic 'level' noise (for instance, a more stringent versus a more lenient case selector) or occasional pattern noise (such as the same selector exhibiting varying standards on different days). They advocate for increased awareness of noise in investigative contexts and draw upon recent research to suggest ways in which personal skills can be developed and organizational strategies implemented to mitigate various forms of noise. Among the personal skills emphasized is open-mindedness, which they define as the ability to reframe information and engage in counterfactual thinking – both crucial for reducing noise in decision-making. On the organizational front, the authors discuss the ambiguities associated with using standards and scales, advocating for the adoption of structured rules, comparative judgments, and the averaging of individual judgments to enhance decision-making consistency. By addressing noise in investigations, they aim to provide practical insights for fostering a more reliable and effective investigative environment.

While 'noise' is inherently unpredictable in its manifestation, other cognitive errors are systematic and, therefore, more predictable; this is the realm of cognitive biases. In Chapter 4, "Beating Biases: An Investigator's Mirage?", examining the prevalence of cognitive biases during investigations, Darren Frey, Tom Willems and Milanka Jug explore the concepts of heuristic thinking and cognitive bias as inevitable byproducts of our intuitive, automatic decision-making processes. They highlight that these biases represent one of two modes of judgment and decision-making, opposing intuitive to the more deliberate and rule-based thinking, commonly referred to as 'dual processing' models. The authors illustrate how these cognitive biases can adversely affect investigative decision-making, particularly under certain conditions – most notably when investigators are pressed for time, prioritizing efficiency, or engaged in suspect-driven, cognitively demanding inquiries such as those seen in PIF investigations. They specifically focus on the pitfalls of 'tunnel vision', which manifests as an automatic inclination to seek out and prioritize information that confirms an investigator's initial beliefs or hypotheses about an event. Echoing the recommendations from the first chapter of this book, the authors emphasize the importance of systematically engaging in falsification and actively considering alternative scenarios to counteract the effects of confirmation bias during investigations. They also propose to incorporate multiple 'judges' or 'decision-makers' throughout the investigative process. This collaborative approach aims to enhance decision-making quality by introducing diverse perspectives, thereby reducing the likelihood of cognitive bias influencing the outcome.

Staying true to the critical perspective embodied in this book, the concepts and standards articulated in the first four chapters serve as the foundation for the subsequent six chapters that comprise the second part of this volume. These chapters systematically traverse the various stages of a typical PIF investigation, encouraging readers to reflect on pertinent quality standards at each step. As in the earlier sections, the emphasis remains on the thinking challenges that investigators may encounter throughout the investigative process. By inviting scrutiny and promoting a deeper understanding of these challenges, the authors aim to foster a culture of continuous improvement in investigative practices, ultimately enhancing the overall quality of investigations. Each contribution not only builds upon the theoretical insights presented previously but also provides practical guidance for addressing the complexities inherent in conducting effective PIF investigations.

In their Chapter 5 on "Initial Reporting", Simon Baechler, Jorick Schreurs and Georgios Kougias explore the various sources of information that can initiate an investigation. They differentiate between voluntary and mandatory reporting, which may come from either official bodies or private entities. When focusing on the intricate reporting framework of OLAF and EPPO, the authors highlight the judgment and decision-making challenges discussed in earlier chapters, proposing strategies to mitigate biases and specifically address noise in the reporting process. Significant attention is devoted to the diverse phrasings associated with numerous reporting obligations, which can hinder the establishment of a coherent and consistent practice. Additionally, the chapter examines the implications of using scales and standards that can lead to varying interpretations across different contexts. To foster more consistent and accurate reporting practices, the authors put forth definitions and descriptions aimed at simplifying and harmonizing the reporting requirements that all participants in the anti-fraud landscape must adhere to. Moreover, they emphasize the importance of understanding informational qualities, which are pivotal themes throughout this volume. The chapter also marks the beginning of an exploration into the fundamental principles of 'burden' and 'standard of proof' as they apply at various stages of the investigative process, laying the groundwork for a more nuanced understanding of these critical concepts in the context of investigation.

Chapter 6 of this book, "Preliminary Examination or Information", focuses on a critical aspect of the investigation cycle: the decision-making process regarding whether to open or not an investigation. In this chapter, Carsten Stahn, Paolo Proli and Pascal Hollevoet delve into the 'preliminary examination' phase, also known as the 'evaluation', 'selection', or 'initial information intake' phase of an investigation. They discuss how investigative bodies exercise discretion in determining the legal grounds and sufficient suspicions necessary to warrant the initiation of a full investigation, as well as the tools and powers available to selectors to make informed decisions. The authors break down these often-challenging assessments into sub-criteria, such as 'reliability' and 'credibility', while acknowledging that 'noise' – the unwanted variability in judgment – can never be entirely eradicated from the process. In addition to 'noise', the chapter highlights the inherent risks posed by various cognitive biases. Notably, the authors point out that the risk of confirmation bias is particularly acute during the preliminary examination phase. In this context, a selector may tend to construct a hypothesis about the events in question and may be tempted to selectively incorporate only the evidence that supports this hypothesis, thereby reinforcing their personal narrative of the situation. To address these challenges, the authors argue that the concept of 'corroboration' of initial information should be reconceptualized as a mindset of 'verification'. While corroboration often implies a focus on positive confirmation, verification serves as a more neutral term aimed at establishing the truth. This shift in perspective encourages a more balanced and thorough evaluation of the evidence, ultimately enhancing the quality of decision-making in the critical early stages of the investigative process.

If an investigation is eventually opened, investigators need to plan how they will proceed. In their Chapter 7 on "Investigation Plans", Antonio Angotti, Kris Vandenberk and Julius Dirma delve into the various functions of this essential tool within the investigative process. They emphasize that an investigation plan necessitates a reassessment of information following the preliminary examination, allowing appointed investigators to identify, plan and pursue both tactical and strategic objectives for the case. Additionally, the plan serves as a mechanism for reporting progress to hierarchy, ensuring ongoing oversight and potentially garnering guidance. The authors caution against the risk of tunnel vision that can occur when investigators develop a case hypothesis, reinforcing the importance of approaching the investigation plan as a dynamic and adaptable resource. They advocate for utilizing the plan as a 'living' knowledge-base and a reflective platform throughout the investigative process, rather than merely a tool for monitoring progress in terms of case duration. To underscore their points, the authors refer to good practices from the ICC and the Norwegian police, highlighting how these organizations integrate flexible planning into their investigative strategies. By doing so, they illustrate the value of maintaining an open and evolving approach to investigation planning, which can enhance the quality and effectiveness of the investigative outcomes.

Chapter 8, "Fact-Finding, at the Core of the Investigation Process" by Anna Sagana, Judit Tátrai and Olivier Coene, underscores the complexity and nuance involved in the fact-finding process during PIF investigations. The authors emphasize the iterative nature of investigations, which necessitates both critical thinking and deliberate actions to uncover facts efficiently. They explain that the distinction between direct and indirect evidence is particularly significant in PIF cases, as the latter, also called circumstantial evidence, is often critical in establishing guilty intent or *mens rea*. A key takeaway from their discussion is the necessity for evidence to not only adhere to legal standards of relevance, reliability and admissibility, but also to possess probative value and persuasive power. The standards of proof, whether it be the criminal threshold of 'beyond reasonable doubt' or the civil standard of 'in the balance of probabilities', set a high bar for the evidence needed to substantiate findings. The authors' recommendation that investigators should not only search for inculpatory, but also exculpatory evidence speaks to the ethical obligation of fact-finders to ensure fairness in the investigative process. By advocating for the importance of falsification and the need to consider alternative hypotheses, the chapter promotes a rigorous analytical framework that encourages investigators to always remain objective and comprehensive in their approaches. In providing insights on review procedures, analytical tools, and adversarial techniques, the authors aim to equip investigative teams with strategies and tools to effectively navigate these challenges. The emphasis on these methodological components supports a robust framework that upholds the principles of justice and accountability within the context of public interest.

At the conclusion of the fact-finding phase, the investigative team is tasked with compiling a comprehensive 'case'. This typically manifests as a final report, which includes a detailed statement of the facts, an analytical overview of the gathered evidence, and culminates in the investigation's conclusions. Chapter 9, "Models of Rational Proof in Investigation" by Daniela-Simona Tatu, Jorick Schreurs and Tom Willems outlines various models for presenting proof, providing compelling arguments for which model may be the most suitable for PIF investigations. The authors begin by reiterating fundamental characteristics of evidence, such as its comprehensiveness, and subsequently delve into the more complex challenge of establishing confidence in their findings. They delineate three distinct models of rational proof – rooted in probabilities, arguments and scenarios – and discuss how these models are currently employed or could be strategically utilized in PIF investigations to achieve either accuracy or persuasive objectives. While highlighting that these methodologies are not mutually exclusive and advocate for an integrated approach to enhance the quality of evaluations, the authors underscore a critical point: no individual approach can guarantee absolute certainty. Particularly pertinent is the principle of defeasibility in claims of intent, which is essential for recognizing PIF offenses. Since the *mens rea*, or guilty intent, of a perpetrator cannot be empirically verified, this principle becomes a crucial element in the investigative process.

In the final Chapter 10, "'To Intend or Not to Intend?', That Is the (Difficult) Question", Tom Willems, Anna Sagana and Jennifer Vanderputten confront the crucial challenge of effectively demonstrating *mens rea*. Instead of depending on an intuitive and holistic assessment of a perpetrator's mindset, they advocate for a structured analytical approach, drawing on the exemplary practices and insights highlighted in previous contributions to the series. Their framework seeks to clarify that, in PIF investigations, the principal hypotheses typically revolve around whether investigators and prosecutors are dealing with a case of error or mistake, a case of irregularity, or, indeed, a deliberate PIF offense characterized by intentional misuse. Echoing the sentiments of the previous chapters, the authors promote an open-minded investigative approach that begins with identifying the primary competing hypotheses and advancing through validation and falsification processes. Once a lead hypothesis or theory emerges, the authors recommend employing argumentation schemes to systematically, deliberately and meticulously evaluate all evidence that may support or contradict the existence of guilty intent. In an innovative next step, they encourage investigators or prosecutors to map the available evidence visually, assigning numerical scores to quantify the persuasiveness of each piece of evidence, both individually and collectively. This method aims to address and mitigate the inherent uncertainties associated with assessing intent. The conclusion drawn from this rigorous analysis is presented as a 'best explanation' – whether that be fraud or irregularity.

Importantly, this 'best explanation' does not always meet the stringent standard of 'proof beyond a reasonable doubt'. However, by making the process of arriving at such a conclusion explicit and transparent, investigators can provide the trier of facts with the necessary tools to make informed decisions, confident in the robustness and rationality of their reasoning. This objective encapsulates the overarching theme of the Quality Control Project,[13] highlighting the importance of quality and systematic analysis in the pursuit of justice.

[13] On the Quality Control Project, see "Preface by the Co-Editors", fn. 5.

1

Investigating Allegations of Fraud and Corruption Affecting the European Union's Budget: A Classic Investigative Process?

Ivar Fahsing, Andon Tashukov and Anton Penneman*

1.1. Introduction

Beginning our analysis of the investigative process, this chapter introduces key concepts and proposes critical definitions concerning the investigative process in general, while also focusing on particularities specific to the investigation of PIF offences.[1] On the one hand, we will claim that the latter are significantly different from 'common' investigations; on the other hand, we will explore the extent to which similar quality parameters apply. The primary questions we address include: what makes for a (criminal) investigation as opposed to, for instance, audit; what role do investigations play in the anti-fraud cycle; and whether the investigation of PIF offences poses particular challenges. A major objective of the chapter is to describe quality parameters for PIF investigations, and to explore what the main challenges are to achieving such quality. As throughout the remainder of the book, the focus is on the investigation as a thinking process.

1.2. Investigating: Between Models and Mind

Most people's perceptions of what an investigator does is based on what they see, hear and read in the media, movies, TV and books. The media portrays

---

* **Ivar Fahsing** is Detective Chief Superintendent of the Norwegian Police and Associate Professor of the Norwegian Police College. Dr. **Andon Tashukov** is a Senior Case Analyst and Team Coordinator of the Expenditure Fraud and Corruption team within the Operation's Unit at the European Public Prosecutor's Office ('EPPO'), after serving as the Legal Adviser on "Protection of the European Union's financial interests" Directorate within the Ministry of Interior of Bulgaria. **Anton Penneman** is investigation officer at the European Anti-Fraud Office ('OLAF'). This chapter is authored in the contributors' personal capacity and does not reflect the views of EPPO, OLAF or other institutions mentioned therein.

1 'PIF' stands for '*Protection des Intérêts Financiers*', or 'Protection of the Financial Interest of the European Union' ('EU'), a crucial concept for the definition of criminal offences like fraud and corruption detrimental to the EU budget and the scope of activity of instances created to protect this budget.

characters ranging from dysfunctional, violent rebels fighting for justice by their own rules, to by-the-book forensic investigators who get the job done clinically, using sophisticated science and technology. The truth is: good investigations and real-life investigators are unlikely to make a captivating story and come in many forms, often bearing little resemblance to the thrilling stories seen in entertainment.

One understanding of 'investigation' is that it embraces a wide range of specialities that aim to determine how events occurred and to establish a documented pattern of evidence to prove or disprove wrongdoing,[2] including the possible guilt or responsibility of the actors involved.[3] Another possible definition is that the investigation is a purpose-governed activity with a progression of activities or steps, moving from the reception and collection of information, to fact-finding via a number of investigative procedures, including analyses and validation processes, to obtain evidence sufficient to warrant investigative conclusions and recommendations.

Administrative investigations share with criminal investigations the core concern for fact-finding, but use different means. They typically do not have coercive statutory powers, but do aim to establish facts and make recommendations in light of their findings.

Both criminal and administrative investigations do not occur in a void. The investigation is typically part of a more comprehensive system of accountability, possibly including other processes within that system, like an audit preceding an administrative investigation, or a criminal investigation following the latter.

Investigations come in many forms and are often fluid endeavours in situations of uncertainty: they are conducted in response to events that are often unpredictable, perhaps even continuously unfolding, and usually with incomplete and potentially unreliable information emerging along the way. Therefore, it is not feasible to prescribe a fixed set of techniques or sources of evidence that will be universally applicable. Nevertheless, there are key principles, guidelines and procedures that might be crucial to every investigation. This chapter presents some generic concepts and practical tools for successful investigative work. They are generic because the success of investigations depends largely on the investigators' ability to make the correct decisions at the right times, and they often face similar challenges that hinder optimal decision-making. These include time constraints, emotional involvement, guilt presumption, information overload, and workplace norms favouring quick resolutions. Subsequent

2 Rod Gehl and Darryl Plecas, *Introduction to Criminal Investigation: Processes, Practices and Thinking*, Justice Institute of British Columbia, New Westminster, 2016, p. 4.

3 *Ibid.*

chapters will elaborate how these challenges can interact with the very nature and shortcomings of human judgments and decisions.[4] We will propose that these systematic biases of human thinking make certain safeguards and procedures essential.

1.3. The Objectives of Investigation

The purpose of investigations varies, depending on the context. Still, investigations should generally include: (a) gathering potential evidence from different sources; (b) establishing facts by (c) cross-checking; (d) identifying responsible parties; (e) ensuring accountability and providing closure for the victims; (f) allowing remedial action; and (g) future learning, prevention and countermeasures.

1.3.1. Gathering Potential Evidence

An essential aspect of investigating is the collection and documentation of information from a range of sources that later can be used as evidence, for example, in a court of law or other judicial proceedings to prove or disprove allegations. Information sources may be classified by their format: human, physical, or digital.

The '6WH' framework[5] is used in investigative processes, problem-solving, or analysis to thoroughly explore a situation, by asking some generic key questions. It helps gather comprehensive information by systematically addressing six fundamental aspects. The questions can vary depending on the context, but they generally include the following:

- *Who*: Identifying the individuals involved is crucial for establishing responsibility. This can include suspects, witnesses, victims, and any other relevant parties. Knowing 'who' helps investigators know where to focus their questioning and evidence-gathering.
- *What*: Understanding what exactly happened is fundamental to establishing the facts of the case. This involves determining the nature of the incident – be it a crime, a violation of company policy, or some other event.
- *When*: The timing of events can be critical in establishing alibis, understanding the sequence of events, and sometimes even the legality of actions (for example, statute of limitations).

4 See also, and in particular, Chapters 3 (on heuristics and cognitive biases) and 4 (on noise) below for more detail.

5 Ivar Fahsing, *The Making of an Expert Detective: Thinking and Deciding in Criminal Investigations*, Ph.D. Thesis, Gothenburg University, 2016.

- *Where*: Location data can provide crucial context and contribute to understanding the 'how' and 'why' of the event. Geographical information can also be vital for gathering additional evidence, like CCTV footage.
- *Why*: Understanding the motive behind an action can be essential for establishing intent, which can be a critical component in both criminal and civil cases.
- *How*: The methods used to act can provide significant insights into planning, intent, and level of expertise, which can all be relevant for understanding the case and deciding on punitive or corrective measures.

The '6WH' provides a structured and logical framework for investigations. By following this method, investigators can work systematically, ensuring no critical details are overlooked. This approach is especially valuable when involving multiple investigators, as it provides a standardized framework that everyone can easily understand and follow. Each of the '6WH' elements helps identify the type of evidence that needs to be gathered. For instance, 'when' and 'where' can guide investigators to specific CCTV footage, while 'who' can lead to background checks or interviews. In short, the '6WH' framework is an essential tool that helps investigators remain thorough and focused throughout the investigative process.

1.3.2. Fact-Finding

Building on the '6WH' framework, we can move more systematically towards the fundamental aim to establish the facts surrounding an incident or situation.[6] Understanding each of these six elements not only provides individual pieces of the puzzle but also helps synthesize the overall narrative of what took place. This is crucial for the decision-making process, whether it involves pressing charges, taking internal disciplinary action, or any other consequential steps. Answering these questions rigorously and thoroughly helps to ensure that the investigation is conducted in adherence to legal standards and ethical guidelines. This is vital for the credibility of the investigation and any subsequent legal proceedings, ensuring that justice is served and human rights are respected. This will typically include testing the evidence for three interlinked dimensions:

- *Relevance*: Is the information relevant to the matter under investigation?
- *Accuracy*: Is the information sufficiently detailed to serve as evidence?
- *Reliability*: Can the information be tested or evaluated across different sources?

[6] See Chapter 8 of this book for more details on fact-finding.

1.3.3. Cross-Checking

Cross-checking is essential in investigations for several reasons, all of which contribute to the reliability, integrity and success of the process.

First, it helps verify the accuracy of gathered information, whether witness statements, timelines, or physical evidence. By comparing data from multiple sources, investigators can either validate or question their initial findings.

Second, cross-checking is crucial for assessing the credibility of different sources, including witnesses. This is especially important because investigators, being human, are prone to biases that can cloud their judgment.[7] Cross-checking may help us safeguard against these biases by requiring verification from independent sources.

Third, consistency is key in building a strong case. Cross-checking helps establish whether the evidence and accounts align to form a coherent narrative or if there are discrepancies that warrant further investigation.

In high-stakes situations like criminal cases, where the outcomes can be life-altering, the importance of cross-checking is amplified. It not only strengthens the case, but is also crucial for ensuring a fair trial and upholding human rights. Overall, a case supported by cross-checked information is more robust and stands up better in court or other decision-making settings.

1.3.4. Identifying Responsible Parties

Another main goal of the investigation is identifying who is responsible for a particular action or event. This could be a criminal suspect, a negligent employee, or any other individual, group or enterprise. Identifying those suspects is a necessary step to take effective action to address their behaviour and ensure accountability. This can take the shape of criminal justice outcomes, civil remedies, or internal disciplinary action within an organization.

1.3.5. Providing 'Closure'

The 'need for closure' is a concept from social psychology, describing the finding that people in general desire a clear, firm answer or peaceful resolution to a question or problem to minimize ambiguity and move beyond the problem.[8] By identifying the perpetrator and holding him or her accountable, an investigation can provide closure for victims or those harmed by the wrongdoing. Knowing that the matter has been diligently looked into and appropriate action has been or will be taken leads to a sense of procedural justice, which is a feeling of

---

7 See Chapter 4 of this book for more details on cognitive bias.

8 See, for example, Arie W. Kruglanski and Donna M. Webster, "Motivated Closing of the Mind: 'Seizing' and 'Freezing'", in *Psychological Review*, 1996, vol. 103, no. 2, pp. 263–283.

having been treated fairly, listened to, and taken seriously, regardless of the outcome of an allocation process (here: of justice).[9]

1.3.6. Remedial Action

The investigation also has more structural objectives, including:

- implementing corrective measures in organizational or systemic contexts: the purpose often extends to identifying flaws or weaknesses in existing systems or procedures and recommending corrective action;
- maintaining public trust and safety in public sectors like law enforcement and regulatory agencies: investigations are a way to demonstrate that misconduct or unsafe practices are taken seriously and dealt with appropriately;[10]
- ensuring legal and regulatory compliance, for instance when businesses conduct an internal investigation to ensure compliance with laws and regulations, as failure to do so can result in hefty fines and legal penalties; and
- identifying risks or potential issues in corporate settings, where understanding and mitigating risks can save the organization from future problems.

1.3.7. Training and Education

Finally, investigations often serve as learning opportunities. The findings can be used to train employees, update policies, or advise the public on preventing similar incidents.

Importantly, research suggests that training on soft skills – think of clear communication and rational thinking in the context of investigations – only leads to better performance when the training is followed by an integration of (parts of) the newly acquired skills in daily practice.[11]

---

9 See, for example, Riël Vermunt and Herman Steensma, "Procedural Justice", in Clara Sabbagh and Manfred Schmitt (eds.), *Handbook of Social Justice Theory and Research*, Springer, New York, 2016, pp. 219-236.

10 'Dealing seriously' with unlawful practices includes an efficient enforcement policy. The 'experiential effect' refers to the view that persons who commit crimes, but have not been caught, will develop lower risks perceptions of certainty and severity. Essentially, experience in getting away with breaking the law is believed to teach offenders to believe that they can continue to get away with crime. Researchers have come to a strong conclusion that, rather than by (increasing) its severity, punishment only deters crime if the punishment is inevitable (see Benjamin Van Rooij and Adam Fine, *The Behavioral Code: The Hidden Ways the Law Makes Us Better ... or Worse*, Beacon Press, Boston, 2021, p. 37).

11 See, for example, Jolanda A. Botke, "*Understanding the Transfer-to-Work of Soft Skills Training: Examining Transfer Stages, the Role of Work Factors and Self-Efficacy*", Ph.D. Thesis, Vrije Universiteit Amsterdam, 2021.

1.4. A Hypotheses-Informed Model for Investigation

1.4.1. The 'ABC' of Investigations

To achieve the objectives of the investigation, an expert-investigator should embrace a so-called investigative mindset,[12] where the terms 'possibly' and 'could' should be the watchwords for use in every investigation. In manuals for investigators, this is often formulated as the 'ABC' principle:[13]

A	Assume nothing
B	Believe nothing
C	Challenge and check everything

Illustration 1.1.: The ABC of Investigations.

In this mind-frame, nothing should be taken for granted or accepted at face value. It can prove fatal to assume that things are what they seem. Expert investigators should always approach anything presented to them sceptically, avoiding placing too much confidence or relying too significantly on the new information. All stories are possible – until they are not. Correlation does not imply causation.

This might seem pretty straightforward, but it is not. To an investigator, the hardest thing is resisting automatic assumptions and seeking immediate closure. Our deeply rooted need for quick cognitive closure[14] might push the investigator to 'freeze' his thinking once having come across a tentative solution, whilst becoming reluctant to consider other alternatives. However, the information gathered in criminal investigations and most other real-life settings is often ambiguous and fragile. Therefore, the burden of proof cannot be understood as a truly deductive elimination of all possible alternatives to guilt. The available data will simply not always allow for this.

1.4.2. The Information Gap

'WYSIATI', the acronym for 'What You See Is All There Is', is a term for a form of bias coined by Daniel Kahneman[15] to describe the fact that we typically make our judgements according to the information we have readily available,

12 See Chapter 2 for more detail.

13 Ivar Fahsing, "Beyond Reasonable Doubt: How to Think Like an Expert Detective", in Paulo Barbosa Marquez and Mauro Paulino (eds.), *Police Psychology*, Elsevier Academic Press, Cambridge, 2022, pp. 267–298; Ivar Fahsing, "How to Think Like a Detective", *Psyche*, 2021.

14 Kruglanski and Webster, 1996, see *supra* note 8.

15 Daniel Kahneman, *Thinking, Fast and Slow*, Farrar, Straus and Giroux, New York, 2011.

no matter how incomplete. We do not seem to realize there are still many things we do not know.

For instance, when we meet someone new, we typically use less than a second to build up an impression of them. Immediately, we decide whether they are bright and nice, or dominant and hostile, and we decide whether we like them. And we do all this based on extremely incomplete information, such as facial features, how they dress or the way they talk. When we make everyday decisions, our mind often only considers the first information available, regardless of its quality and quantity, and it immediately seeks to build a coherent story. The story does not have to be accurate, complete or reliable, it only has to be somewhat coherent.[16]

Making decisions this way is easy, comfortable, intuitive, and even worse, it makes us feel good, confident and competent. Regardless of class or level of IQ (regardless of how it is measured), we are all cognitive 'misers' due to a strong tendency to solve problems in simpler and less effortful ways rather than in more sophisticated and more effortful ways. Hence, there will always be a gap between what you see and think and what is real. If ignored, this overconfidence gap can lead even the most trusted expert astray. This is particularly relevant in investigations since information is often scarce in the early stages.

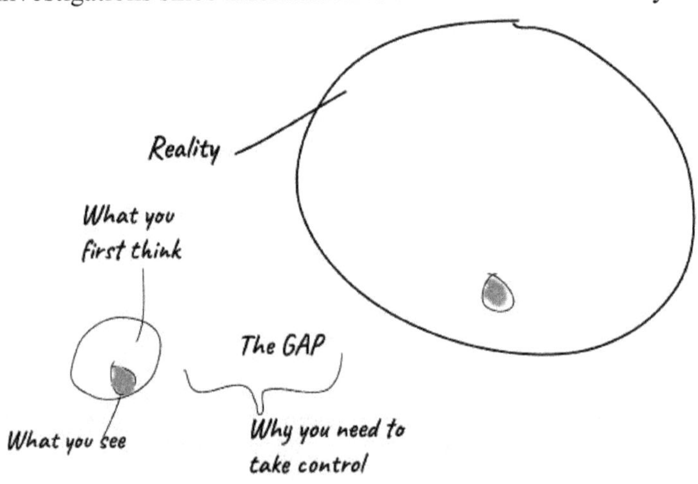

Illustration 1.2.: The information gap.[17]

[16] See also Chapter 9 on the powers of narratives.

[17] See Fahsing, 2021, *supra* note 13.

1.4.3. Hypothesis-Testing and Falsification

Rather than jumping to conclusions, the investigator should practice hypothesis-testing and falsification. As early as 1892, Doyle indeed coined the first true mantra of how to think like an investigator, when his fictional detective Sherlock Holmes asserted that "[w]hen you have eliminated the impossible, whatever remains, however improbable, must be the truth".[18] In this understanding, the (criminal) investigation can be understood as a pragmatic and abductive process to identify the most reasonable explanation for the available information.

Abduction can be described as 'the logic of what might be'. Unlike a deduction, but similar to induction, the conclusions from an abductive argument might be false, even if the premises are true. In other words, abductive logic allows for qualified and pragmatic guessing and is probabilistic in nature. A medical diagnosis is a typical application of abductive reasoning: given a set of symptoms, what diagnosis would best explain most of them? Sometimes, the symptoms are so ambiguous or hard to test that there simply is no clear diagnosis. In this case, the abductive process must (1) generate the best guesses based on the knowledge available and (2) evaluate the competing hypotheses to find the best diagnosis. We can consider both inferences ampliative, selective and creative because, in both cases, the reasoning involved amplifies or goes beyond the information contained in the premises. Such reasoning is particularly useful in investigations, as investigative contexts are often complicated by many potential explanations for a given observation, a constant influx of new information, and many possible ways to combine, test and develop competing hypotheses about the most likely explanation.

In the application of abductive logic, all tentative hypotheses explaining an allegation or event should be formed based on the initially available information, and the investigator's available schemata of potential crimes and their non-criminal alternatives. Not formulating all possible hypotheses is one of the most serious diagnostic mistakes investigating officers can make.[19] Ideally, such hypotheses should subsequently include assumptions about all likely situations, potential perpetrators, modes of conduct and motives behind an offence. The aim is to keep track of alternative explanations of the evidence and to remind the investigator of all the different avenues of enquiry which should be considered.

[18] Arthur C. Doyle, *The Adventures of Sherlock Holmes*, in *The Strand Magazine*, London, 1891–1892.

[19] Ivar Fahsing, Asbjørn Rachlew and Lennart May, "Have You Considered the Opposite? A Debiasing Strategy for Judgment in Criminal Investigation", in *The Police Journal*, 2023, vol. 96, no. 1, p. 47.

When nature (our cognitive set-up) fails, a method or formula is necessary. Without it, there is a huge risk that you will become a slave to your first or seemingly best idea. Key concepts are falsification and hypotheses-testing, essentially seeking alternative scenarios to account for the given fact-pattern.

Falsification involves looking for evidence that can disprove an idea or theory.[20] It is an invaluable process when trying to determine what most likely happened, as failed attempts at disproving a theory can indirectly act as support for the theory.[21] Falsification is closely related to the consideration of alternative scenarios. A scenario can be defined as a chronological or causal description of a central action.[22] Evidence that disproves one scenario may confirm another scenario. Furthermore, trying to find a good alternative scenario for the available evidence can also be considered part of attempting falsification.[23]

1.4.4. The '6 Cs' Model

The '6 Cs' model[24] integrates and summarizes the main questions and steps of the investigative process, as described above, in six essential and sequential steps.

20 Karl Popper, *The Logic of Scientific Discovery*, Routledge, New York, 1959.

21 Hans F. Crombag, Peter J. van Koppen and Willems A. Wagenaar, *Dubieuze zaken: De psychologie van strafrechtelijk bewijs* [*Dubious Cases: The Psychology of Evidence in Criminal Law*], Olympus, Amsterdam, 2006.

22 Peter J. van Koppen and Anne R. Mackor, "A Scenario Approach to the Simonshaven Case", in *Topics in Cognitive Science*, 2020, vol. 12, no. 4, pp. 1132–1151.

23 *Ibid.*

24 Ivar Fahsing and Karl Ask, "Decision Making and Decisional Tipping Points in Homicide Investigations: An Interview Study of British and Norwegian Detectives", in *Journal of Investigative Psychology and Offender Profiling*, 2013, vol. 10, no. 2, pp. 155–165.

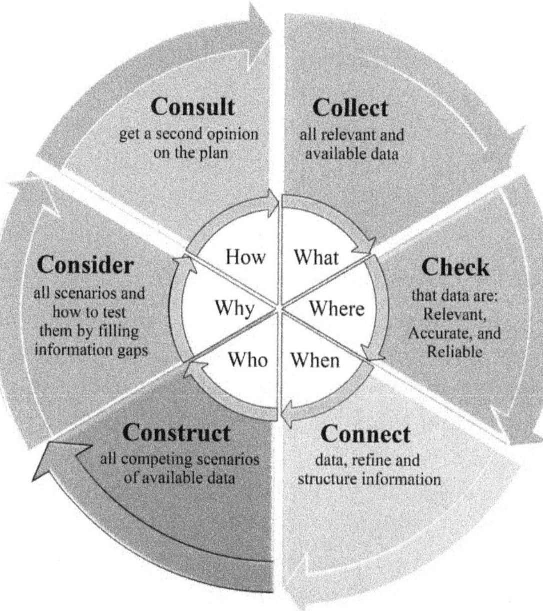

Illustration 1.3.: The '6 Cs' Investigative cycle.

These steps can be summarized as follows. First of all, what do you know? *Collect* available information and *check* the facts. Are they relevant, accurate and reliable? *Connect* the dots. Do different sources say the same thing? Find out what you do not know.

Construct all possible solutions and hypotheses. What does the available information allow? What can already be ruled out? What remains possible? A hypothesis is a proposed explanation for a phenomenon. It is a testable statement about the relationship between two or more variables. This approach often contrasts with exploratory or inductive investigations, which aim to collect data and derive conclusions or theories. Hypothesis-driven investigations are common in scientific research, but should also be applied in investigations and corporate audits.

Consider the information you need to prove or disprove your remaining hypotheses most effectively. Falsification is the process of trying to disprove a hypothesis. In the context of investigations or audits, falsification involves looking for evidence that contradicts each hypothesis. If evidence is found that contradicts a hypothesis, then that hypothesis must be rejected or modified.

Before you implement your plan, always *consult* somebody you trust before you continue to narrow your case by repeating this process from step one. While a sound starting hypothesis provides initial direction, the investigative process is typically iterative. This allows for course corrections based on findings, making the approach adaptable.

Keep going until you have only one solution which best explains the available evidence to fit your needs. As the last 'C' (Consult) suggests, applying a devil's advocate approach, whereby others' dissenting opinions or competence are actively sought, has proven to be an effective debiasing strategy in complex decision-making.[25]

1.4.5. Conditions and Advantages of a Hypotheses-Driven Investigation

Modern societies are becoming more complex, and the amount of information available to investigators in almost any field is growing exponentially. Therefore, it is essential to use a system that acknowledges and documents this complexity. Investigators should adopt tools like matrices or mind-mapping techniques to track their hypothesis-driven investigations. This approach provides a clearer overview, enhances transparency, facilitates collaboration, and encourages second opinions on ideas and judgments.

Using hypotheses and actively attempting falsification helps to reduce the risk of tunnel vision during investigations. It ensures that all relevant explanations for an allegation are considered, minimizing the effects of cognitive biases and emotional involvement.[26] A well-supported set of investigative hypotheses strengthens the investigative conclusions, particularly if the evidence has been systematically collected and analysed with these hypotheses in mind.

This approach fosters better problem-solving and critical thinking. A more systematic approach requires investigators to engage in a deeper mental processing of issues relevant to the enquiry. In legal contexts, a hypothesis-driven approach holds up better under scrutiny, as it demonstrates a systematic and rational process for reaching conclusions, thereby promoting fairness and respecting human rights.

In summary, hypothesis-driven investigations offer a structured, focused and adaptable framework for enquiry. By systematically testing hypotheses, investigators can reach conclusions that are more objective and defensible, making this approach highly valuable in a variety of investigative settings. In view of Canter and Alison's suggestion that "good thinking is represented by a thorough search for alternatives without favouring what one already has in mind",[27]

---

[25] See, for example, Charles R. Schwenk, "Effects of Devil's Advocacy and Dialectical Inquiry on Decision Making: A Meta-Analysis", in *Organizational Behavior and Human Decision Processes*, 1990, vol. 47, no. 1, pp. 161–176.

[26] See Chapter 4 for more details on tunnel vision and other cognitive biases.

[27] David Canter and Laurence Alison, *Profiling in Policy and Practice*, Ashgate, Aldershot, 1999, p. 30.

to have the capacity to *not* make up your mind too soon is probably the best ability a good investigator can have.

1.5. The Investigative Process in PIF Investigations

1.5.1. General Setting

Investigating offences affecting the financial interests of the EU, often referred to as PIF, is a complex endeavour. This multifaceted undertaking encompasses both the revenue and expenditure sides of the EU budget and involves probing into various types of fraud, including customs fraud, VAT fraud, expenditure fraud, active and passive corruption and misappropriation, all of which are often perpetrated by organized crime groups and frequently linked to money laundering and other related offences.

For this reason, PIF investigations differ from most other investigations because of their complexity. This results from not only the diversity of PIF offences, but also the applicability of different legal frameworks (especially when investigating in a transnational way), access to different analytical tools and databases, and ultimately, on how EU money is spent.

Such spending can take place in a direct management mode, through indirect management, or, most often, in the form of shared management with the Members States of the EU. Each of these modes entails the investment of, a large amount of financial resources,[28] creating an unprecedented arena of funds and programmes, each entailing its own set of challenges and fraud risks.

Protecting the financial interests of the EU is also inherently complex due to its 'cross-policy' nature, which involves both revenue and expenditure aspects of the EU budget. The revenue side involves combating customs fraud and VAT fraud. These forms of fraud are distinct in nature and require specialized approaches to investigate. Considering that these offences imply a 'cross-border' element, the investigation process should always provide for appropriate means, procedures and tools to safeguard the admissibility of evidence. Often extensive

[28] See, for example, EUR 1.2 trillion of budget capped by over EUR 800 billion of NextGen Funds for post-Covid Recovery. More than 50 per cent of this budget will go to new priorities, as it will focus on research and innovation, fair climate and digital transitions; preparedness, and recovery and resilience via the Recovery and Resilience Facility. Thirty per cent of this budget will be spent on fighting climate change – the highest share ever, from the largest EU budget ever. Approximately one-fifth (20 per cent) of the funds allocated under the Recovery and Resilience Facility will be dedicated to advancing the EU's digital transformation. Furthermore, during the years 2026 and 2027, a noteworthy portion of the annual expenditures outlined in the long-term budget, specifically 10 per cent, will be directed towards initiatives aimed at stopping and reversing the ongoing decline in biodiversity. For an article on concerns over an enhanced risks of irregularity and fraud in this Recovery and Research Facility, see, for example, Eulalia Rubio, "Balancing Urgency and Control", *Economics & Finance*, Policy Paper No. 262, 2021.

VAT 'carousel' fraud involves numerous fictitious businesses across multiple EU Member States (and abroad), rendering conventional judicial collaboration methods inadequate for combatting this type of fraud.

In sum, the investigative process must therefore be adapted to the transnational nature of these criminal activities and enable the use of all legal means to investigate irregular and fraudulent behaviour, combining national means with international co-operation, and as of 2021 – with the application of the revolutionary Article 31 of the EPPO Regulation.[29] The establishment of the EPPO as a trans-national investigating and prosecuting authority, operating as a 'single office', marks a significant milestone in enhancing the EU's capacity to investigate and prosecute PIF offences, surpassing the investigation process' shortcomings on national level.

1.5.2. Typology of the Authorities Involved in the Investigative Process

The investigative process can also be broken down from the perspective of the authorities involved and the choice of forum.[30] In regard to the protection of the financial interests of the EU, investigation is a multi-tiered and complex endeavour, with authorities operating at both the national and European levels.

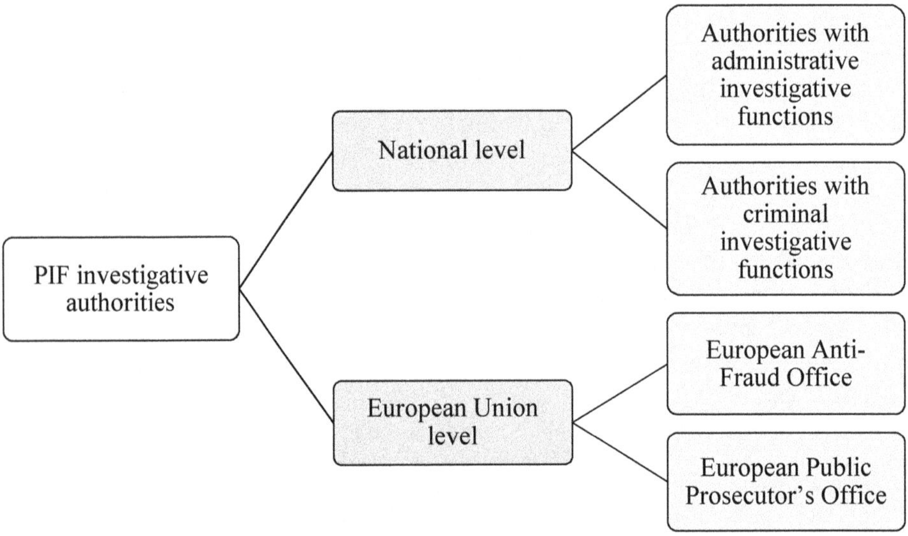

Illustration 1.4.: PIF investigative authorities.

[29] Council Regulation (EU) No. 2017/1939 of 12 October 2017 implementing enhanced co-operation on the establishment of the European Public Prosecutor's Office ('the EPPO') ('EPPO Regulation') (https://www.legal-tools.org/doc/plfszr14/).

[30] Andon Tashukov, *Fraudulent Use of EU Funds in the Field of Agriculture: Current State, Investigation and Challenges*, Policy Brief No. 82, Center for the Study of Democracy, 2019.

At the national level, PIF investigative authorities are responsible for safeguarding the EU's financial interests within individual Member States. These authorities can be broadly categorized into two groups: those with administrative investigative functions and those with criminal investigative functions. Administrative Investigative Authorities are primarily tasked with conducting administrative inquiries and audits to ensure compliance with EU regulations and policies (for example, the national Anti-Fraud Coordination Services ('AFCOS')).[31] Criminal investigative authorities, such as national law enforcement agencies, financial crime units, and prosecution authorities are responsible for probing and prosecuting criminal offences related to fraud of EU funds.

The two European authorities with a PIF-centric mandate are the following. OLAF is an independent investigative body, part of the European Commission, responsible for conducting administrative investigations into irregularities, fraud and corruption that affect EU funds. OLAF has the power to conduct its own administrative investigations (called "external"[32] – on the territory of the Member States and third countries, or "internal"[33] – regarding misconduct by EU staff). Further to conducting its own investigations, OLAF collaborates with national authorities and provides support in gathering evidence and information. However, OLAF's investigations cannot end with bringing criminal charges. Instead, when OLAF identifies facts likely to constitute criminal offences in line with Article 24 of the EPPO Regulation, it shall report these facts to the EPPO without undue delay. Member States are obligated to support OLAF administrative investigations by providing necessary information, access to data, and cooperation during investigations.[34] On the other side, OLAF will follow up with

[31] According to Article 12a of the 'OLAF Regulation' (Consolidated text of Regulation (EU, EURATOM) No. 883/2013 of the European Parliament and of the Council of 11 September 2013 concerning investigations conducted by the European Anti-Fraud Office (OLAF) and repealing Regulation (EC) No. 1073/1999 of the European Parliament and of the Council and Council Regulation (Euratom) No. 1074/1999 (https://www.legal-tools.org/doc/6f0ede/)), every EU Member State has the obligation to designate a service (the "anti-fraud coordination service") to facilitate effective co-operation and exchange of information, including information of an operational nature, with the Office. The AFCOS have a particularly important role to overcome resistance and gain access to the premises by economic operators when OLAF conducts an on-the-spot-check (see Articles 3(4), 3(5) and 3(6) and 12a of the OLAF Regulation).

[32] See Article 3, *ibid.*

[33] See Article 4 in relation with Article 1, para. 4, *ibid.*

[34] See Council Regulation (Euratom, EC) No. 2185/96 of 11 November 1996 concerning on-the-spot checks and inspections carried out by the Commission in order to protect the European Communities' financial interests against fraud and other irregularities ('Regulation 2185/96') (https://www.legal-tools.org/doc/j91442n3/).

the Member States, who are competent to enforce the recommendations that arise from its investigations.

EPPO represents a groundbreaking development in the EU's investigative landscape. It has the authority and responsibility to investigate, prosecute, and bring perpetrators of PIF offences to justice before national courts. Up until EPPO started its operations in 2021, only national authorities could investigate and prosecute PIF crimes, but their powers stopped at the borders of their country. EPPO was granted with a mandatory competence over the protection of the financial interests of the EU. This competence now bounds both national authorities and EU institutions, bodies, offices and agencies ('IBOAs') to report to the EPPO, without undue delay, any criminal conduct in respect of which it could exercise its competence.[35] The competence of EPPO spans over the offenses affecting the EU's finances, such as expenditure fraud, which includes procurement fraud, non-procurement fraud, misappropriation, corruption, revenue fraud like VAT fraud and customs fraud, as well as money laundering, organized crime and other inextricably offences to those. The ability of EPPO to function in a no-border zone, so-called 'EPPO Zone', is a revolutionary aspect of Article 31 of the EPPO Regulation, which allows European Delegated Prosecutors ('EDPs') to exercise their investigative powers across participating Member States without the need for traditional mutual legal assistance procedures.

From the perspective of law enforcement at EU level, *Europol* serves as a crucial partner to the EPPO in combating PIF fraud by providing operational and analytical support. While Europol does not have the authority to conduct criminal investigations or prosecutions, it enhances the EPPO's investigations by facilitating information-sharing, analytical support, cross-border co-ordination, and access to specialized databases. EPPO and OLAF co-operate on the basis of the principles of complementarity and non-duplication.[36] *National inspection services* are crucial in the accomplishment of OLAF's independent power to conduct on-the-spot-checks in its administrative investigations.[37]

In essence, all these (investigative) authorities create a comprehensive and collaborative framework for protecting the EU's financial interests. They contribute unique strengths to the investigative process, collectively working

[35] Article 24 of the EPPO Regulation, see *supra* note 29.

[36] See the OLAF Regulation, *supra* note 31, and specifically Articles 12d and 12e.

[37] Article 4 of Regulation 2185/96, see *supra* note 34, provides that on-the-spot checks and inspections shall be prepared and conducted by the Commission in close cooperation with the competent authorities of the Member State concerned. In practice this will often be the AFCOS, presented in footnote 31 above.

towards the common goal of preserving the integrity of EU funds and deterring financial misconduct.

1.5.3. The Different Steps of a PIF Investigation

Similar to other investigations and integrating parts of the '6 Cs' model presented earlier, the investigative process in PIF investigations involves a systematic series of steps designed to detect, prevent and address financial misconduct, irregularities and fraud. These steps are crucial for ensuring that EU funds are used in accordance with legal and regulatory frameworks. The pursuit of truth, justice, and the preservation of the EU's financial integrity always remain at the core of the investigative process.

The typical steps of a PIF investigation follow the logic of any investigation, with specific accents common to financial investigations.

The journey of a PIF investigation often begins with the receipt of initial information for suspicions of irregularity or fraudulent behaviour. The *preliminary examination* of this initial information involves a careful assessment of the provided information to determine if there are credible reasons to believe that financial misconduct may have occurred. Experts of the investigation service must evaluate the source and reliability of the information and determine if further action is warranted.

Once suspicions are substantiated during the preliminary examination, investigators move into the *planning and preparation* phase. Here, they develop a comprehensive *investigative plan* that outlines the scope, objectives and strategies for the investigation. Planning includes defining investigative goals, identifying resources, and establishing a timeline. Adequate preparation ensures that the investigation proceeds effectively and efficiently.

At the heart of any financial investigation is the *identification and collection of evidence*. Investigators meticulously gather relevant information and evidence to build a strong case. This includes reviewing financial records, conducting interviews, analysing documents, and engaging forensic accounting techniques when necessary. The goal is to establish a clear understanding of the irregularities or fraud and gather evidence to support legal action if needed.

Review is an essential step in the investigative process, where investigators assess the collected evidence, analyse findings, and verify their accuracy and relevance. This phase involves evaluating the strength of the case and identifying any gaps or areas that require further exploration. Thorough review ensures that the investigation is sound and that the evidence can withstand legal scrutiny.

The final step of a PIF investigation is the *reporting* of investigative results. Investigators compile their findings, evidence and conclusions into a comprehensive report. This report serves as a critical document that communicates the results of the investigation to relevant authorities and stakeholders. It includes details on the irregularities of fraud identified, the evidence collected, and any recommendations for corrective action or legal prosecution.

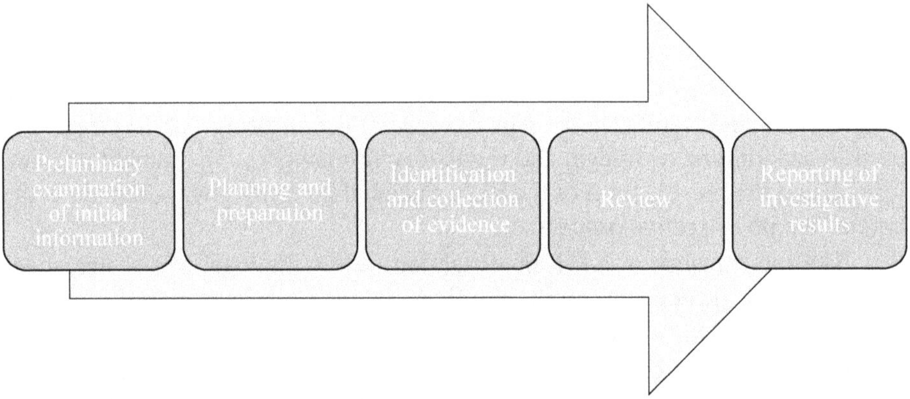

Illustration 1.5.: The different steps of the investigation process.

1.5.4. Goals of the PIF Investigation

The overarching goal of PIF investigations is to uncover the truth to protect the financial interests of the EU. To this end, the investigation of crimes affecting the financial interests of the EU serves a critical purpose. These investigations primarily aim to combat procurement fraud, non-public procurement fraud, misappropriation, corruption, VAT fraud, customs fraud and other illegal activities that undermine the financial stability and governance of the EU. By targeting such offenses, PIF investigations not only seek to recover misappropriated funds but also to deter potential wrongdoers. Other important objectives include (a) restoring trust in the EU and its Institutions and (b) implementing corrective measures.

When PIF investigations are performed by EU IBOAs, this fosters additional trust in the EU, which is paramount. Upholding the highest standards in financial investigations not only safeguards EU funds, but also strengthens the confidence in the EU's ability to protect its financial interests.[38]

[38] To uphold public trust in the investigative authorities, the seizure and confiscating of the proceeds of criminal activity and the recovery of unduly paid sums, are of a particular importance. Quite alarming in this respect is that in a 2020 report, Europol asserts that "today, more than 98% of criminal assets are still not recovered" (see Europol, European Financial and Economic Crime Centre, "Enterprising Criminals: Europe's Fight Against the Global Networks of Financial and Economic Crime", 2020, p. 37). Even the best performing agencies, such as the American Securities and Exchange Commission, collect only about 45 per cent of their outstanding fines and penalties (see Van Rooij and Fine, 2021, p. 37, see *supra* note 10).

In addition to uncovering fraud through PIF investigations, prosecution and bringing to judgement of the perpetrators, implementing asset-recovery measures is also crucial to remedy the established wrongdoings and deter potential fraudsters. Other corrective measures include establishing mechanisms for addressing deficient legislation, correcting procedural errors, and perpetually monitoring for possible improvements to the investigative processes. Such remedial action does not only enhance the quality of individual investigations but also contributes to the overall integrity and trustworthiness of the EU's financial oversight system.

Overall, the investigation should ensure that EU funds are safeguarded, wrongdoers are held accountable, and that the integrity of the financial system is maintained, while being guided by the principles of accuracy, legality, and ethical conduct.

1.5.5. The Distinctive Nature of PIF Investigations

PIF investigations are classified as financial investigations. They differ from other forms of enquiries, such as common criminal investigations or audits, due to their specific focus on financial irregularities and fraud. This distinction typically makes for a demanding investigative environment, including:

- a specific regulatory setting: PIF investigations are guided by EU law and policies, which necessitate a deep understanding of EU laws and compliance requirements;
- a cross-border element: PIF investigations typically transcend national borders in terms of place of damage and fraudulent activity, thus becoming transnational investigations by nature;
- a revolutionary legal provision: Article 31 of the EPPO regulation creates a no-border zone, in which no need for traditional mutual assistance measures arises;
- complex financial constructs: PIF investigations often involve intricate financial constructions and transactions, making them more complex than traditional criminal investigations. The need to decipher convoluted financial schemes adds an additional layer of intricacy, such as in complex VAT schemes;
- an enhanced need for subject-matter expertise: investigators must possess expertise in financial matters, including forensic accounting and financial analysis. This specialized knowledge also extends to other domains like procurement rules and is essential for unravelling complex financial schemes and identifying irregularities effectively.

By contrast to other investigations, PIF investigations might seem less prone to a falsification and hypotheses-testing approach, as presented above.

The main alternative scenarios are indeed often reduced to either a case of irregularity (a violation of a rule with financial implications), or a case of fraud (including guilty intent). The suspect(s) of the alleged offence or irregularity is (are) typically known at an early stage and the motive involved is often financial. These characteristics might seem to undermine the efficiency of extensive hypotheses development and testing, especially compared to cases in which different suspects and motives for a crime exist.[39] However, regardless of the outcome of such debate,[40] there is no doubt that an open, evidence-based mindset will always contribute to the quality of any investigation.

1.5.6. Specific Knowledge and Skillsets

The '6 Cs' model is a systematic approach to investigation informed by critical and iterative thinking. Applying this model correctly, helps ensure investigators perform at the very highest levels throughout the life cycle of the investigation. This includes correctly interpreting relevant law and recognizing offences, effectively handling evidence, using appropriate forensic tools for evidence analysis, interviewing effectively, and preparing and presenting solid cases.

The complex nature and demands of PIF investigations require significant specialized knowledge, expertise, and sophisticated skillsets. This necessitates specialized training and continuous capacity building, in particular regarding EU rules and practices, forensic accounting, and cross-border co-operation.

1.6. Concluding Remarks

In this first chapter, we introduced a number of foundational concepts and proposals concerning the investigative process in general, and the specificities of PIF investigations in particular. Some of these propositions are further developed in subsequent chapters, and many of our proposals are invitations for further consideration, research and debate.

The highlights of the previous chapter are as follows:

- Investigating is a sequence of progressive activities to determine how events occurred, and to establish an evidence-based fact-pattern to prove or disprove wrongdoing and responsibilities of the actors involved. Ultimately, we need to know 'Who, What, Where, When, Why and How?'.

---

39 However, see the United Nations handbook for prosecutors and investigators of corruption cases, holding that (emphasis added) "[i]nvestigators develop *theories* about what an individual item of information may mean and how the various pieces may fit together, but such theories may require refinement as an investigation proceeds" (see United Nations, "United Nations Handbook on Practical Anti-Corruption Measures for Prosecutors and Investigators", 2004, p. 39)

40 See Chapters 7 and 10 for sections revisiting the question of hypotheses testing in PIF investigations.

- As opposed to criminal investigations, administrative investigations do not entail the use of coercive measures, but both of them use a fact-finding approach.
- A typical investigation entails a preliminary examination of initial information, a planning- and preparation-phase, the collection and analysis of evidence, and the formulation of investigative results.
- The '6 Cs' model provides for an iterative analytical process meant to guarantee a sound investigative process and efficient structuring of the essential fact-finding procedures. It compensates for the limitations of the human brain – which often pushes us to 'quick and messy' decision-making – by, among other things, using abduction and cross-checking as key operating principles.
- PIF investigations are marked by complexity. This includes the regulatory setting, the various modes of expenditure and revenue, and the intricate landscape of all national and European actors involved. Such complexity places very high demands on investigative authorities, who are also expected to restore public trust and propose remedial action as an outcome of their investigation.
- Key legal concepts in PIF investigations are (suspicions of) irregularity and fraud. These two competing hypotheses are divided by guilty intent.
- Conducting PIF investigations requires the investigator to have high standards across various domains, including solid (legal) knowledge, expertise in financial investigations, and sound, critical thinking skills. Continual training and regularly updated standard operating procedures should ensure such quality.
- A good start is to visualize and document ideas, actions, findings and judgements, writing everything down and then looking for patterns without jumping to conclusions. This will foster especially systematic briefings and productive interactions with others.
- The protection of EU's financial interests has recently evolved into the creation of a transnationally operating EU body, EPPO, with mandatory competence over PIF crimes. National authorities and EU IBOAs co-operate and are bound to report criminal conduct in respect of which EPPO can exercise its competence.

2

The Investigative Mindset

Tom Willems, Milanka Jug and Marian-Vladut Cozma*

2.1. Introduction

Investigators need to plan their investigation, make strategic and tactical decisions, prepare for interviews, and write a comprehensive report, supported by the facts. In sum, they need to think well before acting. This does not come easy. Investigators are often confronted with a large set of complex, ambiguous and sometimes even contradictory information. Not only must they make sense of this multifaceted information, they must also use it as a basis for making decisions with often significant consequences.

In this chapter, we explore the nature of this type of thinking and examine what constitutes a good investigative mindset. We address a number of questions related to the particularities of investigation contexts, including whether there are any specific qualities of thinking an investigator should master, about the basics of the way investigators think, and the role of intuition.

2.2. Thinking

In order to gain a better understanding of the investigation process, it is important to study the psychological underpinnings of an investigator's judgment and decision-making.[1] Judgment and decision-making are forms of conscious and directed thinking, when our flow of thoughts is aimed at a particular goal (as opposed to, for instance 'day-dreaming'). Other forms of directed thinking are reasoning and problem-solving.[2]

Judging, as understood here, happens when a person has to assign odds or estimate the likelihood of a given event in an uncertain context, as in: 'What is

---

* **Tom Willems** is co-ordinator for inter-institutional relations at the European Anti-Fraud Office ('OLAF'). Dr. **Milanka Jug** is Senior Case analyst and Team Coordinator at the European Public Prosecutor's Office ('EPPO'). **Marian-Vladut Cozma** is Senior Financial Investigator at EPPO. This chapter is authored in the contributors' personal capacity and does not necessarily reflect the views of EPPO, OLAF or other institutions mentioned therein.

1 Ivar Fahsing, "Beyond Reasonable Doubt: How to Think Like an Expert Detective", in Paulo Barbosa Marquez and Mauro Paulino (eds.) *Police Psychology*, Elsevier Academic Press, Cambridge, 2022, p. 267.

2 Henry Gleitman, James J. Gross and Daniel Reisberg, *Psychology*, 8th ed., W.W. Norton & Company, New York, 2011.

the likelihood this person is telling us everything he knows?' or 'Do we need to investigate more or do we have enough information about the offence?'. In other words, judging involves probabilities. These are often subjective probability assessments, as is the case when individuals are trying to assess the credibility of new information or the likelihood of an event, given their previous information and experience.

Reasoning refers to the application of decision-making rules like induction, deduction or abduction.[3] It is the process of figuring out the implications of particular beliefs, which helps predict what will happen under new conditions.[4] When a person behaves based on reasoning, he or she knows what they are doing and why they are doing it. He or she has a conscious access to the operative rule, the rule that maps the relevant features of the situation onto a suitable behaviour.

A decision is a commitment to a course of action taken to achieve a certain point. The field of decision-making explores what people do after they form some judgment – after they knew, or thought they knew, the odds.[5] Not every judgment is followed by a decision, but every decision implies some judgment.[6] It concerns thinking prior to action.

Finally, when our thinking is aimed at a particular goal and we are considering the sequence of steps that will lead us to it, we are problem-solving. Its objective is to resolve problems with a definite and recognizable solution, using effective methods.

Conscious thinking[7] relies on processes of attention, memory and language, and is continuously influenced by our immediate context. A typical sequence is that our attention is triggered by a perceptual cue (for example, hearing a question during interview), we think about ('process') the request, and decide what to do before we act (for example, tell the truth or lie). This decision is influenced by circumstances like (remaining with the example of an interview) fatigue, social expectations or the behaviour of the interviewer. Emmerling summarizes the process in his behavioural circle.[8]

---

3 See Chapter 1.

4 Steven Sloman and Philip Fernbach, *The Knowledge Illusion: Why We Never Think Alone*, Riverhead Books, New York, 2017, p. 11.

5 Michael Lewis, *The Undoing Project*, New York, W.W. Norton and Company, 2017, p. 252.

6 *Ibid.*, p. 251.

7 See Chapter 3 for the impact of unconscious thinking on our judgment- and decision-making.

8 Torben Emmerling, "D.R.I.V.E.: A Practical Framework for Applying Behavioural Science in Strategy", in Alain Samson (ed.), *The Behavioral Economics Guide 2018*, 2018, p. 38.

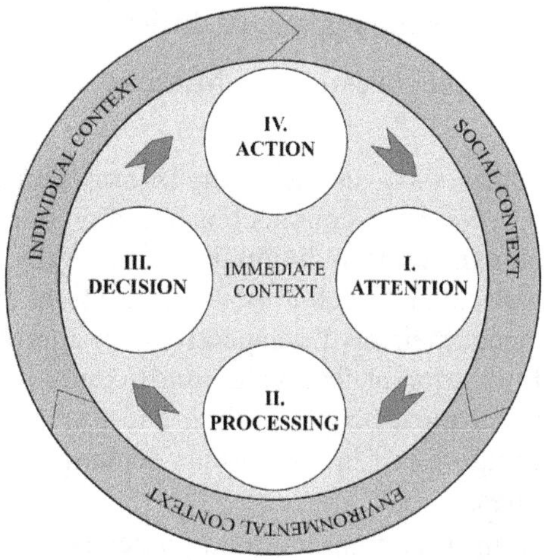

Illustration 2.1.: The behavioural cycle.

2.3. Thinking During Investigations

Any investigation, whether complex or straightforward, involves answering three interrelated questions: (a) what happened; (b) who did it; and (c) can it be proven (beyond reasonable doubt)?[9] In essence, the investigator must assess the validity of the information available to guide the investigative process, strive to move from a position of mere suspicion to one of reasonable certainty, and ultimately articulate evidence upon which the court can make a finding of guilt (beyond a reasonable doubt). This makes for a multifaceted thinking challenge, entailing a continuous series of judgments (for example, 'can I trust the source?'), decision-making (for example, 'should we conduct the search now?') and reasoning (for example, 'can we infer guilty intent from the pattern that we see?'). This thinking is often based on limited information and occurs in a dynamic environment.

Thus, in addition to a set of specific investigative skills, investigators need thinking capabilities enabling them to cope with complex situations, typically embedded in a great deal of uncertainty. To become an effective investigator, these skills need to be consciously understood and internalized so that they become deliberate, consistent aspects of the problem-solving process of fact-finding that is an investigation. Because our everyday thinking tends to be much less formal and evidence-based than what is required of an investigation,

[9] Fahsing, 2022, p. 270, see *supra* note 1.

internalizing the necessary reasoning habits, making these skills necessary aspects of our investigative repertoires, can be difficult.

2.4. In Search of the Right Investigative Mindset

2.4.1. The Challenges

People are constantly processing and assessing information to build their understanding of the world.[10] We draw conclusions based on our perceptions and the information we encounter. Some individuals are naturally inclined to adopt a fairly critical and analytical approach to new information, actively seeking evidence to support or reject their own perspectives. In contrast, others are more inclined to accept information at face value until contradicted by facts. Either approach may suffice for most people in their day-to-day interactions, but the rigour and discipline required of investigations demand more developed thinking skills and procedures.

While investigating, investigators often gather large and complex sets of data, find ambiguous and contradictory information, and develop theories of what happened. This analysis and its interpretation establish reasonable grounds to believe a given assertion[11] that then informs follow-up recommendations and decisions. To succeed in this challenging thinking task, practitioners need to develop and maintain a productive 'investigative mindset'. The latter term is used to describe a systematic mental attitude of investigators underpinning an effective investigation, and entails a number of critical thinking skills, both 'soft' (for example, open-mindedness) and 'hard' (such as deductive reasoning).

So far, both research and applied guides, including investigative manuals, have emphasized the particular importance for investigators to, for instance, be open-minded and consider ideas and opinions that are new or different from their own. They are also regularly counselled to be aware that their judgments are works in progress,[12] and so they should actively search for information that contradicts their pre-existing hypotheses[13] and be willing to change their opinion based on new facts and pieces of evidence.[14] Additionally, strong analytical thinking skills are key. They are crucial, for instance, in recognizing the possible

---

[10] Keith S. Taber, "Beyond Constructivism: The Progressive Research Programme into Learning Science", in *Studies in Science Education*, 2006, vol. 42, no. 1, pp. 125–184.

[11] Rod Gehl and Darryl Plecas, *Introduction to Criminal Investigation: Processes, Practices and Thinking*, Justice Institute of British Columbia, New Westminster, 2016, p. 47.

[12] Daniel Kahneman, Olivier Sibony and Cas Sunstein, *Noise: A Flaw in Human Judgment*, William Collins, London, 2021, p. 234.

[13] *Ibid.*

[14] Christer Sturmark, *The Flame of Reason: Clear Thinking for the Twenty-First Century*, Head of Zeus, London, 2022, p. 7.

offence depicted by the fact pattern ('offence recognition') and critically analysing all available information and evidence.

Another important aspect of the investigative mindset is the capacity to draw correct conclusions, given competing, often even conflicting, information and evidence.[15] The investigator must be able to evaluate the likelihood of different possible inferences based on the evidence at hand, and apply sound logic to reach the most appropriate conclusion.[16] In this respect, it is also important for criminal investigators to be able to articulate their thinking process. This enables them to illustrate their evidence-based path, leading from often disparate pieces of information to the formation of reasonable grounds for a given belief and subsequent action.

An *assumption* is something we usually take for granted or presuppose ("*I believe that...*"), while	an *inference* is a conclusion you draw depending on your observations. The main difference between assumption and inference is that we make assumptions without any evidence or facts, while we make inferences based on facts and evidence.

Illustration 2.2.: To infer or to assume?

In sum, a productive investigative mindset can be summarized in four terms: (a) open, (b) critical, (c) strategic, and (d) evidence-based.

Yet, multidisciplinary scientific research suggests that humans, including investigators, often fail to apply such characteristics, and that this can have serious negative consequences. For example, in criminal investigations it can result in wrongful suspicions or dismissals of guilty individuals as suspects, inefficient use of resources (money as well as time), and ultimately it can also undermine the legitimacy of the criminal case procedure, as this should be guided by objectivity and neutrality.

2.4.2. 'Open' Thinking

Criminal investigations should be conducted in a broad and neutral way, not just because legal principles guiding criminal investigations require this, but also

[15] Teresa Curmi, "Investigative Decision Making and Its Association With Critical Thinking Skills, Thinking Styles, and Law Enforcement Experience", Ph.D. Thesis, City University of New York, 2021, p. 117.

[16] *Ibid.*, p. 121.

because it is most likely to lead to accurate results.[17] Although the investigator should refrain from drawing conclusions until the facts have been established, psychological research and reviews of investigative processes demonstrate that criminal investigators often do not have an open mindset. For example, they sometimes form a hypothesis about the identity of a perpetrator or a criminal conduct very early on in an enquiry (for example, 'this is a case of fraud! Not an irregularity!') and thereafter the investigation's purpose is simply to confirm that the hypothesis is correct, a tendency referred to as *confirmation bias*.[18]

Confirmation bias can occur in relation to any hypothesis, regardless of whether it is correct. On the face of it, it would seem the interest of preventing confirmation bias is greater when it leads investigators to believe an incorrect hypothesis. However, whether a hypothesis is incorrect or correct is rarely known during the investigation, and the legal duty criminal investigators have to remain open-minded, to consider both incriminating and exonerating circumstances, and to presume innocence, applies throughout the investigation. Specifically, applicable laws require that judgment on the veracity of the hypothesis is postponed during the investigation. Hence, preventing confirmation bias is not only about ensuring appropriately rigorous investigative reasoning standards, but also about safeguarding the integrity of the procedure.

2.4.3. Any Role for Intuition?

In the realm of law enforcement, the 'police hunch' has long been a mysterious but crucial aspect of decision-making.[19] Contemporary reasoning scholars insist confirmation bias is one of the most common ways that intuitive decision-making can lead to judgment errors,[20] and should therefore be avoided in matters of investigation. One understanding of intuition is that it concerns a form of knowledge that appears in consciousness without obvious deliberation, based

---

17 See, for example, Erik Rassin, Anita Eerland and Ilse Kujpers, "Let's Find the Evidence: An Analogue Study of Confirmation Bias in Criminal Investigations", in *Journal of Investigative Psychology and Offender Profiling*, 2010, vol. 7, no. 3, pp. 231–246.

18 See Chapter 3 for more details on confirmation bias.

19 Gareth Stubbs and Karl Friston, "The Police Hunch: The Bayesian Brain, Active Inference, and the Free Energy Principle in Action", in *Frontiers in Psychology*, 2024, vol. 15, p. 1.

20 Reference can be made to two competing schools of thought. On the one hand the 'heuristic-cognitive biases' school of Kahneman and others holds that intuitive thinking can be efficient, but at the expense of accuracy and often leading to systematic thinking errors. On the other hand, there is the 'fast and frugal' school of Gigerenzer, claiming intuitive decision-making via heuristics is, in fact, very performant (see, for example, Daniel Kahneman, *Thinking, Fast and Slow*, Farrar, Straus and Giroux, New York, 2011, and Gerd Gigerenzer, *Gut Feelings: Short Cuts to Better Decision Making*, Penguin Books, London, 2007).

on the recognition of patterns gained through experience.[21] These 'gut feelings' are believed to arise through rapid and holistic associations from cues in the environment, when the brain makes a substantial match (or mismatch) between a lived experience and the current experience.[22]

Research on confirmation bias hence connects to what is referred to as 'skilled intuition', a label used to indicate instances of efficient intuitive decision-making.[23] Researchers seem to agree that even when decision makers are unaware of the cues that guide them, they can make accurate decisions when three conditions are satisfied: (a) an environment providing adequately valid cues to recognize later; (b) adequate opportunity to learn the relevant cues; and (c) practice of the skill.

Researchers found that after at least 10,000 hours of practice, chess masters acquire a repertoire of up to 100,000 immediately recognizable patterns, enabling them to identify a good move without having to calculate all possible contingencies.

Illustration 2.3.: Skilled intuition at play.[24]

The example above helps to understand the limitations of intuition in investigation. The learning environment of the investigator is significantly different from the chess grandmaster. A chess-player who learns to intuitively identify the best next move has done so on the basis of a large number of 'trial and error' runs, receiving feedback about the merits of their moves relatively immediately, at least by the end of the match. By contrast, the investigator rarely gets direct feedback on whether his or her intuition was correct. So even if an experienced

21 See, for example, Hugo Mercier and Dan Sperber, *The Enigma of Reason: A New Theory of Human Understanding*, Allen Lane, London, 2017, p. 133; Robert J. Girod, *Logical Investigative Methods*, CRC Press, Taylor and Francis Group, Boca Raton, 2015, p. 3; Mathilda Gerber, B.L. William Wong and Neesha Kodagoda, "How Analysts Think: What Triggers Insight?", presented during the thirteenth International conference on Naturalistic Decision Making in 2017.

22 Erik Dane and Michael Pratt, "Exploring Intuition and Its Role in Managerial Decision Making", in *Academy of Management Review*, 2007, vol. 32, no. 1, p. 40.

23 Daniel Kahneman and Gary Klein, "Conditions for Intuitive Expertise: A Failure to Disagree", in *American Psychologist*, 2009, vol. 64, no. 6, pp. 515–526.

24 William G. Chase and Herbert Simon, "The Mind's Eye in Chess", in William G. Chase (ed.) *Visual Information Processing*, Academic Press, New York, 1973, pp. 215–281.

criminal investigator spends over 10,000 hours working on investigations, he or she will have received far less immediate feedback than the chess player. This is partly because of completely different time frames and partly because of differences in availability of the 'ground truth' between a game of chess and a criminal investigation.

Moreover, the skilled intuition one develops in a given domain might not generalize to another, though both are included in the investigative field. For example, auditors who have expertise in 'hard data', like evaluating accounts receivable, may do less well with 'soft' data such as indications of fraud.[25]

Concluding on this topic, we thus propose that intuition is not always bad, in the sense that it always results in the wrong answers. However, relying significantly on intuition in criminal investigations puts the integrity of the procedure at risk.

2.4.4. Critical Thinking

There is consensus that investigations should be based on 'critical thinking'.[26] While many definitions have been suggested, most researchers agree that this refers to a person's ability to regulate their judgments and reasoning, analytically evaluating and incorporating information and evidence into their thought processes, while maintaining an open mind for new ideas and alternative perspectives.[27]

Some initial dispositions that are key to critical thinking include attentiveness, a habit of inquiry, willingness to suspend judgment, trust in reason, and wanting evidence for one's beliefs, among many others. It also implies the willingness to persist in a complex (cognitive) task and to abandon non-productive strategies in an attempt to self-correct.

Key qualities of critical thinking include:[28]

- critical enquiry, including argument evaluation, clarifying meanings of terms and statements, evaluating authorities and sources, and examining plausible alternatives;

---

25 Kahneman and Klein, 2009, p. 522, see *supra* note 23.

26 See, for example, Curmi, 2021, p. 22, see *supra* note 15; Gehl and Plecas, 2016, pp. 7–8, see *supra* note 11; see also Chapter 1.

27 Peter A. Facione, "Critical Thinking: A Statement of Expert Consensus for Purposes of Educational Assessment and Instruction", Committee on Pre-College Philosophy of the American Philosophical Association, California Academic Press, Millbrae, 1990, p. 3.

28 *Ibid.*, p. 3; Peter A. Facione, "The Disposition Toward Critical Thinking: Its Character, Measurement, and Relationship to Critical Thinking Skill", in *Informal Logic*, 2000, vol. 20, no. 1, pp. 61–84.

- reflective judgment, demonstrated by, for instance, being honest in facing personal biases, prudent in drawing conclusions, and diligent in seeking relevant information;
- cognitive skills that include analysis, interpretation, inference-making, explanation and evaluation; and
- the open-mindedness to monitor and correct one's own reasoning.

Echoing a claim made earlier concerning the 'ABC' of investigation,[29] routines and procedures can mitigate the risks of erroneous individual thinking. Tools with acronyms like the 'RED' model of critical thinking[30] can be useful in providing hands-on practical guidance to a sound thinking stance, where the acronym means:

R	Recognizing assumptions;
E	Evaluating arguments;
D	Drawing conclusions.

Illustration 2.4: The 'RED' Model.

2.4.5. Challenges for Open and Critical Thinking

The rigorous critical thinking skills depicted above are very demanding and may, at points, be beyond the investigator's capacities. Although we all think we are able to be honest, prudent, diligent, *et cetera*, in our judgments and decisions, research demonstrates time and again that investigators, like all other humans, are prone to error.[31] Open and critical thinking does not necessarily come easily. Regardless of education, most of us have never actually learned how to think formally or to explicitly explain how we came to make our choices. Most people are, in general, not particularly good at rigorous, formal reasoning, and critical thinking skills are not part of most traditional learning curriculum for investigators. The latter are expected to develop investigative thinking skills through field experience, learning from mistakes, and on-the-job mentoring.[32]

However, open-mindedness and metacognition, the ability to think about thinking, can be learned.[33] Every investigator can work towards developing and refining the skills necessary to be (more) conscious of his or her own thinking

---

29 See Chapter 1 for the recommendation for investigators to '**A**ssume nothing', '**B**elieve nothing' and '**C**hallenge and **C**heck' everything.

30 Goodwin Watson and Edwin Glaser, *Watson-Glaser II Critical Thinking Appraisal: Technical Manual and User's Guide*, Pearson, London, 2010.

31 See Chapter 3 on bias.

32 Gehl and Plecas, 2016, p. 3, see *supra* note 11.

33 Kahneman, Sibony and Sunstein, 2021, p. 234, see *supra* note 12.

processes and, consequently, become a better investigator.[34] Active open-mindedness is a teachable skill and essentially involves actively searching for information that contradicts one's pre-existing hypotheses.[35] Likewise, critical thinking is a learned skill, and investigators can – and must – develop it in light of the accelerating complexity facing the criminal justice system.[36]

But even if investigators were fully capable of continuously engaging in open and critical thinking, this process remains a conscious one. Since biases, including confirmation bias and the like, often operate on a subconscious level,[37] conscious efforts to counteract them will often simply not be enough. This means that even criminal investigators and prosecutors who have high standards of professionalism, motivation, and skill are not immune to occasional narrow-mindedness and various cognitive biases.

2.4.6. Strategic Thinking

'Open thinking' should not be confused with naivety or gullibility. Balancing between keeping an open mind – that is, being willing to accept that there might be other explanations than those which your brain pushes you to accept – and critical thinking is challenging enough on its own. It becomes even more complicated when adapting the clinical concept of '*thinking dirty*'[38] to investigations, which involves taking a sceptical stance towards what is coming from the suspect by default.[39]

---

[34] Gehl and Plecas, 2016, see *supra* note 11, p. 8.

[35] Kahneman, Sibony and Sunstein, 2021, p. 234, see *supra* note 12; Jonathan Baron, "Actively Open-Minded Thinking", in *id.*, *Thinking and Deciding*, 4th ed., Cambridge University Press, 2008, pp. 199–232.

[36] Wesley E. Phillips and Darrell N. Burrell, "Decision-Making Skills That Encompass a Critical Thinking Orientation for Law Enforcement Professionals", in *International Journal of Police Science and Management*, 2009, vol. 11, no. 2, pp. 141–149.

[37] See Chapter 3 for more detail.

[38] In a setting of therapeutic conversations (with psychiatric patients), 'thinking dirty' is described as "recognizing hidden motivations and being alert to unseemly, distressing, or even pathologic reasons for patients to deceive or withhold information from their providers. It is essentially a maxim to take nothing at face value, to be alert to the presence of deception, and also to be interested in the patient's motives. Thinking dirty also means recognizing that many patients deceive clinicians for reasons involving stigma, shame, and fear that are not necessarily pathologic", see Scott Beach, John B. Taylor and Nicholas Kontos, "Teaching Psychiatric Trainees to 'Think Dirty': Uncovering Hidden Motivations and Deception", in *Psychosomatics*, 2017, vol. 58, no. 5, pp. 474–475.

[39] Irena Bošković, "Trust, Doubt, and Symptom Validity", in Sara Landström, Pär Anders Granhag and Peter J. van Koppen (eds.), *The Future of Forensic Psychology*, Routledge, Abingdon, 2022, p. 136.

The middle ground can be found in the concept of 'strategic thinking'. This term is used to refer to methodical thinking that takes into account the possible decisions, actions and reactions of another actor. It relates to game theory, which underscores the necessity of putting yourself in the other player's shoes in order to obtain your objective(s).[40] From this perspective, the investigator should think strategically throughout the investigation and consider (all) possible behaviours by the suspect. For example, when an investigator prepares questions for an interview, she should anticipate in some depth the possible answers and counter-strategies of the interviewee.[41] Such an approach is particularly relevant in PIF interviews, which have suspects that are typically eloquent, assertive and persuasive, often leading to strategic and 'negotiated' but conclusive interviews at the end of the investigation.[42]

While the ability to think strategically is in part related to training, as for example in interviewing, it is also, in part, contingent on the investigator's emotional intelligence, the ability to understand and predict emotional reactions of others.[43]

2.4.7. Evidence-Based Thinking

Criminal evidence is by its very nature multidisciplinary. There are a number of scientific disciplines that are directly relevant to criminal investigations but that investigators often know little about, especially psychology, forensic genetics, forensic medicine, and digital forensics. To learn about and actively integrate such knowledge in decision-making during criminal investigations, is as crucial to criminal law as staying abreast of medical literature is to physicians prescribing medicines. Investigative fields in which such an evidence-based approach is particularly productive include interviewing, forensics and digital investigations.

As regards the first, interviewing should be approached with an investigative mindset and communication that establishes rapport and trust, aiming to

---

[40] See, for example, Avinash K. Dixit and Barry J. Nalebuff, *The Art of Strategy*, W.W. Norton & Company, New York-London, 2007.

[41] For an interviewing technique embracing this approach, see, for example, Maria Hartwig, Pär Anders Granhag and Timothy Luke, "Strategic Use of Evidence During Investigative Interviews", in David C. Raskin, Charles R. Honts and John, Kircher (eds.) *Credibility Assessment: Scientific Research and Applications*, Academic Press, Waltham, 2014. For a recent article proposing Game Theory as an appropriate canvas to analyse interviewing behaviour of the suspect and develop contingent interviewing tactics, see Andréanne Bergeron, Francis Fortin and Nadine Deslauriers-Varin, "Toward a New Theoretical and Methodological Understanding of Investigative Interviews", in *Research and Practice*, 2023, vol. 13, no. 1, pp. 59–78.

[42] See, for example, Manon Hoekstra, *Investigative Interviewing of High-Status Fraud Suspects: Distinctive Features*, Dutch Ministry of Finance, 2017.

[43] Daniel Goleman, *Emotional Intelligence*, Bantam Books, New York, 1997.

facilitate memory retrieval and to properly assess the credibility of the information. When dealing with human sources like victims, witnesses or suspects, investigators must avoid making judgements about their reliability and the credibility of the information they provide, based solely on lifestyle or previous offence history or associates, as these may not be relevant to the investigation. Such factors have the potential to adversely affect the quality of the evaluation. Researchers have identified three fundamental challenges to eliciting the truth in these contexts: (i) investigative biases, (ii) the frailty of human memory, and (iii) resistance to providing information.[44] Therefore, the accounts obtained from the interviewee should always be cross-checked for independent corroboration. Research has shown that the mindset of an investigator with tunnel vision, and in particular their investigative hypothesis, can dramatically influence the way they question a subject, the information and behaviours they elicit from the subject in response, and their assessments of the subject's credibility.[45] Moreover, suggestive or leading questions by an interviewer can produce errors in memory reporting by witnesses.

Like any other investigative measure, interviews should be well planned and prepared, taking into account the risks and pitfalls of narrow-minded and biased thinking. Moreover, the interviewer should always remain open-minded without becoming gullible, critically assessing every piece of information in support of a corroboration or disproval of the information already available.

2.5. Concluding Remarks

Investigating puts high demands on clear and sound thinking. This is particularly the case in PIF investigations, which tend to be very complex. Thus, defining the 'right mindset' of a good (PIF) investigator is not an easy task. He or she should aim to remain critical, always questioning his or her own assumptions while carefully evaluating the evidence, constantly striving for open-mindedness, which even includes searching for explanations contrary to those that come easily to mind.

The above-mentioned research and practical field experience underscore the qualities that characterize excellent investigators, which include being a

44 Christian Meissner *et al.*, "Investigative Interviewing: A Review of the Literature and a Model of Science-Based Practice", in David DeMatteo and Kyle C. Scherr (eds.) *The Oxford Handbook of Psychology and Law*, Oxford University Press, 2023, pp. 582–603.

45 Karl Ask and Ivar Fahsing, "Investigative Decision Making", in Ray Bull and Iris Blandon-Gitlin (eds.), *The Routledge International Handbook of Legal and Investigative Psychology*, Routledge, Abingdon, 2019, pp. 84–101.

flexible thinker who is aware of the risks of intuitive responses and trained in the process of critical thinking.[46]

The key points to keep in mind include the following:

- Our thinking is influenced to a large extent by subconscious thinking processes and our own subjective states. Intuitive thinking is automatic and comfortable; however, it tends to lead to good decision-making only in conditions of regularity and predictability. Such patterned contexts allow investigators to develop real expertise, but can lead to overconfidence.
- Good investigative thinking builds on four pillars:
  a) being open to all hypotheses;
  b) being critical;
  c) being strategic; and
  d) relying on scientific, empirical findings (evidence-based).

  These factors are mutually reinforcing. For example, an investigator who knows that there are very few, if any, reliable cues to deception is more likely to maintain an open mindset in relation to a suspect during interviewing.
- The ability to draw conclusions and to justify and articulate the reasoning process that leads to them is a particularly important quality for the investigator.
- By applying the 'ABC' of investigations, investigators may be more critical in their job than people usually are in daily life, but this should not close their mind. Rather than 'thinking dirty', they should think strategically.
- Anyone can work towards developing and refining his or her thinking skills to become a good investigator.
- Critical thinking (in complex investigations) sets thinking challenges which often exceed the limits of our mental capacities. We need to acknowledge this and, in order to further safeguard the investigative mindset, the investigation process should provide methods, tools and structures to help us overcome these frailties of human judgment and decision-making.

[46] Gehl and Plecas, 2016, see *supra* note 11, pp. 7–8.

3

'Noise' in Investigations

Darren Frey, Charidimos Chaloftis and Tom Willems[*]

3.1. Introduction

Research on human judgment and decision-making suggests that objectivity is essentially impossible in most contexts, and that most people, most of the time, act in ways that systematically depart from strict, normative, logical and rational[1] considerations, even when they know the relevant reasoning rules in the abstract.[2] From a vast body of scientific literature, two phenomena affecting rational thought deserve particular attention: (a) unwanted variability (or 'noise') in judgments and decisions, due to individual subjectivity and group processes (explained in this chapter), and (b) automatic or reflexive thinking based on intuitive cognitive shortcuts (or 'heuristics'), which leads to cognitive biases.[3]

The investigative process, and investigators themselves, are not immune to these sorts of reasoning errors and so sometimes violate the expectations of fairness and consistency required of all investigative and judicial bodies.[4] For

[*] Dr. **Darren Frey** is Lecturer in Behavioral Economics and Cognitive Sciences (Sciences Po). **Charidimos Chaloftis** is a Senior Financial Investigator at the European Public Prosecutor's Office ('EPPO'). **Tom Willems** is co-ordinator for inter-institutional relations at the European Anti-Fraud Office ('OLAF'). This chapter is authored in the contributors' personal capacity and does not necessarily reflect the views of EPPO, OLAF or other institutions mentioned therein.

[1] The concept of rationality has changed over time. It was often assumed in social science and economics that people know what they want, take into account all (and only) relevant information, make accurate use of the rules of probability and logical inferences, and carefully consider all options before making decisions maximizing the satisfaction of their desires (Eyal Zamir and Doron Teichman, *Behavioral Law and Economics*, Oxford University Press, 2018, p. 10). This rational choice theory (Gary S. Becker, *The Economic Approach to Human Behavior*, University of Chicago Press, 1976) has given way to a different, real world standard of rationality, to be measured by 'the extent decisions achieve the goals and objectives set' (Ken Manktelow, *Reasoning and Thinking*, The Psychology Press, Hove, 1999).

[2] Ivar Fahsing, "Beyond Reasonable Doubt: How to Think Like an Expert Detective", in Paulo Barbosa Marquez and Mauro Paulino (eds.) *Police Psychology*, Elsevier Academic Press, Cambridge, 2022, p. 272.

[3] See Chapter 4.

[4] For research indicating how judicial decision-making deviates from 'rational' standards, see, for example, Mandeep K. Dhami and Ian K. Belton, "On Getting Inside the Judge's Mind", in

example, the assessment of the credibility of a given complaint or the determination of a financial sanction[5] are often matters about which equally competent, reasonable investigators might disagree. Furthermore, any investigator may be affected by tunnel vision.

Although it is tempting, even admirable, to seek to completely avoid these hard-wired thinking flaws, decades of research across countless geographies and cultures demonstrates the impossibility of this ideal. A more fruitful and feasible tactic is to educate for awareness of their occurrence and work toward devising adequate remedial actions and structures aimed at mitigating their impact.

In this chapter, we set out recurrent challenges for objective, consistent and coherent judgment and decision-making during investigations. The primary questions we address here include: Why are there so many differing interpretations of the information in front of us? How much variation is acceptable? Is there a way of avoiding too much unwarranted variation in the approach of the investigation?

3.2. Noise

3.2.1. Description

Matters of judgment[6] (for example, reporting allegations or opening an investigation) are characterized by an expectation of bounded disagreement.[7] Perfect accuracy and consistency are never achieved, but there is a limit to how much disagreement is admissible. A 'judgment call' implies the possibility of disagreement in a setting where people believe they should agree. It sets it apart from matters of preference, opinion or taste, in which unresolved differences are entirely acceptable.[8]

Unwanted variability in judgments that should be identical, or at least relatively close, is called 'noise'.[9] An illusion of agreement in organizational contexts causes noise to be systematically underrated: professional judges and the

Translational Issues in Psychological Sciences, 2017, vol. 3, no. 2, pp. 214–226, and research quoted there.

5 Michael D. Risinger, "Unsafe Verdicts: The Need for Reformed Standards for the Trial and Review of Factual Innocence Claims", in *Houston Law Review*, 2004, pp. 1281–1321.

6 Note, here as elsewhere, that the term 'judgement' refers to the pronouncement of a decision, not necessarily a legal judgment, as the term is often used.

7 Daniel Kahneman, Olivier Sibony and Cas Sunstein, *Noise: A Flaw in Human Judgment*, William Collins, London, 2021, pp. 43-44.

8 *Ibid.*

9 Kahneman, Sibony and Sunstein, 2021, p. 363, see *supra* note 7.

organizations that employ them maintain an illusion of agreement while in fact disagreeing in their daily professional judgments.[10]

The intensity of noise (and bias)[11] can vary across cultures and correlate with personality traits, but their impact is considered to be universal and almost unavoidable.[12] However, Henrich (2021) points out that some of these phenomena are most common among 'WEIRD' populations; that is, specific to people from 'Western, Educated, Industrialized, Rich and Democratic' societies.[13]

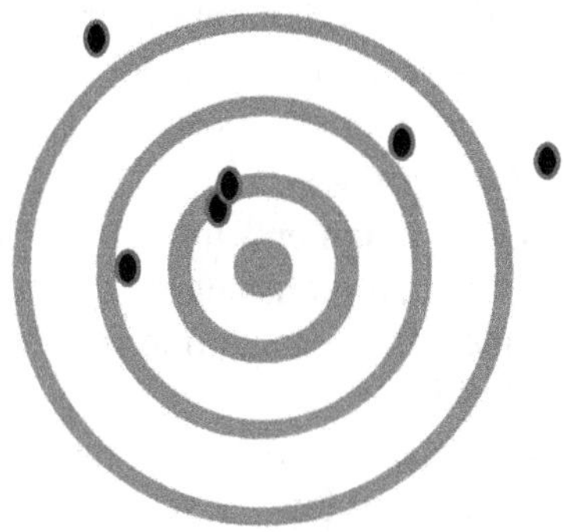

Illustration 3.1.: Noise, or the unwanted variability in judgments.

3.2.2. Different Kinds of 'Noise'

Research has found that judicial decisions are affected by a myriad of extra-legal factors, such as those related to the personal characteristics of the defendant or plaintiff, including his or her gender, race and age. Judges' own gender, race and age have also been found to influence their decisions. Studies have also

[10] *Ibid.*, p. 30.

[11] See Chapter 4.

[12] See, for example, Zamir and Teichman, 2018, p. 585, see *supra* note 1; Chris Guthrie, Jeffrey J. Rachlinski and Andrew J. Wistrich, "Blinking on the Bench: How Judges Decide Cases", in *Cornell Law Review*, 2007, Paper 917, no. 1, pp. 1-12.

[13] Joseph Henrich, *The Weirdest People in the World: How the West Became Psychologically Peculiar and Particularly Prosperous*, Penguin Random House, Westminster, 2021.

demonstrated that judicial decisions are distorted by factors such as fatigue,[14] temperature[15] and hunger.[16]

In addition, there is evidence of intra-judge inconsistency, that is, an individual judge's own decisions differ from test to re-test on substantively equivalent matters.[17]

Finally, there is ample evidence of inter-judge inconsistency as well, situations in which judges disagree on a decision for the same case or fact pattern.[18]

The unwanted variability in judgment observed in organizations that employ interchangeable professionals to make decisions (for example, selectors, investigators, prosecutors and magistrates) is called *system noise.* It can be divided into level noise and pattern noise.[19]

Variability of the average judgments made by different individuals is called *level noise.*[20] If one evaluator in a preliminary examination unit is, for instance, generally more ready to open an investigation relative to a different colleague, this is an example of level noise.

Pattern noise occurs when, regardless of the average level of their judgments, two judges[21] differ in their views. It results from differences in how people see the world.[22] Think of a prosecutor who considers white-collar crime as a priority, hence always prosecutes such matters; whereas another prosecutor,

---

14 Kyoungmin Cho, Christopher M. Barnes and Cristiano L. Guanara, "Sleepy Punishers Are Harsh Punishers: Daylight Saving Time and Legal Sentences", in *Psychological Science*, 2016, vol. 28, no. 2, pp. 242–247.

15 Anthony Heyes and Soodeh Saberian, "Temperature and Decisions: Evidence from 207,000 Court Cases", in *American Economic Journal: Applied Economics*, 2019, vol. 11, no. 2, pp. 238–265.

16 Shai Danziger, Jonathan Levav and Liora Avnaim-Pesso, "Extraneous Factors in Judicial Decisions", in *Proceedings of the National Academy of Sciences*, 2011, vol. 108, pp. 6889–6892. Interestingly, a recent study found that hunger made judges not less, but more lenient, thus contradicting this often cited research (see Sultan Mehmood, Avner Seror and Daniel L. Chen, "Ramadan Fasting Increases Leniency in Judges From Pakistan and India", in *Nature Human Behaviour*, 2023, vol. 7, pp. 874–880.

17 Kahneman, Sibony and Sunstein, 2021, p. 91, see *supra* note 7.

18 See Dhami and Belton, 2017, see *supra* note 4, and research quoted there.

19 The following classification is based on Kahneman, Sibony and Sunstein's taxonomy.

20 Kahneman, Sibony and Sunstein, 2021, p. 365, see *supra* note 7.

21 Except when specifically indicated (and then we will refer to 'magistrates'), we take the term here as to refer to 'the person who judges', not as a legal profession.

22 Donn Levie, Jr., "Managing Troubled Projects", in *Fraud Magazine*, May-June 2022, pp. 58–60.

even though perhaps generally more severe, applies a different ranking of cases and decides not to bring charges in certain white-collar matters.[23]

Pattern noise typically has more impact than level noise and can be stable or occasional. The former type, *stable pattern noise,* refers to the unique differences individuals have with regard to the same case, a collection of personal and idiosyncratic responses that vary between individuals. These sorts of differences result from differing worldviews based on personal beliefs, experiences, expectations and assumptions (for example, categories, concepts and stereotypes). Such worldviews frame the way individuals consider various situations but are also one source of variability between their judgments.[24]

Occasional pattern noise occurs when the same judge renders different judgments on the same decision, often influenced by factors unrelated to the judgment context. Examples include when:

- the same DNA sample is evaluated as a positive or negative match, depending on the fatigue or good mood of the forensic expert;[25]
- a judge is more severe after his favourite team unexpectedly loses;[26]
- a judge gives harsher pronouncements when time has lapsed since a break;[27]
- experts disagree with their own previous judgments of the same fingerprints.[28]

---

[23] See "Beyond Bias with Olivier Sibony", *The Decision Lab*, 24 May 2021.

[24] Kenneth Cukier, Viktor Mayer-Schönberger and Francis de Véricourt, *Framers*, W.H. Allen, London, 2021, p. 4.

[25] Kahneman, Sibony and Sunstein, 2021, p. 366, see *supra* note 7.

[26] Ozkan Eren and Naci Mocan, "Emotional Judges and Unlucky Juveniles", in *American Economic Journal: Applied Economics*, 2018, vol. 10, no. 3, pp. 171–205.

[27] Danziger, Levav and Avnaim-Pesso, 2011, see *supra* note 16.

[28] Itiel Dror and David Charlton, "Why Experts Make Errors", in *Journal of Forensic Identification*, 2006, vol. 51, no. 4, p. 4.

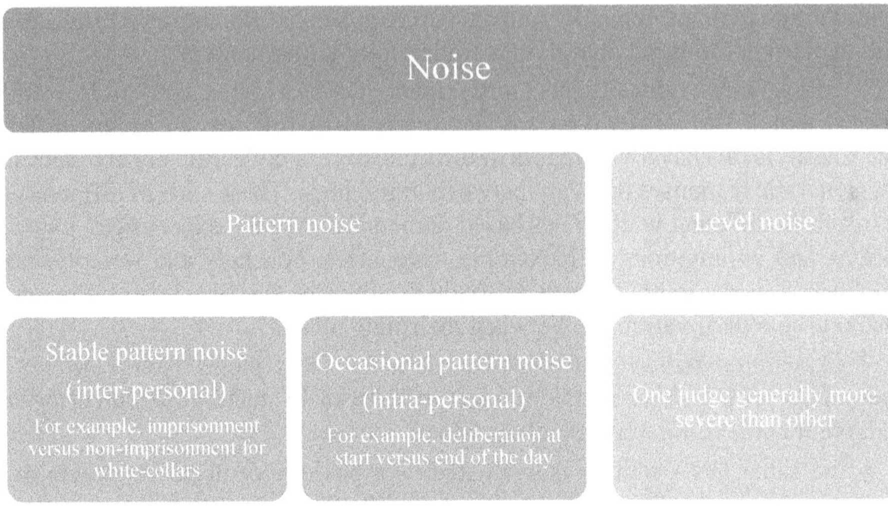

Illustration 3.2.: Different types of noise.

3.2.3. The Impact of Noise

Noise may damage the credibility of the system,[29] which is especially troublesome in the legal context.[30]

Stable pattern noise, or the impact of people's individual mental models, is more significant than the other components of system noise. Noisy judgments that different people make are largely determined by the persistent, personal reactions they have to a multitude of features, influencing their responses to specific cases in diverse ways.[31] "Noise is mostly a by-product of our sense of uniqueness, of our 'judgment personality'."[32]

However, noise is not totally random. Even occasional pattern noise seems to follow some logic. For instance, professional judges who make a series of decisions in sequence, lean toward restoring a form of balance: after a streak, or a series of decisions that go in the same direction, they are more likely to decide in the opposite direction than would be strictly justified.[33] For instance, it was

[29] Kahneman, Sibony and Sunstein, 2021, p. 52, see *supra* note 7.

[30] See the seminal work of Judge Frankel, who in the 1970's established vast discrepancies (for example, a factor of x60 in sentence duration) in the sanctions handed out by American judges in similar cases. See, Marvin E. Frankel, *Current Contents*, 1986, vol. 25, p. 14.

[31] Kahneman, Sibony and Sunstein, 2021, p. 81, see *supra* note 7.

[32] *Ibid.*, p. 216.

[33] *Ibid.*, p. 90.

found that following two positive decisions, asylum seekers in the United States had a 19 per cent greater chance of a negative decision.[34]

3.3. Remedies

Unwanted divergences in judgement are often hidden beneath the illusion of agreement and can never be totally eliminated. Unlike biases, which we can think about causally, isolating and addressing noise in decision-making requires us to think statistically. Correctives should work to address both the sources of, and impediments to reducing noise. This often requires the implementation of systems, rules, or procedures that can feel dehumanizing, in that they reduce the individual's sense of agency.

A necessary first step is to get the organization to recognize that noise in a setting of professional judgement is an issue that deserves attention.[35] The organization should start by determining in what contexts unwanted variability in decision-making is most problematic.

3.3.1. Reducing Noise at the Individual Level

Judgments are less noisy when those who make them are:[36]

a) competent (understood here as 'what you know');
b) intelligent (understood here as 'how well you think'); and
c) have the right thinking style and skills (understood here as 'how you think').

There will be cases in which variability can be attributed to incompetence: some judges know what they are talking about, others do not. When there is a knowledge[37] or skill gap, the priority should be to educate, addressing the deficient knowledge and skills.[38] The knowledge and skill level of judges should be as equal as possible. Although much of intelligence is inherited, training and

[34] Andrew I. Schoenholtz, Jaya Ramji-Nogales and Philip G. Schrag, "Refugee Roulette: Disparities in Asylum Adjudication", in *Stanford Law Review*, 2007, vol. 60, no. 2, pp. 295–412.

[35] Kahneman, Sibony and Sunstein, 2021, p. 221, see *supra* note 7.

[36] *Ibid.*, p. 225.

[37] When an evaluator of initial information does not appreciate that 'misappropriation' is, on the one hand a material component of the offence of fraud (Article 3(2)(a)(i), Directive (EU) No. 2017/1371 of the European Parliament and of the Council of 5 July 2017 on the fight against fraud to the Union's financial interests by means of criminal law ('PIF Directive') (https://www.legal-tools.org/doc/3lsm7y4u/)), to be distinguished, on the other hand, from the criminal offence of misappropriation by a public official (Article 4(3) PIF Directive), a case might be dismissed by one and accepted by another evaluator.

[38] Kahneman, Sibony and Sunstein, 2021, p. 221, see *supra* note 7.

education are likely to foster it, especially fluid intelligence which enables individuals to better solve novel problems.[39]

The point that a good judge is actively open-minded and has great thinking skills has already been made in other contributions.[40] We add here the important quality of re-framing, which is to say the capacity to change the cognitive template through which we look at a situation.[41] By deliberately trying out alternative frames (for example, seeing a complaint as a genuine act of righteousness instead of a manoeuvre to harm a competitor) and creating counterfactuals ('*what if?*'), we demonstrate open-mindedness and get a better picture of options for an effective course of action.[42] Forcing oneself or others to consider counterfactuals can be a productive way to reframe and depart from indoctrinated perspectives.

Scotland's jury system uses three possible verdicts: 'guilty', 'not guilty' or 'not proven'. In light of an ongoing reform, researchers studied the possible effects of a shift from that system to a binary system of 'proven' and 'not proven', comparing it also with the binary Anglo-American 'guilty' or ' not guilty' verdict system.

They found that:

- legal professionals significantly preferred the 'proven' or 'not proven' dichotomy, because such a verdict system might direct jurors to their true role of focusing on the 'proof' provided by the prosecution, rather than their perception of 'guilt' towards the defendant;
- when tested, jury-eligible volunteers were significantly more likely to convict in the Anglo-American 'guilty' and 'not guilty' verdict system when compared with the 'proven' – 'not proven' or existing three-tiered Scottish jury system.

The words 'proven' and 'not proven' seem to help jurors to focus on the prosecution's evidence and evaluate whether it met the required standard of proof beyond reasonable doubt. This caused them to acquit more frequently than jurors only provided with the options of guilty and not guilty. In other words, consistent with the first study, the word choice of 'proven' in a verdict system may prime jurors to think about how much proof the prosecution really has.

Illustration 3.3.: Re-framing choices.[43]

[39] *Ibid.*, p. 228.

[40] See Chapter 2.

[41] Cukier, Mayer-Schönberger and de Véricourt, 2021, pp. 4 and 10, see *supra* note 24.

[42] *Ibid.*, p. 46.

[43] Lee Curley, Lara Frumkin, James Munro and Jim Turner, "Not Proven and Back Again: An Academics' Tale", in *Journal of the Law Society of Scotland*, 2022, vol. 67, no. 7.

Finally, recent research captures some of the principles most likely to minimize unwanted judgment noise in considerations of 'decision hygiene'.[44] The guiding principles here suggest that a good judge should:

- remember that the goal of judgment is accuracy, and not individual expression;
- think statistically, and take an outside view of the case: instead of focusing firmly on the case at hand and embedding it in a causal story, it is better to consider the case as a member of a reference class of similar cases rather than as a unique problem;[45]
- resist premature intuitions (see below);
- sequence information, and avoid premature exposure to irrelevant information early in the judgment;
- structure complex judgments by decomposing them into their component parts and delaying the holistic discussion and the final judgment until all inputs have been collected;[46]
- reduce occasion noise by making a first judgment and re-visiting the issue later for a second look.[47]

3.3.2. Reducing Noise at the Organizational Level

Better judges make better judgments in organizational settings that (a) provide adequate, clear and unambiguous judgment guidelines, and (b) employ measures of 'decision hygiene' in group decision processes.

3.3.2.1. Judgment Guidelines

Noise is a natural feature of any imprecise measurement context and measurable even in contexts without a clear right or wrong outcome.[48] Judgment guidelines aim to reduce between-judge variability in (final) judgments. These might include rules or standards.

Rules eliminate discretion by those who apply them. Those who apply rules must answer a question of fact: '*How fast did the driver go?*' or '*When was the*

---

44 Kahneman, Sibony and Sunstein, 2021, pp. 222–223 and 370–374, see *supra* note 7.

45 *Ibid.*, p. 372.

46 *Ibid.*, p. 223.

47 Research found that the average of two numerical guesses was the best guess, and the second guess was the furthest off-mark. However, the same researchers found that seeking an independent second opinion from another person was 10 times better than this wisdom-of-crowds effect within a single person. See Edward Vul and Harold Pashler, "Measuring the Crowd Within: Probabilistic Representations Within Individuals", in *Psychological Science*, 2008, vol. 19, no. 7, pp. 645–647.

48 Darren Frey, presentation during OLAF's conference on judgement and decision-making in investigations, Brussels, 7 and 8 December 2022.

alleged offence committed?'.[49] Whenever rules are in place, noise ought to be reduced significantly, as this decreases the role of judgment and, therefore, unwanted variability.[50]

As opposed to rules, *standards* grant discretion and allow people to adjust to the particulars of the situations.[51] Those who devise standards effectively export decision-making authority to others. They delegate power.[52] When standards are in place, judges have to do a lot of work to specify the meaning of open-ended terms. They might have to make numerous judgments to decide what counts as, for example, 'beyond a reasonable doubt' or 'clear and convincing evidence'.

Setting standards without specifying details can lead to noise. This is why standards often imply the informal integration of a set of cues to produce a judgment on a scale. *Scales* express (and compare) a subjective value or impression and come as probability percentages (for example, 'a 10 per cent chance'), a ranking (for example, 'on a scale of 0 to 6') or a verbal expression of uncertainty (for example, 'likely' or 'very likely', 'serious').

A sizeable body of research has focused on determining how people interpret various verbal expressions of uncertainty and found that there is substantial variability between individuals in their interpretation and application of various scales.[53] Matching a subjective impression to a scale is necessarily noisy, because this process requires projecting a private, internal impression onto an external scale, which individuals interpret differently. One person's '2 out of 10' is another person's '3 out of 10'. Individuals often differ on their interpretation of labels even when they agree on the substance of the judgment.

---

49 For example, November 2017 marks the starting point of the EPPO's temporal competence. However, offences that occurred prior that date may still fall under the body's mandate. This could be because the wrongdoing was continuous or its effects took place after that date.

50 Kahneman, Sibony and Sunstein, 2021, p. 351, see *supra* note 7.

51 *Ibid.*, p. 360.

52 *Ibid.*, p. 351.

53 See, for example, Dominic A. Clark, "Verbal Uncertainty Expressions: A Critical Review of Two Decades of Research", in *Current Psychology*, 1990, vol. 9, no. 3, pp. 203–235; David V. Budescu Han-Hui Por and Stephen B. Broomell, "Effective Communication of Uncertainty in the IPCC Reports", in *Climate Change*, 2012, vol. 113, no. 2, pp. 181–200; David V. Budescu and Thomas S. Wallsten, "Processing Linguistic Probabilities: General Principles and Empirical Evidence", in *Psychology of Learning and Motivation*, 1995, vol. 32, pp. 275–318; Marek Jozef Druzdzel, *Verbal Uncertainty Expressions: Literature Review*, Carnegie Mellon University, Pittsburgh, 2009.

'Given the lack of supporting documents and the ambiguous explanations given during the meeting with X, *it cannot be excluded*, and is in fact very likely, that his hesitations reflect his involvement in serious and systematic fraud'.	'The evidence suggests that X could not have ignored the presence of several companies of the same group in the winning consortia at the end of that procurement round. Hence, *serious doubts exist* as regards his integrity'.	'The allegations *clearly indicate* criminal intent. How else to explain that X did not notice that company A and company B were part of the same group? He must have had an interest in not reporting this. Claiming negligence is not very serious'.

Illustration 3.4.: Examples of expressing uncertainty in investigations.

One solution to decrease variability in interpretation could be to transpose or supplement verbal expressions with numeric information with clear, shared thresholds or anchors: research has demonstrated that this can be effective in increasing alignment between people's interpretation and the intended meaning of words in a predefined categorization.[54]

However, the same research suggests that whereas one person would interpret a word such as 'likely' similarly across different encounters (for example, meaning 'at least 50 per cent chance'), another person could have a very different interpretation of what 'likely' means (for example, 'at least 75 per cent').[55]

[54] David V. Budescu, Han-Hui Por, Stephen Broomell and Michael Smithson, "The Interpretation of IPCC Probabilistic Statements Around the World", in *Nature Climate Change*, 2014, vol. 4, pp. 508–512.

[55] Anne Marthe Van der Bles, *et al.*, "Communicating Uncertainty About Facts, Numbers and Science", in *Royal Society Open Science*, 2019, vol. 6, no. 5, p. 22. For an extreme case of diverging interpretations of the word 'possible', see David V. Wallsten *et al.*, "Measuring the Vague Meanings of Probability Terms", in *Journal of Experimental Psychology: General*, 1986, vol. 115, no. 4, pp. 348–365. For differences between men and women in interpreting probabilistic words: see Andrew Mauboussin and Michael J. Mauboussin, "If You Say Something Is 'Likely', How Likely Do People Think It Is?", *Harvard Business Review*, 3 July 2018. Interestingly, the same study found no meaningful differences in interpretation across age groups or between native and non-native English speakers.

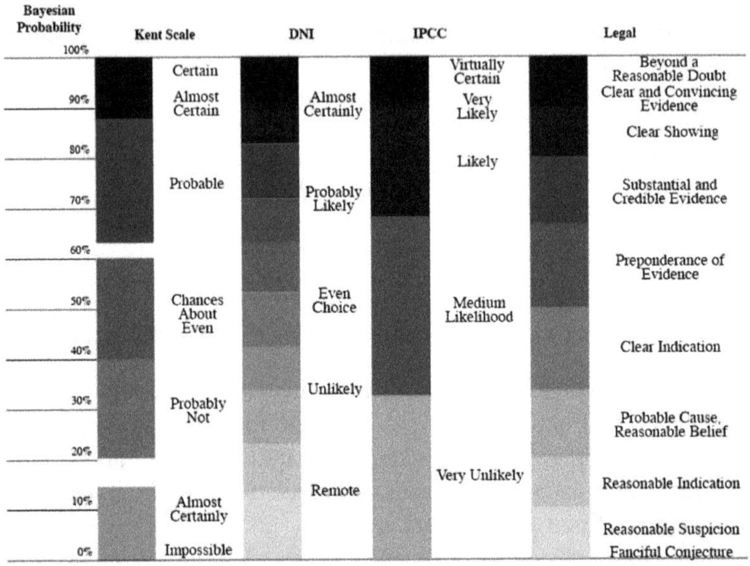

In March 1951, the Central Intelligence Agency published a report suggesting that a Soviet attack on Yugoslavia within the year was a "serious possibility". Sherman Kent, a professor of history who was called to run the Office of National Estimates, was puzzled about what, exactly, "serious possibility" meant. He interpreted it as meaning that the chance of attack was around 65 per cent. But when he asked members of the Board of National Estimates what they thought, he heard figures from 20 per cent to 80 per cent. His first attempt to quantify the terms used in percentages, was followed by others, as can be seen in the table above.[56] It is clear that the scales are interpreted in various ways.

Illustration 3.5.: A 'serious' possibility.

A simple rule to reduce noise is to shift from open-ended discretion or a vague standard to a rule or something close to it, including tight guidelines or decision-making algorithms. When guidelines are tightened to eliminate any discretion, they turn into rules.[57] The choice between rules and standards depends on (a) the costs of decisions (standards need interpretation and require

[56] See Charles Weiss, "Communicating Uncertainty in Intelligence and Other Professions", in *International Journal of Intelligence and Counterintelligence*, 2008, vol. 21, no. 1, p. 61. In this table, 'DNI' refers to the scales used by the American Director of National Intelligence after 11 September 2001, and 'IPCC' to those corrected by the Inter-Governmental Panel on Climate Change in 2001, after critics on the vagueness of scales used in their 1996 report.

[57] Kahneman, Sibony and Sunstein, 2021, pp. 221 and 351, see *supra* note 7.

more efforts from the organization than the application of rules) and (b) the cost of errors (number and magnitude of mistakes).

Research suggests that our ability to categorize objects on a scale is limited, while our ability to make pairwise comparisons is much better.[58] Comparative or relative judgments are more sensitive than categorical or absolute ones (but also more effortful and time-consuming).[59] Hence, it might be fruitful to explore how relative judgments (for example, '*Do these allegations show criminal intent and hence need to be prosecuted?*') could complement scales. Such explicit comparisons between objects of judgment support much finer discriminations than do ratings of objects evaluated one at a time.

Compare the three similar allegations below. Which one holds sufficient elements to report to the judicial authorities as such, or rather needs further enhancement?

Case A:	Case B:	Case C:
An anonymous letter alleges that company X has claimed and received European Union ('EU') funding for providing vocational training, but has only delivered half of the scheduled classroom trainings.	An anonymous letter alleges that company Y has claimed and received EU funding for providing vocational training, but has only provided this training to half of the persons selected for this training.	An anonymous letter alleges that company Z has claimed and received EU funding for providing vocational training, and has delivered a certificate to a person the author asserts never to have been present during the course.

Illustration 3.6.: Comparative judgments.

When people are asked to assess cases that fall within a particular category of actions and harms (for example, fraud), people's judgments tend to be both shared and coherent. When evaluating cases within a category, diverse people are likely to agree on how to rank a set of fraud cases or libel cases by their "punishable merit".[60]

However, comparative or relative judgments have their own intricacies and pitfalls. When people make judgments in isolation, they produce a pattern of outcomes that they would themselves reject, if only they could see that pattern as a whole. A major reason is that human thinking is category-bound. When people see a case in isolation, they spontaneously compare it to other cases that

58 *Ibid.*, p. 374.

59 *Ibid.*, pp. 184–185.

60 Cas Sunstein, Daniel Kahneman, David Schkade and Ilana Ritov, "Predictably Incoherent Judgments", in *Stanford Law Review*, 2002, vol. 54, p. 1158.

are mainly drawn from the same category of harms. When people are required to compare cases that involve different kinds of harms, judgments that appear sensible when the problems are considered separately often appear incoherent and arbitrary in the broader context.[61]

In an experiment, test groups were to assign a sanction for a case of serious fraud and a separate case of minor physical injury.	
When evaluated separately, subjects assigned higher punitive damage awards for the financial crime than the physical injuries: They implicitly compared each case to what they perceived as a typical version of the same type of injury. Because the serious fraud case was so much worse than the typical financial injury, it thus produced a high award. Conversely, because the physical injury was relatively minor, it produced a low award.	When evaluated simultaneously, subjects assigned higher punitive damage awards for the physical injuries than the financial crime: Presenting both cases together, caused the subjects to recognize that the physical harm was more serious than the financial harm. By presenting the cases together, rather than separately, the assessors changed the focus of comparison from serious/minor to fraud/physical injury.

Illustration 3.7.: Category-bound thinking.[62]

3.3.2.2. Decision Hygiene in Group Decisions

Investigative decisions do not occur in a vacuum. The impact of individual qualities and efforts of the selector, investigator, registrar or analyst on the outcome of a case can hardly be overstated. Still, these judgments and decisions tend to be consistent with the decision dynamics (routines and corporate culture) of the organization. Research has identified a number of 'decision-hygiene' measures aimed at improving the quality of judgment and decision-making at the organizational level, which include countering some adverse effects of group decisions.

The organizational measures focus on the need to enable and structure real dialogue between the different actors, and these boil down to:[63]

- Conditions for a productive dialogue:
  - diversity of cognitive skills and frames around the table;
  - sufficient time;
  - an agenda distinguishing points 'for discussion' and 'for decision'.

---

61 *Ibid.*, p. 1153.

62 *Ibid.*

63 See, for example, Kahneman, Sibony and Sunstein, 2021, see *supra* note 7; Olivier Sibony, *Vous allez commettre une terrible erreur*, Flammarion, Paris, 2019.

- Rules on dialogue process:
  - for example, no PowerPoints to persuade but short memoranda;
  - 'as simple as possible … but not more';[64]
  - use of discussion agendas to ensure that different aspects of the problem are considered separately and that the formation of a holistic judgment is delayed;
  - avoiding immediate reactions after a presentation but 'cold' decision the day after;
  - obtain independent judgments from multiple judges, then consider aggregating those judgments systematically and impartially.
- The systematic use of some decision tools:
  - designate decision observers to reduce judgment errors;
  - devil's advocate or 'red teams';[65]
  - mandatory alternatives (with 'vanishing options': if option A is not possible, what then?);
  - alternative narratives: presenter is asked to bring two scenarios, which lead to a different outcome;
  - pre-mortem:[66] just before the final decision, deciders are asked to project a total failure of the project and formulate what went wrong (also called: prospective hindsight).

However, it is important to keep in mind that group decisions entail their own, specific risks. For example, research found that internal discussions often lead to polarized positions.[67] When people talk with one another, they often end up at a more extreme point compared to their original inclination (for example, more severe or lenient) and are more confident in this conclusion.[68] As a result, deliberating groups tend to be noisier than groups that merely average individual judgments.[69]

---

64 Quote attributed to Einstein.

65 Sibony acknowledges this role is often too demanding for staff and does not equate to real, testing dissent (Sibony, 2019, p. 264, see *supra* note 63).

66 Gary Klein, "Performing a Project Premortem", *Harvard Business Review*, 2007, vol. 85, no. 9, pp. 18–19.

67 See, for example, Serge Moscovici and Marisa Zavalloni, "The Group as a Polarizer of Attitudes", in *Journal of Personality and Social Psychology*, 1969, vol. 12, no. 2, pp. 124–135; Daniel J. Isenberg, "Group Polarization: A Critical Review and Meta-Analysis", in *Journal of Personality and Social Psychology*, 1986, vol. 50, no. 6, pp. 1141–1151.

68 Sibony, 2019, p. 159, see *supra* note 63.

69 Kahneman, Sibony and Sunstein, 2021, p. 103, see *supra* note 7.

Moreover, research also suggests that a more competent person will often match his opinion to that of a less competent person, if the latter expresses his opinion with more confidence.[70] The idea that everyone deserves an equal say in a debate can thus lead to suboptimal results. To make optimal decisions, group members should weight their differing opinions according to how competent they are relative to one another; whenever they differ in competence, an equal weighting is suboptimal.[71] Finally, our brain can trick us into believing that members of our group are more intelligent than others, and it tends to process the opinions we already agree with as if they are facts.[72]

Additional risks in group decisions include:

- *diffusion of responsibility*: because group interactions enable individuals to feel less personally responsible for the consequences of their decisions and they therefore become more daring;[73]
- *group think*: because of strong group cohesiveness and directive leadership,[74] groups may tend to prematurely reach consensus, overshadowing the rational decision-making procedures;[75]
- *escalation of commitment*: the more resources, time or efforts an organization has already invested in a given endeavour (for example, opened and started an investigation, whereas it should not have done so), the more it is inclined to pursue it.[76]

3.4. Concluding Remarks

The study of unwanted variability in decisions, or 'noise', underscores that complete objectivity, though a worthwhile ideal, is unattainable. However,

---

70 Dan Bang and Chris D. Frith, "Making Better Decisions in Groups", in *Royal Society Open Science*, 2017, vol. 4, pp. 170-193.

71 Ali Mahmoodi, *et al.*, "Equality Bias Impairs Collective Decision-Making Across Cultures", in *Proceedings of the National Academy of Sciences*, 2015, vol. 112, no. 12, pp. 3835–3840.

72 Michael Gilead, Moran Sela and Anat Maril, "That's My Truth: Evidence for Involuntary Opinion Confirmation", in *Social Psychological and Personality Science*, 2019, vol. 10, no. 3, pp. 393-401.

73 See, for example, Moscovici and Zavalloni, 1969, p. 126, see *supra* note 67; Michael A. Wallach and Nathan Kogan, "The Roles of Information, Discussion, and Consensus in Group Risk Taking", in *Journal of Experimental Social Psychology*, 1965, vol. 1, no. 1, pp. 1–19.

74 Brian Mullen, Tara Anthony, Eduardo Salas and James E. Driskell, "Group Cohesiveness and Quality of Decision Making: An Integration of Tests of the Groupthink Hypothesis", in *Small Group Research*, 1994, vol. 25, no. 2, pp. 189–204.

75 See, for example, Irving L. Janis, *Groupthink: Psychological Studies of Policy Decisions and Fiascos*, Houghton Mifflin, Boston, 1982.

76 Zamir and Teichman, 2018, pp. 56-57, 538, see *supra* note 1; Sibony, 2019, p. 161, see *supra* note 63.

especially in matters of investigation, prosecution and adjudication, professionals should strive to meet the highest standards of objectivity, consistency and coherence available to them. This chapter sheds light on the phenomenon of 'noise' and its key messages include:

- As opposed to matters of taste or opinion, investigations can allow only for a small margin of divergent judgments and decisions.
- 'Noise' occurs when similar cases have significantly different outcomes depending on the overall severity of the decision maker (level noise), his or her personal take on the seriousness of the crime (stable pattern noise), and the mood of the day (occasional pattern noise) or any number of irrelevant influential factors.
- 'Noise' can be exacerbated in group decisions when:
  - a person in authority takes the floor first;
  - group discussion engenders polarization;
  - pursuing consensus overrules critical thinking.
- The elimination of 'noise' requires decision makers to maintain uniformity:
  - in their use of cues;
  - in the weights they assign to these cues;
  - in their use of scales.
- In this respect, relative and comparative judgments are more reliable than absolute ratings on a scale defined by numbers or adjectives (for example, 'very likely').
- Although rules avoid noise, they are often too rigid to be applied in complex evaluative contexts. However, noise-reducing alternatives like standards are often useful, so long as the scales they are built on are as clear, unambiguous and precise as possible, understood in the same way by all judges using them.
- Noise can be significantly reduced by organizational measures focused on ensuring real dialogue and adopting mechanisms to avoid premature convergence, like segmenting and structuring exchanges so individuals only evaluate discrete, manageable parts of complex decisions, rendering judgments in isolation before being exposed to group-wide prejudices.
- On an individual level, re-framing is a cognitive skill particularly useful in departing from mental models leading to noise.

4

Beating Biases: An Investigator's Mirage?

Darren Frey, Tom Willems and Milanka Jug[*]

4.1. Introduction

Even a good understanding of what critical thinking looks like and the conviction that an investigative mindset is beneficial for the investigation does not exempt the investigator from thinking-mistakes. In this chapter, we discuss a major challenge to sound judgment and decision-making in investigations: cognitive bias. Arguably most notorious in its manifestation as tunnel vision, several other biases are almost certain to affect the investigator's decision-making in both mundane and critical ways. The questions we address here include: what kind of thinking mistakes are likely to occur; are we any good in making prognoses and estimates; can we avoid these thinking traps and, if so, what are the best strategies and tactics to mitigate the risks.

4.2. Dual Processing

4.2.1. The Duality of Mind

Human thinking comes in many varieties and relies on a number of related processes, from executive decision-making capacities to language processing, from attention and perception to memory. These processes are continuously influenced by our immediate and social contexts. For example, our attention might be triggered by a perceptual cue (for example, hearing the question of an interviewer), we think about the request (we 'process' the information), and decide (for example, to lie) what to do before we act (state: '*I don't know*').[1]

While traces of the idea are present even in ancient philosophical texts, many modern researchers have converged on the idea that people have two distinct processing mechanisms for reasoning and decision-making tasks. These processes are supposed to employ different procedures and may yield different,

---

* Dr. **Darren Frey** is Lecturer in Behavioral Economics and Cognitive Sciences (Sciences Po). **Tom Willems** is co-ordinator for inter-institutional relations at the European Anti-Fraud Office ('OLAF'). Dr. **Milanka Jug** is Senior Case analyst and Team Coordinator at the European Public Prosecutor's Office ('EPPO'). This chapter is authored in the contributors' personal capacity and does not reflect the views of EPPO, OLAF or other institutions mentioned therein.

[1] See, for example, Scott E. Fruehwald, *How to Teach Lawyers, Judges, and Law Students Critical Thinking: Millions Saw the Apple Fall, but Newton Asked Why*, Amazon Distribution, Leipzig, 2020. See also Chapter 2 for more detail on this so-called 'directed thinking'.

and sometimes conflicting, results when evaluating the same decision.[2] Although there are various formulations of the idea, in general these 'dual process' theories distinguish between two distinct modes of processing information, a fast, effortless mode, and a slower, more deliberative and rule-based mode.

Scholars theorize that an evolutionarily old system of decision-making (most often referred to as '*System 1*') operates automatically and quickly, with little or no effort and with no sense of voluntary control, using mental shortcuts, or 'heuristics', to come to spontaneous, intuitive, associative, context-dependent and holistic judgments and decisions. '*System 2*' is supposed to be an evolutionarily more recent and largely human information processing mechanism, using effortful, hence slow, mental activity to perform conscious, deliberative, analytic and rule-based thinking. The popular terms System 1 (the fast, intuitive system) and System 2 (the slow, deliberative system)[3] are generally accepted across a number of different fields. This classification, and especially the interaction of these two systems, explains many otherwise curious behaviours.

4.2.2. System 1

System 1 ('S1'), or the intuitive decision-making system, operates with *heuristics*, that is, thinking shortcuts that reduce complex problems into simple rules of thumb. These minimize cognitive effort by focusing on a few signals ('cues') in the decision-making context that immediately generate an impression without having to retrieve and store much information in memory.[4] The quick stereotyping of someone you have just met as a party animal or an introvert is an example of S1 at work.

Confronted with an overload of information and a lack of resources, our brain uses these mental shortcuts all the time to cope with cognitive challenges. This is summarized in the simplified table below:

2 We refer to the seminal work of Kahneman and Tversky, summarized in Daniel Kahneman, *Thinking, Fast and Slow*, Farrar, Straus and Giroux, New York, 2011. For an overview of the emergence of these insights of so-called 'dual processing', see, for example, Keith Frankish and Jonathan S. Evans, "The Duality of Mind: An Historical Perspective", in *id.* (eds.), *Two Minds: Dual Processes and Beyond*, Oxford University Press, 2009.

3 Keith E. Stanovich and Richard F. West, "Individual Differences in Reasoning: Implications for the Rationality Debate", *Behavioral and Brain Sciences*, 2000, vol. 23, no. 5; Kahneman, 2011, see *supra* note 2.

4 See, for example, Anuj K. Shah and Daniel M. Oppenheimer, "Heuristics Made Easy: An Effort-Reduction Framework", in *Psychological Bulletin*, 2008, vol. 134, no. 2, pp. 207–222.

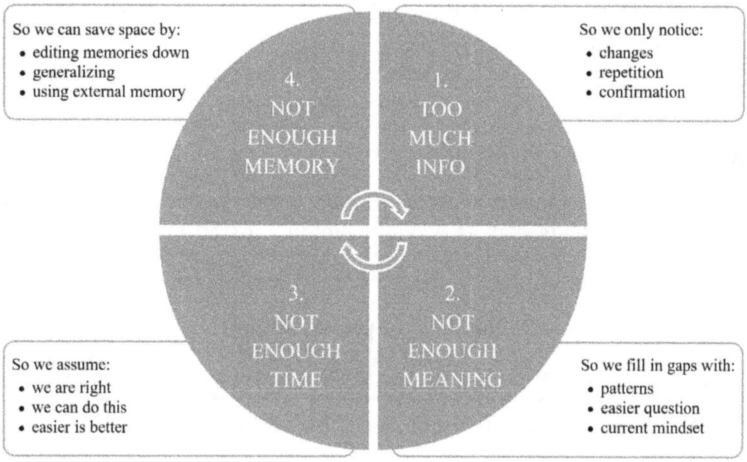

Illustration 4.1.: Heuristic mechanics.[5]

In essence, heuristics often replace a difficult question with another, easier question.[6] The table below provides some examples of these sorts of substitutions in daily life:

The difficult question	The heuristic	The simple question
Which laptop is best quality?	Known = good Expensive = good	Which brand do I recognize? Which laptop is most expensive?
Who should I give my vote?	HALO-effect	Who looks most competent and well-dressed?
Can I trust the salesman?	Authority	Is he an expert?
What takes more lives, traffic or cancer?	Availability heuristic	What examples can I remember most?
What medication should I buy abroad?	Social proof	What do most people buy here?

Illustration 4.2.: Everyday heuristics.

5 Adapted from Buster Benson, "Cognitive Bias Cheat Sheet", *Medium*, 1 September 2016.

6 Russel Korobkin, "Daniel Kahneman's Influence on Legal Theory", in *Loyola University Chicago Law Journal*, 2013, vol. 44, no. 5, pp. 1352–1353.

'MINDSPACE'[7] captures the different heuristics and cognitive biases in nine summarizing phrases:

Capture	Description
Messenger	we are heavily influenced by who communicates information
Incentives	our responses to incentives are shaped by predictable mental shortcuts such as strongly avoiding losses
Norms	we are strongly influenced by what others do
Defaults	we 'go with the flow' of pre-set options
Salience	our attention is drawn to what is novel and seems relevant to us
Priming	our acts are often influenced by sub-conscious cues
Affect	our emotional associations can powerfully shape our actions
Commit-ments	we seek to be consistent with our public promises, and reciprocate acts
Ego	we act in ways that make us feel better about ourselves

Illustration 4.3.: The 'MINDSPACE' categorization of heuristics.

These intuitive judgments and decisions come to mind with an aura of rightness or plausibility, but without clearly articulated reasons or justifications. This 'knowing but without knowing why' is based on an internal signal of judgment completion, a self-administered reward when people reach closure on a judgment: all the pieces of the jigsaw puzzle seem to fit into a coherent story (often by hiding or ignoring pieces of evidence that do not fit).[8]

People are especially likely to resort to intuitive decision-making in situations that they perceive as highly uncertain. When the facts deny them the immediate sense of understanding and confidence they crave, they turn to their intuition to provide it.[9]

7 Paul Dolan *et al.*, "Influencing Behaviour: The Mindspace Way", in *Journal of Economic Psychology*, 2012, vol. 33, pp. 264–277. For another list and categorization of 180 heuristics and cognitive biases, see John Manoogian and Buster Benson, "Cognitive Bias Codex", 2017 (available on the *Wikimedia* web site).

8 Daniel Kahneman, Olivier Sibony and Cas Sunstein, *Noise: A Flaw in Human Judgment*, William Collins, London, 2021, pp. 137–138 and 367.

9 *Ibid.*, p. 145.

4.2.3. System 2

System 2 ('S2') is characterized as slower, rule-based, or deliberative reasoning, as when one reasons analytically, applying a series of logical or probabilistic standards to a given question. It includes hypothetical thinking and making inferences based on facts or propositions.[10] Such deliberation (for example, solving anagrams such as 'vaeertidebli')[11] makes people not only conscious of the response but also of the thinking process that got them there.[12]

The downside of S2 use is that it requires much more cognitive capacity, mental effort and time than S1.[13] If we tried to use our generally logically superior but relatively ponderous S2 formal reasoning capabilities to analyse every piece of information with which we interact in a day, we likely would not manage to get out of our beds. We are simply bombarded with too much information to puzzle through each and every decision we must make throughout the course of our lives.

Intuitive system (System 1)	**Deliberative system (System 2)**
Evolutionary old	Evolutionary recent
Independent of general intelligence	Linked to general intelligence
Automatic	*Controlled*
Always working (habitual)	Target-orientated
Unavailable for conscious introspection	available for conscious introspection
Fast and impulsive	*Slow and prudent*
Considers what automatically comes to mind (narrow frame)	Considers a broad set of relevant factors (wide frame)
Effortless (relatively undemanding on working memory)	*Effortful*
Works on the basis of single associations	Based on reasoning

10 Eyal Peer and Eyal Gamliel, "Heuristics and Biases in Judicial Decisions", in *Court Review*, 2013, vol. 49, p. 114.

11 'Deliberative'.

12 Steven A. Sloman and Philip Fernbach, *The Knowledge Illusion: Why We Never Think Alone*, Riverhead Books, New York, 2017, p. 77.

13 See, for example: Peer and Gamliel, 2013, p. 114, see *supra* note 10; Phil Barden, *Decoded: The Science Behind Why We Buy*, John Wiley & Sons, Hoboken, 2013, p. 38; Ap Dijksterhuis, *Het slimme onbewuste* [*The Smart Unconscious*], Prometheus, Amsterdam, 2016, p. 24.

Heavy contextualized	Abstract (de-contextualized)
Holistic	*Analytic*
Emotional	*Deductive*

Illustration 4.4.: Differences between S1 and S2.

4.2.4. Efficiency

The right way to think in any given situation is often a hard question. It is regularly difficult, sometimes even impossible, to determine whether it is better to use your head (S2) or listen to your gut (S1) in a given context. In daily life, both systems interact, with feelings and impressions quickly generating explicit beliefs and deliberate choices (S1), which slower, rule-based reasoning may correct or revise (S2).[14]

Research tends to agree that people readily violate the most elementary logical, mathematical or probabilistic rules when a task cues an intuitive response that conflicts with these principles.[15] However, in certain contexts heuristics are claimed to produce better decisions and judgments than complex decision rules. This would particularly be the case in the event of limited information (for example, first impressions of whom to trust)[16] or when speed and efficiency of the decision are crucial.[17]

In any case, S1-thinking cannot be automatically equated with inferior thinking and S2 does not always lead to correct answers. Intuition (S1) can be seen as an obstacle, but also as a basis for insight.[18] An individual who uses his or her intuition well while remaining self-critical gains speed and efficiency.[19]

[14] All dual process models suggest some form of interaction between S1 and S2, where S2 often acts as a 'corrector' of S1 processes. A main distinction is made between models that propose a parallel-competitive setting and models that present a default-interventionist model. For a recent. new take on the debate, see Wim De Neys, "Advancing Theorizing About Fast-and-Slow Thinking", in *Behavioral and Brain Sciences*, 2022, vol. 68, no. 1 (online ahead of press).

[15] *Ibid.*, p.7.

[16] Eyal Zamir and Doron Teichman, *Behavioral Law and Economics*, Oxford University Press, 2018, p. 26.

[17] Harald F. Crombag, "Over tunnelvisie" [About Tunnel Vision], in Peter van Koppen, J.W. de Kejser, Robert Horselenberg and Marko Jelicic (eds.) *Routes van het recht: Over de rechtspsychologie,* Den Haag, Boom juridisch, 2017, p. 385.

[18] See in particular Gerd Gigerenzer, *Gut Feelings: Short Cuts to Better Decision Making*, Penguin Books, London, 2007.

[19] Guillaume Calus, *Beslissen is menselijk: Denkfouten, heuristieken en vooroordelen bij rechters* [*Deciding Is Human: Thinking Mistakes, Heuristics and Prejudices of Judges*], Master Thesis, University of Ghent, 2017. See also the section on 'skilled intuition' in Chapter 2 of this book.

4.3. Cognitive Biases

The use of S1 heuristics is inevitable, but may result in systematic and predictable deviations from the axioms of rational decision-making. Such deviations from rational thinking are called cognitive biases.[20] 'Cognitive bias' is an umbrella term that refers to a variety of inadvertent but predictable mental tendencies which can impact perception, memory, reasoning and behaviour.[21] They tend to involve systematic deviations from the axioms of rational decision-making, where most errors in a type of judgments are in the same direction (for example, systematically under-estimating the time needed to finish a project).[22] Consequently, bias can often be predicted and the systemic source of the error can be explained.

Cognitive biases need to be distinguished from 'biases' in common parlance, because they do not imply any emotional or intellectual predisposition toward a certain judgment (like prejudices or stereotypes). They are natural and automatic features of human cognition that often occur in the absence of conscious self-interest[23] and operate without awareness.[24] The word 'bias' does not imply an ethical issue but simply suggests a probable response pattern. They occur involuntarily, and it is hence difficult or impossible to avoid them by mere willpower.

---

20 Paul Slovic, Baruch Fischoff and Sarah Lichenstein, "Behavioral Decision Theory", in *Annual Review of Psychology*, 1977, vol. 28, pp. 1–39; Louise Almond *et al.*, "Heuristics and Biases in Decision-Making", in *Policing Critical Incidents: Leadership and Critical Incident Management*, Willan Publishing, Devon, 2008.

21 Vanessa Meterko and Glinda Cooper, "Cognitive Biases in Criminal Case Evaluation: A Review of the Research", in *Journal of Police and Criminal Psychology*, 2022, vol. 37, no. 1, p. 101.

22 Kahneman, Sibony and Sunstein, 2021, p. 362, see *supra* note 8.

23 Raymond S. Nickerson, "Confirmation Bias: A Ubiquitous Phenomenon in Many Guises", in *Review of General Psychology*, 1998, vol. 2, no. 2, pp.175–220.

24 Keith A. Findley and Michael S. Scott, "The Multiple Dimensions of Tunnel Vision in Criminal Cases", in *Wisconsin Law Review*, 2006, vol. 291, pp. 291–397; Ziva Kunda, "The Case for Motivated Reasoning", in *Psychological Bulletin*, 1990, vol. 108, no. 3, pp. 480–498.

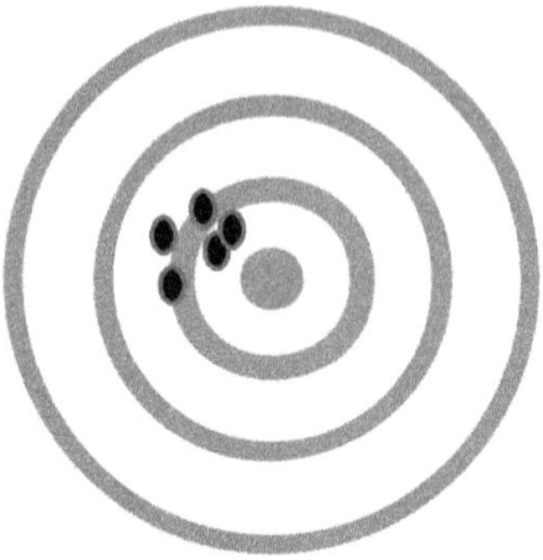

Illustration 4.5.: Bias as a systematic and predictable deviation from an optimal result.

Many different cognitive biases have been categorized on the basis of the main cognitive functions involved (for example, attention or memory-based), the nature of the thinking process (for example, reasoning or judgment skills), the triggering mechanism (for example, contamination or self-preservation effects), and the mental challenge addressed (for example, information overload or lack of meaning).[25] They are explained mainly by reference to our cognitive architecture, but are conditioned by personal factors (for example, high need for closure)[26] and context (for example, cognitive fatigue and time constraints).[27]

Cognitive biases are sometimes caricatured as mainly due to personality traits, something that happens to 'bad apples' and does not impact experts.[28] Interestingly, research in fact suggests the latter are particularly vulnerable to cognitive biases, because the formation of expertise creates and underpins many of the biases.[29] Experience and training make experts engage in more selective attention, use chunking and schemas (typical activities and their sequence), and rely on heuristics and expectations arising from past experiences which create *a priori* assumptions and expectations, essentially making them more likely to be biased in certain contexts.[30]

25 See, for example, Dolan *et al.*, 2012, see *supra* note 7; Manoogian and Benson, 2017, see *supra* note 7; Rüdiger F. Pohl, "Introduction", in *id.* (ed.), *Cognitive Illusions: Intriguing Phenomena in Thinking, Judgment and Memory*, Routledge, London, 2017, pp. 3–21.

26 See Chapter 1.

27 Itiel Dror, "Cognitive and Human Factors in Expert Decision Making: Six Fallacies and the Eight Sources of Bias", in *Analytical Chemistry*, 2020, vol. 92, no. 12, pp. 7998–8004.

28 *Ibid.*

29 See, for example, Zamir and Teichman, 2018, p. 585, see *supra* note 16.

30 Dror, 2020, p. 7999, see *supra* note 27.

Researchers tend to agree that it is very hard, if not impossible, to escape our cognitive biases.[31] People are generally not aware of these biases because of how fundamental intuition is in our daily lives.[32] They tend to identify themselves subjectively with S2 and believe their convictions and decisions are based on arguments or evidence, though ample experimental evidence tells a different story in many cases.[33] Even when people are aware of potential bias, they still underestimate its impact. The bias blind spot[34] makes us assume that everybody else is more susceptible to thinking errors than we are.

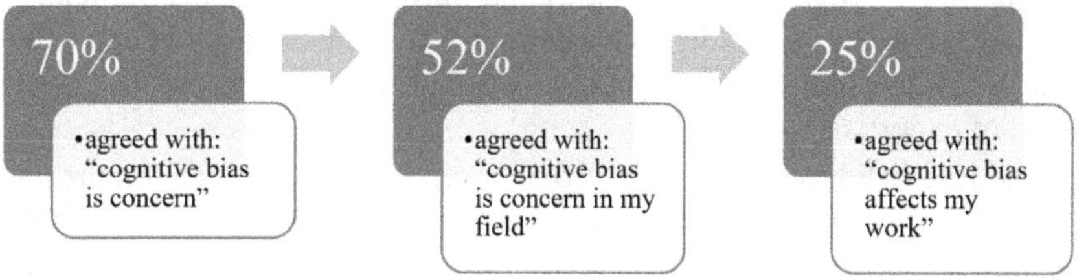

Illustration 4.6.: The bias blind spot of forensic experts.[35]

What is worse, when biases are pointed out, willpower alone is generally inadequate to counter them.[36]

[31] Olivier Sibony, *Vous allez commettre une terrible erreur*, Flammarion, Paris, 2019, p. 203. See, however, Carey K. Morewedge *et al.*, "Debiasing Decisions: Improved Decision Making With a Single Training Intervention", in *Behavioral and Brain Sciences*, 2015, vol. 2, no. 1, pp. 129–140 for training-interventions reducing cognitive biases in intelligence analysis; and Esther Boissin, Serge Caparos, Matthieu Raoelison and Wim De Neys, "From Bias to Sound Intuiting: Boosting Correct Intuitive Reasoning", in *Cognition*, 2021, vol. 201, for training-interventions increasing correct intuitive (S1) thinking. We underline here again that these cognitive biases should be distinguished from social biases, such as racial bias or gender bias, which are mental models (see Peer and Gamliel, 2013, p. 114, see *supra* note 10).

[32] Sibony, 2019, pp. 198–199, see *supra* note 31.

[33] Daniel Kahneman, "La pensée à deux vitesses", in Jean-François Marmion (ed.), *Psychologie de la connerie*, Sciences Humaines Editions, Auxerre, 2018, p. 99.

[34] See, for example, Emily Pronin, Thomas Gilovich and Lee Ross, "Objectivity in the Eye of the Beholder: Divergent Perceptions of Bias in Self Versus Others", in *Psychological Review*, 2004, vol. 111, no. 3, pp. 781–799.

[35] Dror, 2020, p. 8001, see *supra* note 27.

[36] *Ibid.*, p. 7999.

Mitigation strategies focus on mechanisms embedding individual choices in organizational processes or supported by automated decision tools,[37] highlighting the need for a collective and methodical approach.[38]

4.4. Heuristics and Cognitive Biases in Legal Decision-Making

The occurrence and impact of dual processing during investigation, prosecution and adjudication has received increasing attention the last years. Researchers, practitioners and lay people are coming to recognize that judgment is not and cannot be fully rational, that heuristics and biases also influence judicial decision-making. Numerous studies have demonstrated the ubiquity of cognitive biases in legal decision-making[39] and shown that these biases are largely independent of expertise.[40]

Past research has found judges sometimes decide intuitively on the admissibility of proof, the probability of guilt, the fairness of sanctions, and that they rationalize *ex post*.[41] Judicial decisions were found to have been distorted by cognitive illusions such as framing effects, anchoring, and hindsight bias. Unsurprisingly, judges were found to use the same reasoning shortcuts characterized above that are common to all humans, sometimes employing simple

---

[37] See, for example, presentation of the Team Information Decision Engine for intelligence analysist, in Centre for Research and Evidence on Security Threats ('CREST'), "Crest Guide: A Sea Change for Intelligence Analysis?", and Ashraf Labib *et al.*, *Taking Decisions About Information Value*, CREST, 2020.

[38] Sibony, 2019, p. 205, see *supra* note 31.

[39] See, for example, Birte Englich, "Heuristic Strategies and Persistent Biases in Sentencing Decisions", in Margit E. Oswald, Steffen Bieneck and Jörg Hupfeld-Heinemann (eds.), *Social Psychology of Punishment of Crime*, John Wiley & Sons, Hoboken, 2009, pp. 295–314; Jeffrey J. Rachlinski, Chris Guthrie and Andrew J. Wistrich, "Heuristics and Biases in Bankruptcy Judges", in *Journal of Institutional and Theoretical Economics*, 2007, vol. 163, no. 1, pp. 167–186.

[40] See, for example, Andrea L. Miller, "Expertise Fails to Attenuate Gendered Biases in Judicial Decision-Making", in *Social Psychological and Personality Science*, 2019, vol. 10, no. 2, pp. 227–234.

[41] See, for example, Chris Guthrie, Jefferey J. Rachlinski and Andrew J. Wistrich, "Blinking on the Bench: How Judges Decide Cases", in *Cornell Law Review*, 2007, vol. 917, no. 1, pp. 1–12; Calus, 2017, p. 10, see *supra* note 19; Shai Danziger, Jonathan Levav and Liora Avnaim-Pesso, "Extraneous Factors in Judicial Decisions", in *Proceedings of the National Academy of Sciences*, 2011, vol. 108, pp. 6889–6892; Peer and Gamliel, 2013, see *supra* note 10; Rick P. Thomas and Ashley Lawrence, "Assessment of Expert Performance Compared Across Professional Domains", in *Journal of Applied Research in Memory and Cognition*, 2018, vol. 7, no 2, pp. 167–176 ; Anna Sagana and Dave A.G. van Toor, "The Judge as a Procedural Decision-Maker Addressing the Disconnect Between Legal Psychology and Legal Practice", in *Zeitschrift für Psychologie*, 2020, vol. 228, no. 3, p. 226.

heuristic strategies to make decisions that ignore much of the available, relevant information.[42]

4.5. Heuristics and Cognitive Biases in Investigations

4.5.1. Occurrence

Early studies on the occurrence of cognitive biases in investigation outlined risks of bias in analysing and evaluating forensic evidence.[43] This body of research examines how contextual information, such as information found on a digital device (for example, internet search logs)[44] influences the digital forensics practitioners' perceptions of images, documents, or chat conversations found on the same digital device.[45] Likewise, when the digital expert learns that a suspect confessed, this would seem to bias the analysts' judgments.[46] Handwriting experts (erroneously) concluded that handwriting samples from the defendant and perpetrator were authored by the same person, after they heard the latter had confessed.[47] And finally, we must note again the above-mentioned *bias blind spot*, which suggests that experts seem more vulnerable to cognitive biases than lay people in certain contexts, which seems especially pertinent in the case of complex investigations.

Although cognitive biases in forensic science have received the most attention from researchers to date, the second most substantial amount of scholarship is focused on case evaluation (that is, integrating and drawing conclusions based on the totality of the evidence in a case) by investigators and

[42] See Mandeep K. Dhami and Ian Belton, "On Getting Inside the Judge's Mind", in *Translational Issues in Psychological Sciences*, 2017, vol. 3, no. 2, pp. 214–226 and research quoted there. For a study indicating how cognitive bias influenced German magistrates, see Bettina von Helversen and Jörg Rieskamp, "Predicting Sentencing for Low-Level Crimes: Comparing Models of Human Judgment", in *Journal of Experimental Psychology: Applied*, 2009, vol. 15, no. 4, pp. 375–395, quoted in Susanne M. Schmittat, Birte Englich, Lyane Sautner and Petra Velten, "Alternative Stories and the Decision to Prosecute: An Applied Approach Against Confirmation Bias in Criminal Prosecution", in *Psychology, Crime & Law*, 2021, vol. 28, no. 6, pp. 608–635.

[43] See, in particular, the work of Itiel Dror, *supra* note 27.

[44] Nina Sunde and Itiel E. Dror, "Cognitive and Human Factors in Digital Forensics: Problems, Challenges, and the Way Forward", in *Digital Investigation*, 2019, vol. 29, pp. 101–108.

[45] Moa Lidén, "Confirmation Bias in Investigations of Core International Crimes: Risk Factors and Quality Control Techniques", in Xabier Agirre, Morten Bergsmo, Simon De Smet and Carsten Stahn (eds.), *Quality Control in Criminal Investigation*, Torkel Opsahl Academic EPublisher, Brussels, 2020, p. 491 (https://www.toaep.org/ps-pdf/38-qcci/).

[46] *Ibid.*

[47] Jeff Kukucka and Saul M. Kassin, "Do Confessions Taint Perceptions of Handwriting Evidence? An Empirical Test of the Forensic Confirmation Bias", in *Law and Human Behavior*, 2014, vol. 38, no. 3, pp. 1–15.

prosecutors.[48] Other research reports biases affecting other actors in the investigation process, including accountants and lawyers, disqualifying them, respectively, as whistle-blowers in fraud cases[49] or investigators for the defence.[50] One of the present co-authors explored how insights of dual process theories might enhance the efficiency of interviewing.[51] In general, the attention to the occurrence of cognitive biases – and their consequences – in investigations is growing, but the influence of this research on day-to-day investigative (and prosecutorial) decisions remains limited.[52]

4.5.2. Evaluation

Psychological heuristics are an adaptive part of human cognition, helping us operate efficiently in a world full of complex stimuli. However, these mental shortcuts also have the potential to undermine the search for truth in a criminal investigation.[53]

The demands of critical thinking clearly call for a dominant S2 processing of investigations. An investigator should pursue reflective judgment, encompassing cognitive skills that include analysis, interpretation, inference, explanation and evaluation, and practice the monitoring and correcting of one's own reasoning.[54] However, S1, our intuitive judgements, is always present and is, in fact, often explicitly endorsed by some practitioners, who continue to prioritize their intuitions or 'gut-feelings'. Despite the bad press, 'expert intuition' and 'gut feeling' were[55] and remain dominant strategies in investigative matters.[56]

---

48 Meterko and Cooper, 2022, see *supra* note 21. The researchers reviewed 30 social science research papers on cognitive biases in criminal investigations and prosecution, published between December 2016 and again in January 2020.

49 Inez Verwey and Yvonne Vlasman, "De eigen perceptie van accountants ten aanzien van fraude: (on)bewust (on)bekwaam?" [The Self-Perception of Accountants in Regard to Fraud: (Un)consciously (In)competent?], in *Maandblad voor Accountancy en Bedrijfseconomie*, 2020, vol. 94, nos. 1–2, pp. 55–63.

50 Frank J. Erkens, "'Checks and balances' in het proces van waarheids- en rechtsvinding" ['Checks and Balances' in the Process of Finding the Truth and Justice], in *Tijdschrift voor Sanctierecht & Onderneming*, 2021, vol.1, no. 2, p. 26.

51 Tom Willems, *Behaviorally Informed Interviewing*, Maklu Uitgevers, Antwerpen, 2020.

52 Sagana and van Toor, 2020, p. 226, *supra* note 41.

53 Meterko and Cooper, 2022, p. 101, see *supra* note 21.

54 See Chapter 2.

55 Anthony J. Pinizzotto, Edward F. Davis and Charles E. Miller, "Intuitive Policing: Emotional/Rational Decision Making in Law Enforcement", in *FBI Law Enforcement Bulletin*, 2004, vol. 73, no. 2, pp. 1–6.

56 Simon Baechler *et al.*, "Un modèle continu, non linéaire et collaboratif de l'enquête" [A Continuous, Non-Linear and Collaborative Model of Investigation], in *Criminologie*, 2020, vol. 53, no. 2, p. 44.

According to some authors, the reliance on heuristics in investigation is unavoidable and even necessary, given the limitations of human rationality as described above. In this view, we can only hope to make an incomplete reconstruction of the objective 'truth' to capture and approximate what really happened.[57] Thus, heuristics are not to be considered essentially erroneous, but as reasoning strategies that may be valid or invalid, depending on a number of factors, including the context and expertise of the observer.[58] And, indeed, some limited research does suggest training can produce better intuitions.[59]

One likely acceptable compromise is to explicitly monitor heuristic thinking to the extent possible, whether with institutional or personal safeguards, especially acknowledging its shortcomings when investigating matters with critical outcomes.[60] In high-stakes situations, where information is limited or uncertain, heuristics, may be just as fatal as they are helpful.[61] A good starting point is to identify risk factors linked to an investigator relying on 'gut feelings' and establish relevant mitigating measures.

4.5.3. Risk Factors

If not counterbalanced, heuristics and cognitive biases have the potential to undermine criminal investigations and lead to wrongful convictions.[62] Therefore, it is important to understand environmental, individual and case-specific factors that may exacerbate these risks. Building on earlier work,[63] Metterko and Cooper propose a taxonomy of different sources of potential bias that may contaminate decisions (mainly case evaluations) during investigation and prosecution. The broad base of this organizing pyramid is 'human nature', and as the pyramid narrows to its peak, potential sources of bias become increasingly

---

57 Guillaume Louis, "Enquête policière et techniques d'enquête: un regard scientifique" [Police Investigation and Investigative Techniques: A Scientific View], in *Criminologie*, 2021, vol. 53, no. 2, p. 6.

58 Barbara O'Brien, "Recipe for Bias: An Empirical Look at the Interplay Between Institutional Incentives and Bounded Rationality in Prosecutorial Decision Making", in *Missouri Law Review*, 2009, vol. 74, no. 4, pp. 999–1050.

59 See Boissin, Caparos, Raoelison and De Neys, 2021, see *supra* note 31.

60 Rod Gehl and Darryl Plecas, *Introduction to Criminal Investigation: Processes, Practices and Thinking*, Justice Institute of British Columbia, New Westminster, 2016, p. 8.

61 Ivar Fahsing, "Beyond Reasonable Doubt: How to Think Like an Expert Detective", in Paulo Barbosa Marquez and Mauro Paulino (eds.), *Police Psychology*, Elsevier Academic Press, Cambridge, 2022, p. 272.

62 Ivar Fahsing, Asbjørn Rachlew and Lennert May, "Have You Considered the Opposite? A Debiasing Strategy for Judgment In Criminal Investigation", in *The Police Journal*, 2023, vol. 96, no. 1, p. 46.

63 Dror, 2017, see *supra* note 27.

dependent on environmental, individual and case-specific circumstances and characteristics.[64]

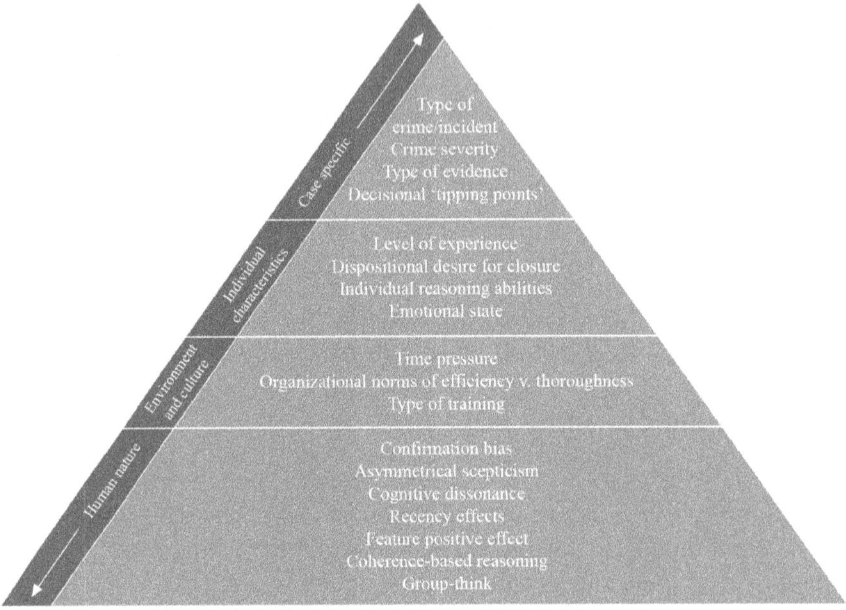

Illustration 4.7.: Pyramid of explanations for cognitive bias during investigation.

4.5.3.1. Human Nature

The 'human nature' factor refers to universal psychological phenomena and their underlying mechanisms in the context of evaluating a criminal case. Several studies in this vein focus on confirmation bias (also tunnel vision, asymmetrical scepticism), detailed later on.

'Order effects', like the primacy or recency effect, refer to the finding that the sequence of presentation of events or information influences judgments downstream, though it should not. A number of psychological and cognitive scientific studies illustrate that in some cases earlier events are heavily weighted, while in others the most recent event is overweighted.[65]

Research found that the order in which evidence was presented influenced beliefs of guilt. When police officers encountered exculpatory evidence prior to

[64] Meterko and Cooper, 2022, p. 106, see *supra* note 21.

[65] See for example, Christine L. Ruva, "Pretrial Publicity's Effects on Juror's and Judges' Decisions", in Monica K. Miller, Logan A. Yelderman, Matthew T. Huss and Jason A. Cantone (eds.), *The Cambridge Handbook of Psychology and Legal Decision-Making*, Cambridge University Press, 2024, p. 104.

inculpatory evidence, guilt belief scores decreased, suggesting their final decisions were influenced by their initial impressions.[66]

4.5.3.2. Environment and Culture

Some aspects of the investigative process make it particularly prone to S1 processing. Research revealed three 'environment and culture' factors which can push an investigation toward more biased thinking[67]: (a) time pressure; (b) a focus on efficiency; and (c) training.

Even though an essential standard for quality in investigations is that they ought to be carried out within a reasonable timeframe,[68] the negative effects of time pressure on human decision-making are well known. Apart from leading to selectivity in information processing (so-called 'filtering'), time pressure seems to decrease flexible thinking. This deteriorates the ability to generate alternative hypotheses and strategies, and it makes people rely more heavily on their previous views and stereotypes and less likely to assimilate new information.[69] Ask and Granhag observed that induced time pressure influenced officers' decision-making, creating a higher tendency to stick with initial beliefs and a lower tendency to be influenced by the evidence presented.[70]

Interestingly, research has shown that even a merely perceived expectation to work quickly, rather than actual time pressure, might have negative effects. Professional investigators exposed to social norms promoting efficiency (vs. thoroughness) were less systematic in their processing of case-relevant information and less aware of this influence.[71]

Organizational culture can impact the integrity of an investigation as well. Ask and colleagues concluded that a focus on efficiency – as opposed to thoroughness – produces more cursory processing among police participants, which

---

66 Wayne A. Wallace, "The Effect of Confirmation Bias in Criminal Investigative Decision Making", Ph.D. Thesis, Walden University, 2015.

67 Meterko and Cooper, 2022, p. 107 and research quoted there, see *supra* note 21.

68 Tor-Geir Myhrer, "The Importance of Successful Co-operation Between Police Investigators and the Prosecution Service to Secure Efficient and Fair Court Proceedings and Verdicts", in Agirre, Bergsmo, De Smet and Stahn (eds.), 2020, p. 1025, see *supra* note 45.

69 Lidén, 2020, p. 527, see *supra* note 45.

70 Karl Ask and Pär Anders Granhag, "Motivational Bias in Criminal Investigators' Judgments of Witness Reliability", in *Journal of Applied Social Psychology*, 2007, vol. 37, no. 3, pp. 561–591.

71 Fahsing, 2022, p. 275, see *supra* note 61.

could be detrimental to the accurate assessment of evidence found later in an investigation.[72]

Finally, the type of training investigators have, appears to impact their ability to generate a variety of relevant hypotheses and actions in an investigation.[73]

4.5.3.3. Individual Characteristics

Research has also identified individual characteristics that make investigators more or less prone to cognitive biases. These personal attributes include:[74]

- varying amounts of professional experience when it comes to assessments of potential criminal cases and assumptions about guilt;
- differences in reasoning skills in relation to the evaluation of evidence;
- dispositional need for cognitive closure;
- negative emotions: when asked to make judgments about a criminal case, sad participants were better able to substantively process the consistency of evidence or lack thereof, whereas angry participants used heuristic processing.

4.5.3.4. Case-Specific

Some studies examined case- and evidence-specific factors:[75]

- the perceived reliability of some types of evidence (DNA versus photographs versus witnesses) is more malleable than others;
- the affinity for incriminating evidence increases with crime severity.

Surprisingly, in one study, police recruits who were presented with a scenario including a clear 'tipping point' (an arrest) did not actually produce significantly fewer hypotheses than those who were not presented with such a tipping point. Regardless of the vividness of such instance, this did not seem to affect their openness to possible other narratives of what happened.[76]

---

[72] Karl Ask, Pär Anders Granhag and Anna Rebelius, "Investigators Under Influence: How Social Norms Activate Goal-Directed Processing of Criminal Evidence", in *Applied Cognitive Psychology*, 2011, vol. 25, no. 4, pp. 548–553.

[73] See Ivar Fahsing and Karl Ask, "The Making of an Expert Detective: The Role of Experience in English and Norwegian Police Officers' Investigative Decision-Making", *Psychology, Crime & Law*, 2016, vol. 22, no. 3, pp. 203–223.

[74] Meterko and Cooper, 2022, p. 108 and research quoted there, see *supra* note 21.

[75] *Ibid.*

[76] Ivar Fahsing and Karl Ask, "In Search of Indicators of Detective Aptitude: Police Recruits' Logical Reasoning and Ability to Generate Investigative Hypotheses", *Journal of Police and Criminal Psychology.*, 2017, vol. 33, no. 1, pp. 21–34.

4.5.4. Debiasing

Research into so-called debiasing techniques has suggested a few different ways to address the vulnerabilities of criminal investigations to cognitive biases. Due to the subconscious nature of many biases and the 'bias blind spot', criminal investigators are unlikely to be able to detect the biases themselves. Instead, proactive remedies are needed. A number of empirically informed options are available to investigators. Specifically, research suggests certain solutions to protect against these vulnerabilities, including: (a) the consideration of alternative scenarios; (b) systems of alternation of the decision maker; or (c) instances of (blind peer) review.

One way to avoid tunnel vision, in particular, is to engage in falsification and to consider alternative scenarios.[77] Explanations that consider alternative scenarios are often indicative of a less biased process of decision-making.[78] Some even argue that the 'active judge' should not just try to exclude an alternative scenario to confirm the original scenario, but make serious efforts to consider evidence for and against all possible scenarios. This should entail investigating whether there is any evidence for any alternative scenario that was "not necessarily explicitly brought forward" by any of the parties.[79] Such endeavours do not seem to correspond with the current practice of magistrates[80] and would likely significantly overstretch the capacity of 'PIF' investigative services (as mentioned earlier in the book, 'PIF' stands for '*Protection des Intérêts Financiers*', or 'Protection of the Financial Interest of the European Union').

If one and the same prosecutor is in charge of an investigation from start to end, without ever even consulting other investigators or another prosecutor, it is likely that the prosecutor's ability to see shortcomings in his or her own reasoning is reduced. A second decision maker does not have the same personal involvement and also has greater cognitive distance from the task.

Furthermore, in the context of forensic investigations, 'contextual information management' has shown debiasing potential. This entails blinding forensic examiners to irrelevant contextual information that might bias them. Importantly, this is not about shielding forensic examiners completely from the

[77] See Chapter 1.

[78] Enide Maegherman, "Tunnel Vision and Falsification in Legal Decision-Making", in Sara Landström, Pär Anders Granhag and Peter J. van Koppen (eds.), *The Future of Forensic Psychology*, Routledge, London, 2022, p. 148.

[79] *Ibid.*, pp. 149–150.

[80] See *ibid.*, p. 150 for a survey of Dutch magistrates, and Pieter Tersago, Miet Vanderhallen, Joëlle Rozie and Sarah-Jane McIntyre, "From Suspect Statement to Legal Decision Making: How Do Judges Weigh the Evidence?", *Zeitschrift für Psychology*, 2020, vol. 228, no. 3, p. 181, for a survey of Belgian magistrates.

world in which they live, but rather for a manager to assess what information they need to know (and when) to be able to most accurately do their work.

Other researchers have suggested the investigative mindset should shift to merely gathering facts, rather than building a case,[81] or institutionalizing the role of a 'contrarian' in a criminal investigation.[82] However, regarding the latter, researchers found that, in practice, these contrarians appear to exert slight influence on investigations without bringing a radical change in case trajectories. Similarly, members of criminal investigation teams in the Netherlands reported that, in practice, designated devil's advocates tend to provide sound advice but do not fundamentally change the course of investigations.[83] Interestingly, O'Brien[84] found that when participants expected to have to persuade someone of their hypothesis, this anticipation actually worsened bias.

4.5.5. Salvation from Artificial Intelligence?

The degree of complexity that marks modern day life may simply exceed our cognitive capacities and require a greater reliance on technological decision aids, like artificial intelligence ('AI'), even, perhaps especially, in investigative and legal decision-making contexts.

In a publication from the French Gendarmerie,[85] the (anonymous) author holds that there is no doubt that the investigation of tomorrow will necessarily rely on the algorithms offered by AI to handle the massive amount of data the investigator and prosecutor are confronted with. AI is better at classifying this data, makes better and faster connections, never forgets anything, and is unbeatable at producing quick outputs. The article praises its expected impact on the quality of operational analysis, the detection of incoherence, and its probability assessments. At the same time, the author echoes a general concern that the authorities should always be capable of explaining how AI came to its results, and – in investigations – be validated by complementary investigative steps.

81 Wallace, 2015, see *supra* note 66.

82 Renze Salet and Jan Terpstra, "Critical Review in Criminal Investigation: Evaluation of a Measure to Prevent Tunnel Vision", in *Policing*, 2014, vol. 8, no. 1, pp. 43–50.

83 Jelle Groenendaal and Ira Helsloot, "Tunnel Vision on Tunnel Vision? A Preliminary Examination of the Tension Between Precaution and Efficacy in Major Criminal Investigations in the Netherlands", in *Police Practice and Research*, 2015, vol. 16, no. 3, pp. 224–238.

84 Barbara O'Brien, "Confirmation Bias in Criminal Investigations: An Examination of the Factors That Aggravate and Counteract Bias", Ph.D. Thesis, University of Michigan, 2007; *id.*, "Prime Suspect: An Examination of Factors that Aggravate and Counteract Confirmation Bias in Criminal Investigations", in *Psychology, Public Policy and Law*, 2009, vol. 15, no. 4, pp. 315–334.

85 Pôle judiciaire de la gendarmerie nationale, "L'impact de l'intelligence artificielle dans la conduite de l'enquête judiciaire", 16 December 2020 (available on its web site).

4.6. Confirmation Bias

4.6.1. Description

Investigators are vulnerable to many biases that may shape their processing of information. The most common type in investigative contexts is likely confirmation bias, which is considered particularly relevant in legal proceedings.[86] Crime scene officers acknowledged that confirmation bias was the first candidate to potentially negatively affect a criminal investigation.[87]

Confirmation bias is the human tendency to search for, recall and interpret information that is consistent with pre-existing beliefs or hypotheses.[88] It is a form of motivated reasoning in which people automatically:[89]

- selectively search for (only) information that supports their hypothesis;
- do not look for evidence that falsifies it or alternative scenarios;
- evaluate ambiguous or neutral information as supporting their hypothesis;
- interpret new information in line with their hypothesis;
- ignore or explain away information that contradicts their hypothesis ('asymmetrical scepticism');
- give little weight to information that does not support their hypothesis.

Confirmation bias thus affects all basic aspects of fact-finding.

It is part of a more complex phenomenon labelled 'tunnel vision', a cognitive strategy that leads to a single-minded focus on a favourite theory to the extent that other suspects or alternate theories are ignored.[90] In addition to its main component, confirmation bias, tunnel vision also entails a number of other

[86] Maegherman, 2022, p. 148, see *supra* note 78.

[87] Hans Ditrich, "Cognitive Fallacies and Criminal Investigations", in *Science & Justice*, 2015, vol. 55, no. 2, pp. 155–159.

[88] Nickerson, 1998, see *supra* note 23.

[89] See, for example, Peter C. Wason, "On the Failure to Eliminate Hypotheses in a Conceptual Task", in *Quarterly Journal of Experimental Psychology*, 1960, vol. 12, no. 3, pp. 129–140; Rüdiger F. Pohl, "Introduction: Cognitive Illusions", in *id.* (ed.), *Cognitive Illusions: A Handbook on Fallacies and Biases in Thinking, Judgment and Memory*, Psychology Press, Hove, 2004; Lidén, 2020, pp. 483–485, see *supra* note 45.

[90] Gehl and Plecas, 2016, p. 8, see *supra* note 60.

heuristics that may account for judgment and decision mistakes, including escalation of commitment[91] and belief perseverance.[92]

Confirmation bias strongly contradicts legal, ethical and rational ideals of decision-making, such as the presumption of innocence and the duty to investigate both incriminating and exonerating circumstances equally.[93] Judgments made under the occurrence of a confirmation bias can be right, but this is the case only when the initial opinion is right, essentially turning the investigative procedure into a lottery.

4.6.2. Explanations of Confirmation Bias

Accounts of confirmation bias can be broken down into three main categories:[94]

a) cognitive explanations;
b) emotional and motivational explanations;
c) social and organizational explanations.

These explanations are to be considered mutually supportive rather than mutually exclusive.

First and foremost, conformation bias is a result of the human cognitive set-up and does not reflect any prejudice or stereotype. The phenomenon of single-minded reasoning happens more or less subconsciously,[95] because "once information rings a bell, the bell cannot be un-rung".[96] In other words, once you have started thinking about a problem one way, the same mental circuits or pathways are activated and strengthened each time you think about it.[97] These mental paths often make it hard to change a first impression.

'Motivated reasoning' refers to the finding that human behaviour is largely motivated by goals, and these goals can have a strong influence on cognitive

---

91 'Escalation of commitment' refers to the tendency to adhere to a prior course of action, even when there are indications that the previous action was wrong. See, for example, Barry M. Staw, "Knee-Deep in the Big Muddy: A Study of Escalating Commitment to a Chosen Course of Action", in *Organizational Behavior and Human Performance*, 1976, vol. 16, no. 1, pp. 27–44.

92 Belief perseverance refers to the finding that people stick to an opinion even after the evidence on which they are based has been discredited. See, for example, Richards J. Heuer, *Psychology of Intelligence Analysis*, Central Intelligence Agency, Langley, 1990.

93 Lidén, 2020, see *supra* note 45, p. 463.

94 *Ibid.*, pp. 501–509.

95 *Ibid.*, p. 462.

96 Heuer, 1999, see *supra* note 92.

97 For an article indicating brain mechanisms and functional regions that underlie confirmation bias, see, for example, Andreas Kappes *et al.*, "Confirmation Bias in the Utilization of Others' Opinion Strength", in *Nature Neuroscience*, 2020, vol. 23, pp. 130–137.

processes.[98] Affective preferences, for instance, trigger the operation of cognitive processes that shift reasoning to reach the desired conclusion.[99] So, although investigators and prosecutors may claim to rely on 'cold' cognitive mechanisms to serve some kind of legally defined objectivity, it is almost impossible to not be affected by these 'hot' motivational goals.[100] Furthermore, being perceived as an effective criminal investigator likely implies a drive for self-actualization[101] and may lead to a disproportionate focus on efficiency to the detriment of accuracy.[102]

Being involved at several stages of an investigation increases the risk of (subconscious) ego-serving issues. This means that decision makers become less interested in the truth of the matter and more interested in proving to others that their hypothesis is right. Changing decision makers between different situations or investigative stages triggers a more a critical stance and is, therefore, a possible de-biasing technique in this context.[103]

The social explanations of confirmation bias essentially hold that humans do not reason to find the truth but instead to convince others that they are right.[104] People generally reason in a one-sided way in order to convince others that they are right and to defend their ideas and behaviours in order to maintain control, coherence and self-esteem.[105] Consequently, research in this area implies that confirmation bias is stronger in relation to self-generated hypotheses than hypotheses generated by others.[106] Prosecutors who themselves search for, or direct searches for, criminal evidence, may be more prone to bias than prosecutors

98 Arie W. Kruglanski and Donna M. Webster, "Motivated Closing of the Mind: 'Seizing' and 'Freezing'", in *Psychological Review*, 1996, vol. 103, no. 2, pp. 263–283; Kunda, 1990, pp. 480–498, see *supra* note 24.

99 Kunda, 1990, see *supra* note 24.

100 Fahsing, 2022, p. 275, see *supra* note 61.

101 See, for example, Steve M. Jex and Thomas W. Britt, *Organizational Psychology: A Scientist-Practitioner Approach*, John Wiley & Sons, Hoboken, 2015, p. 294.

102 See, for an example in a murder case, Karl Ask, Marc-André Reinhard, Tamara Marksteiner and Pär Anders Granhag, "Elasticity in Evaluations of Criminal Evidence: Exploring the Role of Cognitive Dissonance", in *Legal and Criminological Psychology*, 2011, vol. 16, no. 2, pp. 289–306.

103 Lidén, 2020, p. 527, see *supra* note 45.

104 Hugo Mercier, "The Argumentative Theory: Predictions and Empirical Evidence", in *Trends in Cognitive Science*, 2016, vol. 20, no. 9, pp. 689–700; Hugo Mercier and Dan Sperber, "Why Do Humans Reason? Arguments for an Argumentative Theory", in *Behavioral and Brain Sciences*, 2011, vol. 34, no. 2, pp. 57–111.

105 Moa Lidén, Minna Gräns and Peter Juslin, "From Devil's Advocate to Crime Fighter: Confirmation Bias and Debiasing Techniques in Prosecutorial Decision Making", in *Psychology, Crime & Law*, 2018, vol. 15, no. 12, p. 5.

106 Lidén, 2020, p. 526, see *supra* note 45.

who simply evaluate the evidence presented to them by the police.[107] It was found, for instance, that prosecutors shifted to a more guilt-confirming mindset after pressing charges. Before, they were more able to act as their own devil's advocate in the assessment of evidence and better balance considerations about whether or not to prosecute.[108] This research relates to, and compliments, the already existing research on so-called decisional tipping points, decisions that result in a mindset where criminal investigators become focused on verifying (only) the guilt of a suspect.[109]

4.6.3. Risks of Confirmation Bias During Investigations

A body of research indicates that tunnel vision, in general, and confirmation biases, in particular, can significantly influence the investigation process. For example, studies found that investigators interpret ambiguous witness evidence of the same case in line with the initial scenario fed to them (presenting the murder suspect looking either more or less guilty).[110] Likewise, analysts in counterterrorism cases interpreted information as risk-confirming after finding that a target had purchased a one-way flight ticket.[111]

Other research suggests the risk of confirmation bias is particularly high at the start of the investigation when (perceived) strong evidence (for example, CCTV, DNA or fingerprints, rather than a victim or witness' statement) might colour an investigator's expectations.[112] One might extrapolate that a similar effect occurs when documented evidence (for example, emails or a contract) is given disproportionate evidentiary weight, compared to just witness testimony.

Confirmation bias was also found to affect the preparation and conduct of suspect interviews.[113]

---

107 Lidén, Gräns and Juslin, 2018, p. 3, see *supra* note 105.

108 *Ibid.*

109 Ivar Fahsing and Karl Ask, "Decision Making and Decisional Tipping Points in Homicide Investigations: An Interview Study of British and Norwegian Detectives", in *Journal of Investigative Psychology and Offender Profiling*, 2013, vol. 10, no. 2, pp. 155–165.

110 Ask and Granhag, 2007, see *supra* note 70.

111 Mark Kebbell, Damon A. Muller and Kirsty Martin, "Understanding and Managing Bias: Dealing with Uncertainties in Policing Serious Crime", Canberra, ANU E Press, 2010, p. 90.

112 Minhwan Jang, Timothy J. Luke, Pär Anders Granhag and Aldert Vrij, "The Impact of Evidence Type on Police Investigators' Perceptions of Suspect Culpability and Evidence Reliability", in *Zeitschrift für Psychologie*, 2020, vol. 228, no. 3, pp. 188–198. Interestingly, this experiment with experienced South-Korean police officers included a fraud case.

113 See, for example, Lidén, Gräns and Juslin, 2018, see *supra* note 105; Rebecca Milne and Ray Bull, *Investigative Interviewing: Psychology and Practice*, John Wiley & Sons, Chichester, 1999, pp. 56–58; Richard A. Leo and Deborah Davis, "From False Confession to Wrongful Conviction: Seven Psychological Processes", in *The Journal of Psychiatry and Law*, 2010,

Some investigations seem more prone to confirmation bias than others. Risk factors include (a) a suspect-driven approach and (b) cognitive load.

In suspect-driven[114] investigations, investigators form a guilt hypothesis early on and only collect data that pertains to a particular suspect from a very early stage.[115] This may severely distort the information and evidence collection.[116] Moreover, the collection of evidence can be further skewed when it focuses predominantly on the culpability of the target in question. This makes it, often unconsciously and implicitly, much more difficult to comply with the (statutory) obligations to investigate potentially exonerating leads equally.[117]

In this context, cognitive load refers to the efforts used by working memory to actively process case relevant information. Working memory has a limited capacity and is directly related to the volume of information that needs to be processed.[118] When cognitive load is high, resources for S2-processing are low, and the reliance on heuristic thinking high. Our limited cognitive resources (attention, working memory, long-term memory) make it difficult to seriously consider more than one hypothesis. A demanding cognitive setting thus increases the risk of confirmation bias.[119]

vol. 38, pp. 9–56; Karl Ask, *Criminal Investigation: Motivation, Emotion and Cognition in the Processing of Evidence*, Göteborg University, Department of Psychology, 2006.

114 According to Lidén (2020, p. 479, see *supra* note 45), the term 'target' is not only more assertive in relation to an individual's guilt, but also, to a greater extent than the term 'suspect', it implies that the individual in question is dangerous or blameworthy. Therefore, it seems reasonable to expect that the identification of a 'target', potentially, triggers an even more hypothesis-confirming mindset. The same author also recommends a less assertive phrasing of the allegations under investigation ('the alleged crimes', 'according to source X, target Y was responsible for') than presenting them as established facts ('the crimes committed', 'target Y was responsible for').

115 O'Brien, 2009, see *supra* note 84.

116 Moa Lidén, "Prevention of Factual Confirmation-Bias During Offence-Driven Investigations", CILRAP Film, New Delhi, 22 February 2019 (https://www.cilrap.org/cilrap-film/190222-liden/).

117 Christian Axboe Nielsen, "Analysis of Organisational Structures and Quality Control of Case Development", in Agirre, Bergsmo, De Smet and Stahn (eds.), 2020, p. 286, see *supra* note 45.

118 Nicole Adams-Quackenbush, "Cognitive Barriers to Obtaining Information During Investigative Interviews", in Landström, Granhag and van Koppen (eds.), 2022, pp. 61–62, see *supra* note 78.

119 Wim De Neys, "Dual Processing in Reasoning: Two Systems but One Reasoner", in *Psychological Science*, 2006, vol. 17, no. 5, pp. 428–433.

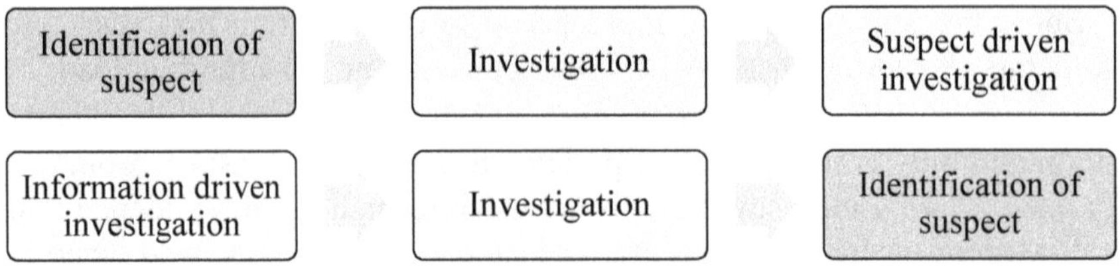

Illustration 4.8.: Suspect- versus information-driven investigations.[120]

Thus, PIF investigations seem to include inherent structural issues which exacerbate the risk of confirmation bias and tunnel vision. Such investigations are typically:

- suspect-driven;
- cognitively very demanding, often requiring the absorption of large amounts of complex information.

Other extraneous factors, like time pressure, work overload, escalation of commitment, and clearance rate might induce more confirmation bias in investigations,[121] and result in a strong (subconscious) temptation to take cognitive shortcuts.[122]

Sometimes a variety of risks for confirmation bias and tunnel vision combine, as is likely the case, for example, in high-profile corruption investigations. Pressure from the media and public opinion push for hasty conclusions and might cause shifts from an evidence-based to a target-based approach.[123]

4.7. Concluding Remarks

Research demonstrates that the human factor – including universal psychological tendencies, predictable responses to situational and organizational contexts, personal traits and characteristics of the crime itself – can unintentionally undermine truth-seeking in the complex evidence integration process. This research demonstrates a number of cognitive biases likely at work in investigative contexts while illuminating some of their risks. However, these findings are partial and cannot fully capture the dynamics of a real criminal investigation.

Better decision-making during investigation (and prosecution) must balance these sorts of insights with the real-life circumstances and constraints

120 Lidén, 2022, see *supra* note 116.

121 See Ask and Granhag, 2007, see *supra* note 70; Ask, Granhag and Rebelius, 2011, see *supra* note 72.

122 See Lidén, 2020, p. 527, see *supra* note 45.

123 Kim Rossmo, "Anatomie d'une enquête criminelle" [Anatomy of a Criminal Investigation], in *Criminologie*, 2020, vol. 53, no, 2, p. 29.

investigators and prosecutors confront. The actionable highlights of these findings are summarized below:

- To cope with and make sense of an overload of information, our brain relies on thinking shortcuts called heuristics. They essentially replace a difficult question with an easier one, and we often refer to them as 'intuition' or 'gut feeling'.
- Heuristics come to mind automatically and quickly, delivering generally acceptable judgments and decisions, but often at the expense of accuracy. Moreover, these heuristics can lead to systematic deviations from accurate, logical (or rational) decision-making. These deviations are called 'cognitive biases'.
- Cognitive biases have nothing to do with being prejudiced or any other negative personal trait, but are universal limitations of human cognition, generally independent of training or experience.
- Investigators should be aware of the mechanisms creating cognitive bias, especially confirmation bias and tunnel vision, as these are particularly likely to endanger the efficiency and fairness of the investigation.
- Mitigating measures involve addressing environmental factors that may be specific to a department or organization, characteristics of individual investigators, or the specifics of the case under review.
- The first step to mitigate the effect of cognitive biases is to acknowledge their existence and the impact they may have on hardworking, dedicated and competent experts. This comes with training.
- PIF investigations have characteristics that make them particularly vulnerable to confirmation bias and tunnel vision: they are typically suspect-driven, cognitively demanding, and often subject to time, media and other pressures.
- Moreover, the expertise of its investigators poses unique risks of bias blind spots.

5

Initial Reporting

Simon Baechler, Jorick Schreurs and Georgios Kougias*

5.1. Introduction

Consider Juan's dilemma: as a European Union ('EU') official responsible for the purchase of office equipment for the European Commission offices in Luxembourg, he has been administering ten supply contracts per year during the last six years. He has now noticed some particularities in the latest procurement he was asked to manage. After a call for offers to supply office chairs, he noticed that:

- the layout of the financial offer of the three competing tenderers is quite similar;
- the prices of the two competitors are exactly 5 per cent and 10 per cent more expensive than the cheapest offer for most parts of the offer;
- during a phone call between one of his colleagues and the most expensive tenderer, the latter referred to a 'courtesy' bid.

The winning offer is made by a company who has been a contractor of his service for many years. Should he report his findings to a controlling instance?

Investigations start with initial information. This is either gathered by investigators on their own initiative or reported to them on a voluntary or mandatory basis. In this chapter, we survey the different sources of initial information, raise challenges related to whether or not one issues an initial report, and propose an understanding of some relevant core concepts. The basic questions we

* **Simon Baechler** is chief of the criminal police, Police neuchâteloise, Neuchâtel, Switzerland; Researcher at the School of Criminal Justice and University of Lausanne; and Associate Professor at the University of Québec in Trois-Rivières. **Jorick Schreurs**, a public prosecutor in the Netherlands, is currently working as National Expert at the European Anti-Fraud Office ('OLAF') where he contributes to the co-operation between OLAF and its external stakeholders, most notably the European Public Prosecutor's Office ('EPPO'). **Georgios Kougias** is the Coordinator of Inter-Institutional Relations and Europol Liaison Officer at OLAF, focusing on co-operation with key partners such as the EPPO and Europol. He previously served as Head of Registry and Operational Stakeholders at the EPPO and worked as a Financial Intelligence Analyst at Europol. This chapter is authored in the contributors' personal capacity and does not necessarily reflect the views of EPPO, OLAF or other institutions mentioned therein.

address here include: Who has to report? What triggers a reporting duty? Are there any thresholds or quality criteria for initial reporting?

5.2. Initial Reporting

Threats to public funding, like the EU budget, come in many varieties and from many sources. Examples abound: overpriced medications purchased by the EU; reimbursements of non-eligible costs in research projects; or restriction of competition in a tender for construction work. These and countless other threats endanger the sound financial management of EU funds. However, these do not necessarily amount to fraud. Such threats can occur unintentionally, by omission (as is the case when one misunderstands the relevant rules), or intentionally.

The detection and reporting of events that might warrant investigative attention involves a great range of actors who have to navigate the applicable legal and procedural frameworks to assess the seriousness and validity of the information, as well as the reliability of its source. This decision constitutes a critical junction in the whole investigative process,[1] as without initial reporting, events may never be investigated.

Standard operating rules or guidelines can help investigators understand and implement legal or ethical obligations to report possible instances of irregular behaviour of fraud, like safeguarding the anonymity or otherwise protecting whistle-blowers; however, the actual reporting will often entail specific and delicate judgement calls and assessments of probability. As explained elsewhere in this book, such judgments and decisions are affected by noise and bias.[2] These often happen in a context of relative entropy,[3] where the level of uncertainty is high and hard to manage and individuals are striving to minimize this disorder.

Organizations may apply risk indicators or 'red flags' to provide guidance to their staff in reporting observations that warrant closer scrutiny, but such indicators do not usually include standards for validating the information.[4]

In the sections below, we focus on the initial reporting framework for PIF[5] offences.

1 Simon Baechler *et al.*, "Un modèle continu, non linéaire et collaboratif de l'enquête", in *Criminologie*, 2020, vol. 53, no. 2, pp. 43–76.

2 See Chapters 3 and 4.

3 Baechler *et al.*, 2020, see *supra* note 1.

4 The 2022 United Nations ('UN') handbook on fraud and corruption awareness for instance refers (pp. 14–15) to general risk indicators ranging from a key employee not taking leave, over a high standard of living and a close personal relationship with contractors, to missing or manipulated electronic and hard copy documents (see UN, *Fraud and Corruption Awareness: A Handbook for Staff*, 2022).

5 'PIF' stands for the 'protection des intérêts financiers' of the EU.

5.3. The Legal Framework

5.3.1. Actors and Offences

Three of the main players in detecting and reporting possible instances of fraud against the EU budget are the European Court of Auditors ('ECA'), OLAF and EPPO.

The ECA examines whether EU revenue and expenditure have been incurred in a lawful and regular manner and whether the financial management has been sound. As a part of its mission, it detects and reports errors. It determines the amount of money that should not have been paid out from the EU budget because it was not used in accordance with EU or national rules. Detecting fraud is not the main focus of ECA audits, but professional audit standards require auditors to carry out specific fraud-related procedures for each audit engagement. The auditor should thus be attentive to inherent risks of fraud in any transaction with financial impact and report it consequently.[6]

OLAF investigates fraud, corruption and any other illegal activity affecting the financial interests of the EU. In this context 'illegal activity' includes irregularities,[7] more specifically, any infringement of a provision of EU law by an economic operator prejudicing the EU budget, either by reducing or losing revenue or by unjustified expenditure.[8]

The EPPO investigates, prosecutes and brings to judgment the perpetrators of (organized) fraud affecting the Union's financial interests, corruption, misappropriation and money laundering in relation to EU expenditure (grants and

---

[6] Article 287(2) of the Treaty on the Functioning of the European Union ('TFEU') (https://www.legal-tools.org/doc/15b8be/) obliges the ECA to report cases of irregularity and Article 325(1) TFEU impells it to contribute to the fight against fraud and any other illegal activity affecting the EU financial interests.

[7] See Article 2(3) of the 'OLAF Regulation', Consolidated text of Regulation (EU, EURATOM) No. 883/2013 of the European Parliament and of the Council of 11 September 2013 concerning investigations conducted by the European Anti-Fraud Office (OLAF) and repealing Regulation (EC) No. 1073/1999 of the European Parliament and of the Council and Council Regulation (Euratom) No. 1074/1999 (https://www.legal-tools.org/doc/6f0ede/).

[8] Article 1(2) of Council Regulation (EC, EURATOM) No. 2988/95 of 18 December 1995 on the protection of the European Communities financial interests ('Regulation 2988/95') (https://www.legal-tools.org/doc/95p8lazw/).

procurement) or EU revenue.[9] EU Member States must ensure that these so-called PIF offences constitute a criminal offence in their national law.[10]

EU fraud consists of any intentional act or omission affecting the EU's financial interests, including the use or presentation of false, incorrect or incomplete statements or documents, or failure to disclose information despite a specific obligation to do so, or the misapplication of funds or benefits.[11]

5.3.2. Rules on Initial Reporting

When suspicions of EU fraud arise, this should be reported to the competent authorities. The new[12] institutional setting for fighting EU fraud entails an intricate framework of reporting duties between the different actors and subsequent preliminary examinations.[13] The modalities and conditions of such exchanges are often specified in bilateral working arrangements, which complement other antifraud reporting duties, under different regimes (for example, in customs cases). This makes for a complex and sometimes overlapping system of reporting channels.

Neither the ECA, nor OLAF or EPPO, have any restriction as regards the sources of initial information. Such information can emerge during or outside audits, come from public or private, known or anonymous sources,[14] whistleblowers,[15] or can even be gathered in a proactive way.

Reporting duties abound. Every member of EU staff has to report to his or her hierarchy or to OLAF directly, "facts which give rise to a presumption of the existence of possible illegal activity, including fraud or corruption […] or

[9] See Article 86 TFEU, *supra* note 6, Article 4 of the 'EPPO Regulation', Council Regulation (EU) No. 2017/1939 of 12 October 2017 implementing enhanced cooperation on the establishment of the European Public Prosecutor's Office ('the EPPO') ('EPPO Regulation') (https://www.legal-tools.org/doc/plfszr14/), and Article 3 of the 'PIF Directive', Directive (EU) No. 2017/1371 of the European Parliament and of the Council of 5 July 2017 on the fight against fraud to the Union's financial interests by means of criminal law (https://www.legal-tools.org/doc/3lsm7y4u/).

[10] Articles 3(1), 4(2) and 4(3) of the PIF Directive, see *supra* note 9.

[11] See *ibid.*, Article 3(2).

[12] EPPO became operational in operational in June 2021.

[13] See Chapter 6.

[14] See Article 5(1) OLAF Regulation, *supra* note 7.

[15] Directive (EU) No. 2019/1937 of the European Parliament and of the Council of 23 October 2019 on the protection of persons who report breaches of Union law, to be implemented in the Member States by 17 December 2021 ('Directive (EU) 2019/1937') (https://www.legal-tools.org/doc/1rhhcqqr/).

professional misconduct, which he or she becomes aware of in the course of or in connection with the performance of his/her duties".[16]

Staff members involved in the financial management and control of transactions, and the external auditors they contract, have an additional obligation to report "events of illegal activity, fraud or corruption".[17]

EU Member States, via their competent authorities (for example, judiciary, customs and national authorities managing EU funds), should report to the EPPO any "conduct in respect of which EPPO could exercise its competence".[18] They may first conduct a preliminary evaluation of allegations,[19] and make use of reporting procedures already in place[20] or set up specifically for reporting to the EPPO.[21]

Member States are also expected to report irregularities and fraud in shared management of EU funds to the Irregularities Management System, managed by OLAF.[22]

EU Institutions, Bodies, Offices and Agencies ('IBOAs') have the obligation to immediately transmit to OLAF "any information relating to possible cases of fraud, corruption or any other illegal activity affecting the financial interests of the Union".[23]

---

16 Article 22(a) of the EU 'Staff Regulations', Regulation No. 31 (EEC), 11 (EAEC), laying down the Staff Regulations of Officials and the Conditions of Employment of Other Servants of the European Economic Community and the European Atomic Energy Community, 1 January 2016, No. 31/2016 (https://www.legal-tools.org/doc/q3tlenb4/).

17 Article 74(8)(1) and (2) of Regulation (EU, EURATOM) No. 2018/1046 of the European Parliament and of the Council of 18 July 2018 on the financial rules applicable to the general budget of the Union (https://www.legal-tools.org/doc/eh3bee5b/). The Regulation was recast in September 2024 (European Commission, "Financial Regulation Applicable to the General Budget of the Union (Recast)", September 2024 ('EU Financial Regulation') (https://www.legal-tools.org/doc/5pjqylsw/)).

18 Article 24(1) of the EPPO Regulation, see *supra* note 9.

19 *Ibid.*, Recital 51.

20 EPPO, "Protecting Taxpayers Against Fraud and Corruption: The European Public Prosecutor's Office", 2019, p. 6.

21 Recital 52 of the EPPO Regulation, see *supra* note 9.

22 The Irregularities Management System is a secure electronic communications tools, which facilitates the Member States' obligation to report irregularities, as envisaged in Article 15(2) of the PIF Directive, see *supra* note 9.

23 Article 8(1) OLAF Regulation, see *supra* note 7.

When they consider their information indicates that a PIF offence has occurred, the same IBOAs should report to the EPPO,[24] either directly or indirectly[25] (after a preliminary assessment by OLAF).[26]

The European Commission shall report to EPPO criminal conduct in respect of which the EPPO could exercise its competence, or inform EPPO when it is not yet clear whether EPPO is competent.[27] In either case, the Commission is expected to send EPPO "any information and evidence" in relation to the alleged PIF offence.

The ECA is expected to send EPPO "any information and evidence which comes to its attention where it considers the existence of possible criminal conduct" under EPPO competence, including in cases of "any suspicion of criminal conduct".[28]

OLAF receives a copy of the reports IBOAs sent to EPPO directly[29] and should itself report to EPPO without undue delay, any criminal conduct in respect of which it could exercise its competence.[30]

Frameworks for whistle-blowing protection add to the complexity of the field of initial reporting.[31]

---

24 Article 24(1) EPPO Regulation, see *supra* note 9.

25 In accordance with Article 5 of the Agreement establishing the modalities of cooperation between the European Commission and the European Public Prosecutor's Office, 18 June 2021, and Article 1 of its annexe (https://www.legal-tools.org/doc/wssxawqq/), the European Commission, as a rule, transmits reports of criminal conduct to EPPO via 'contact point' OLAF.

26 See Article 12c(6) of the OLAF Regulation, see *supra* note 7, and Recital 51 of the EPPO Regulation, see *supra* note 9.

27 Agreement establishing the modalities of cooperation between the European Commission and the European Public Prosecutor's Office, see *supra* note 25.

28 See Article 3 of the Working Arrangement between the European Court of Auditors and the European Public Prosecutor's Office, 3 September 2021 (https://www.legal-tools.org/doc/amwiipmq/).

29 Article 8(1) OLAF Regulation, see *supra* note 7.

30 Article 24(1) EPPO Regulation, see *supra* note 9 and Article 12c(1) OLAF Regulation, see *supra* note 7.

31 In addition to EU-internal whistle-blowing schemes, Directive (EU) 2019/1937, see *supra* note 15, imposes all EU Member States to introduce a whistle-blower protection in their national legislation by December 2021. However, many Member States failed to do so by this deadline (see European Commission, Directorate-General Migration and Home Affairs ('DG HOME'), "Report", 2022, p. 19)

Illustration 5.1.: The reporting imbroglio.

5.4. Levels of Initial Reporting

Figures on actual reporting of suspicions of fraud and corruption are spread over several sources, public and private, based on public surveys or on hard figures, and are hence difficult to compare.[32] As regards institutional reporting, important players in the protection of the EU budget have exposed weak detection and reporting performance by the Member States of the EU. In 2019 already, the ECA exposed weak fraud reporting in cohesion funds,[33] and after its first year of operations (at the end of 2021), EPPO concluded that "it has become clear that the level of detection of fraud affecting the financial interests of the EU is suboptimal and varies significantly from MS to MS".[34]

[32] For example, whereas 'Eurobarometer 2022' reports a decrease in reporting of corruption cases and adds that less than half of respondents knew where to report (European Commission, "Corruption", Special Eurobarometer 523, March–April 2022, p. 84), Eurojust comments that an increase in corruption cases registered year on year "might indicate that this is becoming less of a barrier" (see Eurojust, "Eurojust Casework on Corruption 2016–2021: Insights", May 2022, p. 15). A study of 2022 on the fight against corruption in the EU, reports that there are limited (or ineffective) reporting rules (p. 14) and that reporting of corruption should be boosted by introducing common minimum standards for reporting (see DG HOME, 2022, pp. ix, xiii, see *supra* note 31).

[33] ECA, "Tackling Fraud in EU Cohesion Spending: Managing Authorities Need to Strengthen Detection, Response and Coordination", Special Report No. 06, 2019, p. 36.

[34] EPPO, "2021 Annual Report", 2022, p. 10. In its 2022 report, EPPO writes that: "In 2022, the EPPO's activity brought about a first positive evolution, with regard to the level of detection of fraud affecting the financial interests of the EU in some Member States. Even if a comparable dynamic could not be observed on the side of the institutions, bodies, offices and agencies of the European Union, there are now more investigations into EU fraud initiated in the 22 participating Member States than the historical average before the EPPO's establishment", see EPPO, "2022 Annual Report", 2023, p. 10.

In addition to the inherent uncertainty surrounding reporting duties, the alertness for, and willingness to, report fraud and corruption is tainted by cultural differences.[35] Moreover, the grand public cannot be expected to know whether the conduct they encounter falls within the scope of criminal or non-criminal investigation.[36] Even the authorities under reporting obligations may find it difficult to make this distinction.

Better reporting arguably starts with awareness campaigns and training on prohibited behaviours. Here we set out some additional challenges, linked to confusion about the scales and standards[37] that apply.

5.5. To Report or Not to Report

5.5.1. A Murky Field

The reporting of irregularities and fraud is replete with instances of judgment and decision-making. For instance, a person aware of a situation considered to be 'delicate', has to judge whether this information might indicate a criminal offence or whether it concerns an irregularity. He or she has to consider if a reporting obligation applies, and, if so, how strong suspicions should be to trigger initial reporting. The determinant often concerns the presence of guilty intent, which is often difficult to assess.

Such 'judgment calls' are not computations following exact rules, but are affected by noise, heuristic thinking, and cognitive bias, as described in other contributions of this volume. Noise and bias are understood to be especially prominent in situations that people perceive as highly uncertain. A potential whistle-blower might, for instance, hesitate to come forward and report a suspicion that his boss was bribed, because he just read a press article about how a whistle-blower in another country was arrested for violation of professional secrecy. The *availability heuristic*[38] will have made this presentation very salient in the person's mind and hence disproportionally obstructive (compared to the real efficiency and integrity of existing whistle-blowing schemes).

Although heuristic thinking and cognitive biases can definitely have an impact on judgment and decision-making in relation to initial reporting, in the

[35] See, for example, Fons Trompenaars and Charles Hamden-Turner, *Riding the Waves of Culture: Understanding Diversity in Global Business*, Nicholas Brealey International, London, 2011.

[36] See, however, EPPO's 2022 Annual Report, p. 10, *supra* note 34, for a positive comment on the reporting by private parties: "The proportion of reports from private parties (58%) is very high, and is an expression of great expectations towards the EPPO as a European Union judicial body".

[37] See Chapter 3.

[38] Richards J. Heuer, *Psychology of Intelligence Analysis*, Central Intelligence Agency, Langley, 1999, p. 147.

following we will focus on the influence of 'noise'. The wide variety of terminology present in the entire regulatory framework for reporting PIF irregularities and offences, and its inconsistent use, may hinder a common understanding and implementation of reporting duties. By causing uncertainty among the staff that has to work with these regulations, it risks being a source of unwanted variability in reporting judgments.

5.5.2. Noise in Reporting

In a previous chapter, Frey, Chaloftis and Willems[39] distinguished the concepts of 'rules', 'scales' and 'standards', and highlighted their importance in arriving at consistent and accurate judgement and decision-making processes. Like other legislation, the EU Regulations, and adjacent documents[40] on PIF irregularities and crimes, are replete with terms that aim to qualify human behaviour in terms of its legality. Relatedly, these documents aim to establish values, essentially diagnostic criteria, for differentiating and qualifying the legality of various forms of conduct, and this is typically done in terms of texts or statements. Although many of these terms play a crucial role in the judgment and decision-making processes of PIF investigations, some of them are problematic for the risk of noise they introduce. There are three key types of impediments to making proper decisions about whether or not to report a PIF case: (a) the distinction between information, facts and evidence; (b) the difference between irregularity and fraud; and (c) the 'standards of proof' for initial reporting.

Our first focus will be on the interrelated concepts of 'information', 'fact' and 'evidence'. Although these concepts are obviously not exclusively PIF-related, they are particularly significant in this context. Even at this point, it is worth noting that the different instructions to report refer (inconsistently) to:

- "any *fact* of which they become aware when carrying out their duties";[41]
- "any *information* relating to possible cases of fraud";[42]
- "any information and *evidence* relating to possible cases of fraud";[43]
- "any information and evidence [...] of *possible criminal conduct* [...]";[44]
- "any information and evidence [about] any *suspicion* of criminal conduct";[45]

[39] See Chapter 3.

[40] Such as (internal) guidelines and working arrangements.

[41] Article 15(3) of the PIF Directive, see *supra* note 9.

[42] Article 8(1) of the OLAF Regulation, see *supra* note 7.

[43] Article 4(1) of the working Arrangement between the ECA and OLAF of 22 May 2019.

[44] See Article 3 of the Working Arrangement of 3 September 2021, *supra* note 28.

[45] *Ibid.*

- "criminal conduct".[46]

Then, we focus on the use of the more distinctly PIF-related concepts 'irregularity' and 'fraud', and all of their usual variations. Finally, we will consider different standards of proof mentioned in the various EU regulatory documents.

As we will see, it is not always easy to distinguish 'errors' from 'illegal activity', 'serious irregularities' from 'irregularities', and 'fraud' from other wrongdoings or omissions, all of which are subject to separate but sometimes parallel reporting duties. Furthermore, their assessment during the preliminary examination (see the next contribution in this volume) involves vague standards like "sufficient suspicions",[47] "reasonable grounds",[48] or "manifestly unsubstantiated complaints".[49]

In addition to the complex and often confusing patchwork of standards and scales, there are significant linguistic obstacles. Certain terms may have different meanings among the various linguistic areas in the EU. Related nuances associated with these terms may similarly vary across geographic and linguistic regions.[50] Thus, in the next sections, we propose definitions and descriptions that could contribute to more consistent and accurate reporting.

5.5.3. From Information to Evidence

In relation to initial reporting and investigations, 'information' can be understood as all data[51] that has not undergone a test of validity, that is, a process confirming whether it is real and accurate.[52] This might concern, for example, allegations, articles found on the internet, or the informal information exchanged between colleagues regarding their knowledge of persons reportedly involved.

---

46 Article 24(1) of the EPPO Regulation, see *supra* note 9.

47 Article 5(1) of the OLAF Regulation, see *supra* note 7. In French: 'soupçons suffisants'.

48 Article 24(6) of the EPPO Regulation, see *supra* note 9, and Article 40 of Internal Rules of Procedure of the European Public Prosecutor's Office, consolidated version of College Decision 003/2020, 2022 (https://www.legal-tools.org/doc/yhuues8e/).

49 Article 12c(3) of the OLAF Regulation, see *supra* note 7. In French: 'allégations manifestement non fondées'.

50 We refer in particular to the distinction between data, information, facts, evidence and intelligence, as discussed below.

51 For the purpose of this contribution, we use the categorization of 'data' common in intelligence contexts (for example, human intelligence ('HUMINT'), signals intelligence ('SIGINT')), and forensic analysis (for example, structured, non-structured). Using the conventional sequential logic often applied in this context, most data would precede the status of information, understood as a selection of relevant and purposeful data. See, for example, Jerry Ratcliffe, *Intelligence-Led Policing*, Willan Publishing, Portland, 2008.

52 Eric Shepherd and Andy Griffiths, *Investigative Interviewing: The Conversation Management Approach*, 2nd ed., Oxford University Press, 2013.

In relation to administrative and criminal procedures, 'evidence' can be defined as the information that is used (in court) to try to prove something.[53] Evidence is subject to criteria of admissibility and relevance and relates to a wide range of information sources that might eventually inform the prosecutor, judge, or court in order to prove or disprove, given the applicable standard of proof (see below), that a suspected individual committed (or did not commit) the offence.[54] The same applies to administrative proceedings, in which evidence serves the purpose of proving or disproving that the person concerned committed an irregularity, allowing EU institutions or national administrations to take appropriate measures.

Information only becomes evidence when it has been successfully validated, that is, when its reality and accuracy have been established. Validation entails the possibility of independent verification and makes the information (more) immune to contestation, which is to say factual.[55] A distinction is made between strong evidence (for example, a video-recording of a person entering a European Commission building) and weak evidence, resulting from less stringent forms of validation, and thus somehow ambiguous or open to interpretation (for example, in a witness statement, the bad quality record of a telephone conversation). In some jurisdictions, information generally known to the public (for example, that 'on 25 December, Christians celebrate Christmas' or 'some types of crime involve the use of large sums of cash money') does not need validation to be accepted as a fact. In any case, evidence never ensures full certainty and is always defeasible.[56]

The primary processes of validation are corroboration and consistency. Corroboration signifies positive confirmation[57] and occurs, for instance, when a testimony that a sum was paid is confirmed by a bank statement, or when

[53] Material collected in the field is not, strictly speaking, evidence, as this status can only be determined when it is presented for the purpose of arriving at a decision by its judge(s), who analysed it in the context of the applicable substantive law. See Ewan Brown and William H. Wiley, "International Criminal Investigative Collection Planning, Collection Management and Evidence Review", in Xavier Agirre, Morten Bergsmo, Simon De Smet and Carsten Stahn (eds.), *Quality Control in Criminal Investigation*, Torkel Opsahl Academic EPublisher, Brussels, 2020, p. 537 (https://www.toaep.org/ps-pdf/38-qcci/).

[54] Rod Gehl and Darryl Plecas, *Introduction to Criminal Investigation: Processes, Practices and Thinking*, Justice Institute of British Columbia, 2016, New Westminster, p. 33.

[55] According to the Oxford Learner's Dictionary, a fact is "a thing that is known to be true, especially when it can be proved". A fact thus refers more to a claim of the state of nature (reality) than a state of knowledge (information and evidence).

[56] See more on defeasibility in Chapter 9.

[57] Xavier Agirre Aranburu, "The Contribution of Analysis to the Quality Control in Criminal Investigation", in Agirre, Bergsmo, De Smet and Stahn (eds.), 2020, p. 224, see *supra* note 53.

different people give accounts containing detail supporting the same narrative (inter-statement consistency). Similarly, when the statements of a complainant are consistent over time, this is a form of validation via intra-statement consistency.

A difference is made between substantive and circumstantial corroboration. Substantive corroboration is the most common and compelling understanding of corroboration, and it occurs when two independent sources support the same evidence. Circumstantial corroboration takes place when one source reports the substantive (evidence) fact, and other sources report some accessory (evidence) facts in a way that makes the primary account plausible (for example, an allegation of bribery, followed by the observation of a changed lifestyle of the suspect).[58] When no source reports substantive evidence, but two or more sources report converging accessory pieces of evidence, this makes for a specific form of corroboration, sometimes called a 'cluster of indications' or a 'body of evidence'.[59]

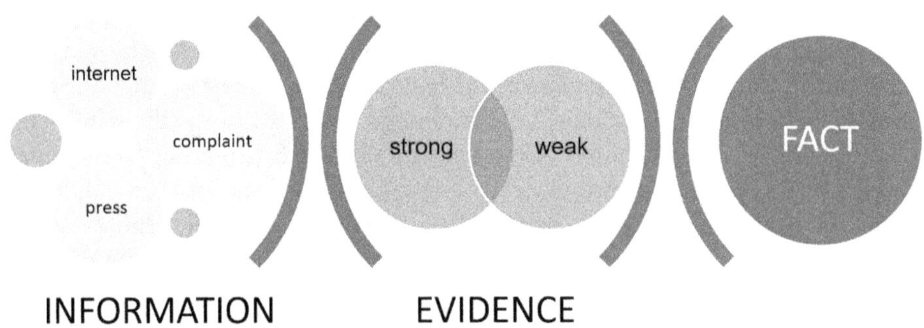

Illustration 5.2.: From information to evidence.

5.5.4. From Error to Fraud

Detection and reporting duties refer to 'errors', 'irregularities', 'misconduct'[60] and 'fraud', without these concepts and reporting rules always being well defined. For example, the difference between an *error* and an *irregularity* is not clear. They both require a negative financial impact, but when the ECA distinguishes both concepts by stating that errors are unintentional misstatements in

[58] *Ibid.*, p. 226.

[59] None of the English terms exactly translates the better term used in French: '*un faisceau d'indices*' (literally: 'a bundle of indications').

[60] In the UN Secretariat "fraudulent acts" are considered to be "misconduct": see UN, 2022, *supra* note 4.

financial statements,[61] this seems to attribute – *a contrario* – intentionality to an irregularity.

The Regulation defining an irregularity itself, confusingly refers to "intentional irregularities or those caused by negligence".[62] An 'intentional irregularity' seems to equate to fraud and could be considered to be a contradiction in terms. In the same vein, annual reports on the protection of the EU's financial interests distinguish between "fraudulent" and "non-fraudulent" irregularities.[63]

The EU Staff Regulation[64] and Financial Regulation[65] both refer to the obligation of staff to report illegal activity to OLAF.[66] However, several other legal acts refer to an obligation to report irregularities. For instance, Regulation (EU) 2021/691[67] lays upon Member States the obligation to report 'irregularities including fraud' to the European Commission. OLAF's Regulation specifies that irregularities are captured in the notion of illegal activity[68] but this might not be clear to all persons subject of the reporting obligation.

The Regulation protecting the NextGeneration EU budget introduces the new concept of "serious irregularities", comprising fraud, corruption and

---

[61] Nikolaos Kilonis, "The ECA Statement of Assurance: Separating Errors From Alleged Fraud", in *ECA Journal*, 2019, p. 45.

[62] Article 5(1) of Regulation 2988/95, *supra* note 8.

[63] See, for example, European Commission, "33rd Annual Report on the Protection of the European Union's Financial Interest and the Fight Against Fraud", 2021.

[64] See Articles 22(a), 22(b) and 22(c) of the Staff Regulations, *supra* note 16.

[65] See Article 74(8) of the 'EU Financial Regulation', European Commission, "Financial Regulation Applicable to the General Budget of the Usssnion (Recast)", September 2024 (https://www.legal-tools.org/doc/5pjqylsw/); see also the previous Regulation (EU, EURATOM) No. 2018/1046 of the European Parliament and of the Council of 18 July 2018 on the financial rules applicable to the general budget of the Union (https://www.legal-tools.org/doc/eh3bee5b/).

[66] We remind that under Article 24(1) of the EPPO Regulation, see *supra* note 9, IBOAs might have the obligation to report the same illegal activity to EPPO when it concerns 'criminal conduct' in respect of which EPPO could exercise its competence.

[67] Regulation (EU) No. 2021/691 of the European Parliament and of the Council of 28 April 2021 on the European Globalisation Adjustment Fund for Displaced Workers (EGF) and repealing Regulation (EU) No 1309/2013 (https://www.legal-tools.org/doc/mzikhdvu/).

[68] See Article 2(3) of the OLAF Regulation, see *supra* note 7, which provides that: "the notion of 'any other illegal activity' shall include irregularity as defined in Article 1(2) of Regulation (EC, Euratom) No. 2988/95".

conflicts of interest.[69] This provides an alternative to the previously used dichotomy of 'criminal' versus 'administrative' acts used consistently in other contexts.[70]

To avoid any confusion, it would seem helpful to clearly distinguish and consistently use the term:

- *irregularity* for an act or omission which does not comply with EU rules and has a potentially negative impact on EU financial interests, committed either:
  - by error (unconscious), for example, a beneficiary of a grant inserting a wrong amount for claiming reimbursement of a cost;
  - by mistake (conscious), for example, a member of EU staff interpreting wrongly an evaluation guideline in a procurement case;
  - by negligence,[71] for example, a Member of the European Parliament delegating his signature to his assistant, who uses it to sign off irregular mission statements;
- *fraud* for a qualified ('guilty') intentional act or omission, involving for instance deliberation, malice or deceit.[72]

69 See Recital 53 of Regulation (EU) No. 2021/241 of the European Parliament and of the Council of 12 February 2021 establishing the Recovery and Resilience Facility (https://www.legal-tools.org/doc/gmqgnds5/).

70 Charlotte Arwidi and Clemens Kreith, "Protecting the EU's Financial Interest in the New Recovery and Resilience Facility: The Role of the European Anti-Fraud Office", in *EUCRIM*, 2021, vol. 3, p. 172.

71 See Articles 4(3) and 5(1) of Regulation 2988/95, *supra* note 8.

72 Examples taken from fraud indicators in audit, more in particular p. 69 of ECA's "Financial and Compliance Audit Manual", 2012; Kilonis, 2019, p. 45, see *supra* note 61, and "International Standard on Auditing 240: The Auditor's Responsibilities Relating to Fraud in an Audit of Financial Statements", 2009, para. 11.

ADMINISTRATIVE	vs.	CRIMINAL
Irregularity		**Fraud**
An act or omission in breach of an EU rule and negatively affecting the Union's financial interest		An act or omission in breach of an EU rule and negatively affecting the Union's financial interest
➔ Not intentional		➔ Intentional
By error, by mistake, by negligence		On purpose (or) willingly and knowingly accepting the possibility that one's behaviour will constitute a criminal offence

Illustration 5.3.: Irregularity versus fraud.

5.5.5. Standards for Initial Reporting

As discussed before, information becomes evidence, and evidence – provided it is sufficiently validated – develops into facts. Any staff member who has the responsibility to decide whether to report a potential irregularity or criminal offence is at the early stage of this sequence. This means that the staff member deals with information that does not have evidential value, at least not at that moment, nor has it been established as a fact. This also means that that the rapporteur is *not* expected to:

- attain "the psychological state of taking a fact for true";[73]
- present 'comprehensive' or 'conclusive' evidence;[74]
- accuse a particular suspect;
- qualifies of the reported offence in legal terms.

[73] Christoph Engel, "Preponderance of the Evidence Versus Intime Conviction: A Behavioural Perspective on a Conflict Between American and Continental European Law", in *Vermont Law Review*, 2009, vol. 33, p. 441.

[74] Matthew E. Cross, "The Standard of Proof in Preliminary Examinations", in Morten Bergsmo and Carsten Stahn (eds.), *Quality Control in Preliminary Examination: Volume 2*, Torkel Opsahl Academic EPublisher, Brussels, 2018, p. 252 (https://www.toaep.org/ps-pdf/33-bergsmo-stahn).

However, an institutional partner may be expected to produce better supported reports than, for instance, reports from private sources.[75]

In addition, the efforts of the rapporteur to provide correct, complete and accurate information should never go so far as to jeopardize the prospective investigation. In some cases, this endeavour might derail into unauthorized investigative activities and complicate the evidence-gathering by formal bodies. It is thus essential to avoid harm to (criminal) investigations in the documentation and collection of information for accountability purposes ('no harm principle').

It was proposed earlier that *standards* are judging guidelines that, as opposed to rules, grant discretion and allow people to adjust to the particulars of the situation.[76] In matters of initial reporting, standards address the level of certainty or assurance that warrants the decision to be made. In other words, and especially applicable here, the question is: 'how sure' should the rapporteur be to denounce suspicions of irregularity or fraud? In adjudication, which is the decision of guilt or innocence and determination of a possible sanction by a judge, the term 'standard of proof' is traditionally used. It is also the threshold of sufficient evidence and persuasive power the prosecutor has to produce in order to convince this magistrate or the trier of facts of the rightness of his or her claim.[77]

Reporting obligations by themselves do not entail independent standards of proof. Standards of proof for adjudication were not conceived for persons or institutions obliged by reporting duties (of PIF offences) and cannot be considered as enforceable standards. The rapporteur does not have to demonstrate 'reasonable grounds' or to be sure 'beyond reasonable doubt'. A superior level standard cannot impose but can inform lower-level standards. Deliberations to report or not can hence benefit from, but are not constrained to, the standards used downstream (for example, during the preliminary examination, investigation and adjudication phases).

When no or open-ended standards are in place, judges might have to make numerous judgments to decide what counts as a duty to report. Setting standards

---

75 Article 24(4) of the EPPO Regulation, *supra* note 9, provides that reports send by IBOA's and authorities of the Member States to EPPO "shall contain, as a minimum, a description of the facts, including an assessment of the damage caused or likely to be caused, the possible legal qualification and any available information about potential victims, suspects and any other involved persons".

76 See Section 3.3.2. of Chapter 3.

77 More technically: "The burden of proof is a party's obligation in legal proceedings to establish an assertion or charge, encompassing the burden of production (provision of sufficient evidence) and the burden of persuasion (preponderance of evidence)", see Fundamental Rights Agency, "Presumption of Innocence and Related Rights: Professional Perspectives", 2021, p. 5.

without details that help support and illustrate them can lead to noise. The provisions in the OLAF and EPPO legal framework support the largest interpretation of a suspicion, triggering a duty to report.[78] Scholars have endorsed this view, commenting that "the notion of suspicion should not be interpreted narrowly".[79] The overarching guideline seems to be to report even in the case of doubt. '*In dubio pro reo*'[80] does not apply at the reporting stage. However, it would seem reasonable to expect that the rapporteur of irregularities or fraud provides information that is not the result of conjecture or mere assertions.[81] In this view, a 'balance of probabilities' criterion could be useful in structuring the reporting duties (more 'yes' than 'no'). Such assessment is contingent on the risks and rates of false positives (reporting when – with hindsight – reporting was not the right decision) and false negatives (not reporting when this would have been the right decision) that the decision maker or system is ready to accept in a given context of operations (here: selection).[82] The notions of false positives and false negatives may also be understood as the risks of over-specification or under-detection, respectively.

The quality of the information provided encompasses:[83]

- *relevance*: this concerns the effectiveness of the information in view of the decision to be made (in initial reporting, opening of an investigation, or adjudication); it entails aspects of:
  - *competence* (for example, the reported case does not have any EU financial interests at stake);
  - *timeliness* (for example, the report is sent soon after an alleged solicitation of a bribe, not four years later).
- *credibility*: this concerns the match with reality and relates to qualities including:

[78] See Article 8(2) of the OLAF Regulation, *supra* note 7, Recital 7 of the European Commission's "Proposal to amend Regulation 883/2013", 2021, and Articles 24(5) and 24(9) and Recital 53 of the EPPO Regulation, *supra* note 9.

[79] Anne Weyembergh and Chloé Brière, "The Future Cooperation Between OLAF and the EPPO, Report for the European Parliament, Budgetary Affairs Policy Department, 2017, p. 18.

[80] '*In dubio pro reo*' is an expression reflecting the presumption of innocence, which implies that any doubt as to the question of guilt is to benefit the suspect. See Council of Europe-European Court of Human Rights, "Guide on Article 6 of the European Convention on Human Rights: Right to a Fair Trial (Criminal Limb)", 31 August 2020, p. 60, para. 317.

[81] Cross, 2018, p. 252, see *supra* note 74.

[82] Baechler *et al.*, 2020, see *supra* note 1.

[83] Remmer W. Starreveld, Heidi B. de Mare and Emanuel J. Joëls, *Bestuurlijke informatie-verzorging, deel 2b: Toepassingen typologie van de bedrijfshuishoudingen* [*Administrative Information Management, Part 2b: Applied Typology of Corporate Accountants*], 4th ed., Samsom, Alphen aan den Rijn-Diegem, 1997, p. 294.

    - *correctness* (for example, the complaint concerns a 'H2020' research project, not an 'FP4' project);
    - *completeness* (for example, all names of the competing tenderers are mentioned in the complaint of bid rigging);
    - *accuracy* or *detail* (for example, the staff member was seen with a contractor on the evening of 7 July 2024 instead of 'last summer') and;
    - *objective* (not reflecting a biased or unilateral stance)
- *format* of presentation (for example, supported by documents);
- *verifiability* of the information (for example, follow-up on request for more detail, traceability).

5.6. Concluding Remarks

There is a clear need for comprehensive and reliable reporting of alleged irregularities and PIF offences. The European legislator has adopted various rules obliging individuals, institutions and Member States to report irregularities and fraud. The reporting system is multi-layered and complex, with various terms and standards which are likely to lead to confusion. This produces 'noise' and may raise reporting thresholds. Furthermore, it increases the uncertainty in which the actor finds himself or herself when deciding to report or not.

Below, some salient observations of this chapter are summarized.

- It would be helpful to promote the understanding that initial reporting does not have to comply with standards for prosecution and adjudication like 'beyond reasonable doubt' and that the status of 'evidence' takes its full meaning in front of the judge or trier of facts, not at the reporting level. Reporting, as an initial step, will be followed by an investigation process meant to gather and assess further information to reach more demanding standards downstream.
- The rapporteur should understand that he or she is not expected to present clear and conclusive evidence, but will enhance the probability of follow-up by being transparent and providing relevant and credible (correct, complete and accurate) information. Ideally, this information is corroborated by supporting documents or other means of validation, but the rapporteur, in doing so, should refrain from actions which may jeopardize the prospective investigation.
- These lowered standards at initial reporting stage should not incite to blind denunciation or manifestly unsubstantiated reporting. Rather, the rapporteur should act responsibly and be driven by the intention to submit his or her information to more in-depth scrutiny and examinations. As long as he or she genuinely considers an irregularity or criminal offence occurred, the reporting obligation stands.

6

Preliminary Examination of Information

Carsten Stahn, Paolo Proli and Pascal Hollevoet*

6.1. Introduction

Decisions to open an investigation cannot be taken lightly. Investigative bodies have hence set up units or teams and approved procedures aiming to make informed and consistent choices in what initial information justifies further inquiry. In this chapter, we explore what these procedures are and if they could be improved. Key questions to consider include: What factors and processes influence the decision to initiate an investigation? What verifications are necessary and/or permissible during the assessment phase? What criteria, such as guidelines, rules and standards, are utilized in this process?

This chapter includes certain parallels between criminal and non-criminal (pre-)investigative activities and bodies, such as between the EPPO and OLAF. However, it does not intend to downplay the fundamentally different legal frameworks and institutional logics between them, including in terms of procedural safeguards, judicial oversight and evidentiary thresholds. Any comparative references are included purely for illustrative purposes and should not be interpreted as conflating their legal mandates or institutional roles.

6.2. The Preliminary Examination

The preliminary examination refers to the phase of the (pre-)investigative cycle where the organization considers whether it should open an investigation, or not. When the organization decides not to open an investigation, the preliminary examination may also entail the assessment of the need for further reporting (outside the organization). Other terms used for this phase include 'selection', 'verification', 'intake', 'assessment' and 'predication'. The preliminary investigation involves exercising discretion in order to determine whether there are legal

* **Carsten Stahn** is Professor of International Criminal Law and Global Justice at Leiden University and Queen's University Belfast. **Paolo Proli** is a former official of the Office of the Prosecutor ('OTP') of the International Criminal Court ('ICC'), and is currently the Head of the Investigation and Analysis Support Sector at the European Public Prosecutor's Office ('EPPO'). **Pascal Hollevoet** is a former investigator of the Belgian Judicial Police and the European Anti-Fraud Office ('OLAF'). He is currently Policy Senior Assistant at OLAF. This chapter is authored in the contributors' personal capacity and does not necessarily reflect the views of EPPO, OLAF or other institutions mentioned therein.

grounds and sufficient suspicions to proceed with the launch of a full investigation.[1]

These pre-investigative evaluations differ from investigations in several ways, including that they typically (a) precede the actual formal investigation and serve essentially as an analytical tool to determine whether there are sufficient grounds to commence an investigation; (b) have no investigative (coercive) powers; and (c) apply different procedural safeguards and standards of proof.[2]

The preliminary examination can thus be conceptualized as a filter in relation to a fully-fledged criminal investigation process.[3] It is primarily a legal and analytical process that is essentially about rules, benchmarks, parameters, and various other safeguards against which information is assessed so consequential decisions can be made.[4]

We remark that whereas the study of the preliminary examination in this chapter is focused on its function as an analytical lens, it does not override or downplay the relevant legal realities. This concerns in particular the obligation to apply the principle of legality where it applies.[5]

---

1 Andrew T. Caley, "Constraints and Quality Control in Preliminary Examination: Critical Lessons Learned from the ICTY, the ICC, the ECCC and the United Kingdom", in Morten Bergsmo and Carsten Stahn (eds.), *Quality Control in Preliminary Examination: Volume 1*, Torkel Opsahl Academic EPublisher ('TOAEP'), Brussels, 2018, p. 35 (https://www.toaep.org/ps-pdf/32-bergsmo-stahn/).

2 See Carsten Stahn, "From Preliminary Examination to Investigation: Rethinking the Connection", in Xabier Agirre Aranburu, Morten Bergsmo, Simon De Smet and Carsten Stahn (eds.), *Quality Control in Criminal Investigation*, TOAEP, Brussels, 2020, pp. 2 and 39–42 (https://www.toaep.org/ps-pdf/38-qcci/).

3 Carsten Stahn, Morten Bergsmo and Chan Ho Shing Icarus, "On the Magic, Mystery and Mayhem of Preliminary Examinations", in Bergsmo and Stahn (eds.), 2018, p. 11, see *supra* note 1.

4 Matilde E. Gawronski, "The Legalistic Function of Preliminary Examinations: Quality Control as a Two-Way Street", in *ibid.*

5 Such as in the case of the EPPO, where legal conditions for exercising competence must be strictly followed. See Council Regulation (EU) No. 2017/1939 of 12 October 2017 implementing enhanced cooperation on the establishment of the European Public Prosecutor's Office ('the EPPO'), Recital 66 ('EPPO Regulation') (https://www.legal-tools.org/doc/plfszr14/): in order to ensure legal certainty and to effectively combat offences affecting the Union's financial interests ('PIF' offences), the investigation and prosecution activities of the EPPO should be guided by the legality principle, whereby the EPPO applies strictly the rules laid down in this Regulation relating in particular to competence and its exercise, the initiation of investigations, the termination of investigations, the referral of a case, the dismissal of the case and simplified prosecution procedures).

6.3. Initial Filtering

Not all information received by an investigative body makes it to the preliminary examination. Organizations are usually not willing to spend capacity or resources in examining information that does not reach a certain threshold of seriousness. Typically, these services apply a gatekeeper approach, processing only information warranting a preliminary examination *prima facie*[6] or – in the negative – which are not manifestly unsubstantiated.[7] The information need not be comprehensive or conclusive, but must amount to something more than an entirely unsupported allegation and should at least comprise some factual foundation to support the allegations.[8] As anonymity raises particular concerns in this respect, some organizations have set up systems to interact anonymously with the initial source to obtain supporting information.[9]

6.4. Criteria of the Examination

The preliminary examination marks the start of the '*juridification*' of the investigative process. That is, the turn towards individualization, accountability and legal characterization of the allegations.[10] Considering the applicable legal framework, such as the obligatory or discretionary nature of criminal

---

6 The ICC refers to information "warrant[ing] further analysis", excluding "matters which are manifestly outside the jurisdiction of the Court" (see ICC-OTP, "Policy Paper on Preliminary Examinations", 1 November 2013, para. 78, pp. 18–19 ('Policy Paper on Preliminary Examinations') (https://www.legal-tools.org/doc/acb906/). Article 1.1. of OLAF's Guidelines on Investigation Procedures for OLAF Staff, 11 October 2021 ('GIP') (https://www.legal-tools.org/doc/tgfdldc7/) provides that its selection unit will verify and analyse "information of possible investigative interest" ('IPII'). *A contrario*, OLAF is not expected to evaluate information that has no potential investigative interest. OLAF's glossary does not provide further guidance on this standard, as it merely specifies that IPII concerns "all information received by OLAF or information gathered on OLAF's own initiative, that could be considered for the opening of an investigation or coordination case and which shall be submitted to the selection procedure for analysis".

7 Article 12c(3) of the 'OLAF Regulation' provides that the Office is not bound to send "manifestly unsubstantiated allegations" to the EPPO, Consolidated text of Regulation (EU, EURATOM) No. 883/2013 of the European Parliament and of the Council of 11 September 2013 concerning investigations conducted by the European Anti-Fraud Office (OLAF) and repealing Regulation (EC) No. 1073/1999 of the European Parliament and of the Council and Council Regulation (Euratom) No. 1074/1999 (https://www.legal-tools.org/doc/6f0ede/).

8 Matthew E. Cross, "The Standard of Proof in Preliminary Examinations", in Morten Bergsmo and Carsten Stahn (eds.), *Quality Control in Preliminary Examination: Volume 2*, TOAEP, Brussels, 2018, p. 222 (https://www.toaep.org/ps-pdf/33-bergsmo-stahn/).

9 See, for example, OLAF's Fraud Notification System (https://fns.olaf.europa.eu/), allowing an anonymous exchange of information and documents via an internet platform.

10 Christine Schwöbel-Patel, "Commissions of Inquiry: Courting International Criminal Courts and Tribunals", in Christian Henderson (ed.), *Commissions of Inquiry: Problems and Prospects*, Hart Publishing, Oxford, 2017, p. 145.

prosecution and whether competencies are exclusive or shared, the following broad aspects can be identified as general reference points for the evaluation:[11] (a) *competence*: do we have competence over the matter reported?; (b) *admissibility*: even if competence is established, does the case warrant the opening of an investigation based on additional relevant factors, such as the severity or the extent of damage caused by the offence?; and (c) *opportunity*: even if all other requirements are met, should an investigation still be initiated, considering the broader context?

6.4.1. Competence

Any preliminary examination includes an analysis and assessment of whether the decision-making agent has the competence to investigate, prosecute or otherwise decide on the reported allegations or suspected wrongdoing.[12] It concerns, in essence, a legal analysis of whether the investigative body has competence to act in terms of:

- *temporal competence*: the timeframe of events;
- *material competence*: the nature of reported wrongdoing;
- *personal competence*: when the competence of the investigative or prosecutorial body is restricted to persons with a certain quality (for example, public officials) or of a specific nationality (for example, that of the State exercising criminal prosecution);
- *territorial competence*: the location where the facts reported took place.

Subject-matter or 'material' competence is often the most crucial and arduous type of jurisdiction that needs to be ascertained. Allegations of corruption or fraud often relate to a complex regulatory setting, where it can be difficult to distinguish possible criminal offences from other, non-criminal offences or 'creative' interpretations of ambiguous rules. Evaluating whether what happened constitutes an irregularity, misconduct or a criminal offence is often more challenging than assessing whether what is reported might be true.[13] The

[11] The terminology used here is heavily influenced by the legal framework of the ICC. The authors are conscious that the same terms could have another meaning in a different legal setting. This chapter will detail the divergences between the various models.

[12] When OLAF receives initial information indicating criminal conduct under EPPO competence, it has to report this to the EPPO, including a description of the facts, an assessment of the damage caused or likely to be caused, the possible legal qualification and any available information about potential victims, suspects and any other involved persons (see Article 24(1) and (4) of the EPPO Regulation, see *supra* note 5, and Article 12c(1) and (2) of the OLAF Regulation, see *supra* note 7).

[13] Maxime Reeves-Latour, "Stratagèmes criminels à la jonction des pouvoirs publics et des milieux d'affaires : les élites délinquantes et le processus d'octroi des contrats publics de construction", Ph.D. Thesis, Université de Montréal, 2007.

criminalization of corruption for instance is focused mostly on bribery-related cases, possibly leaving other 'corruptive' practices outside the scope of criminal sanctioning. Moreover, definitions and concepts differ, enhancing the complexity of clear qualification.[14]

In addition, practical considerations may make some criminal offences more amenable to identification at the preliminary examination stage than others.[15] For example, an examiner may be more inclined to open an investigation when initial documents are reported to be materially forged (for example, two versions of a contract), than when a single document is reported to contain false claims. Likewise, it would require flexible thinking and deeper analysis, to examine whether an alleged conflict of interests in a grant-application amounts to fraud, given that the conflict of interests was not reported and hence led to 'incomplete statements' in the sense of the material element of a fraudulent activity.[16]

6.4.2. Admissibility

When competence over a particular situation or case is positively established, the assessment may encompass an additional admissibility stage; that is, addressing the question of whether the investigative, prosecutorial, or other deciding body should exercise this jurisdiction. Subject to the applicable regulatory framework, admissibility may encompass considerations such as (a) *veracity*: is there any truth in the allegation?; (b) *gravity*: are the reported facts serious enough to warrant an investigation?; and (c) *complementarity*: is somebody else already looking into the matter?

---

14 See Articles 4(2) (corruption) and 4(3) (misappropriation) of Directive (EU) No. 2017/1371 of the European Parliament and of the Council of 5 July 2017 on the fight against fraud to the Union's financial interests by means of criminal law ('PIF Directive') (https://www.legal-tools.org/doc/3lsm7y4u/), and compare with the description of corruption offences in:

- the United Nations ('UN') Convention on Corruption, 21 November 2003, Articles 15–22 (https://www.legal-tools.org/doc/hwuihi/);
- a 2022 report on corruption requested by the European Commission's Directorate-General for Migration and Home Affairs, Ilia Gaglio *et al.*, "Strengthening the Fight Against Corruption: Assessing the EU Legislative and Policy Framework", 15 December 2022, p. 9; and
- European Commission, Proposal for a Directive of the European Parliament and of the Council on combatting corruption, 3 May 2023, 2023/0135 (COD) (https://www.legal-tools.org/doc/1n1lw82a/). See also Articles 4(2) (corruption) and 4(3) (misappropriation) of the PIF Directive, see *supra* note 14.

15 Cross, 2018, p. 216, see *supra* note 8.

16 See Article 3(2)(a)(i) and (ii) of the PIF Directive, *supra* note 14.

6.4.2.1. Veracity

As regards veracity or truthfulness, the preliminary examination typically differentiates between the veracity of the source and the veracity of the information. The terminology for those two parameters has not always been used consistently.[17] One approach is to consider that reliability concerns the source, and credibility concerns the evidence,[18] but authorities also occasionally refer to the credibility of the source.[19] In any case, it is generally accepted that both should be evaluated separately.[20]

When referring to the source of information, *reliability* is usually understood as the 'trustworthiness' of the expected or actual behaviour of the source over time. It has a cognitive (expert authority) and an affective (trustworthiness and goodwill) component.[21] A source may appear competent or knowledgeable, but this does not always mean it can be trusted. Inversely, a complainant can seem trustworthy, but have no expert knowledge. Even honest witnesses may be mistaken, while the worst sounding source may be telling the truth.

When verification opportunities are limited, perhaps because of the complexity of the facts and operational limitations, or when allegations have been expressed by a single source, the source-specific indicators become indispensable.[22] The ICC applies a semi-structured approach in this context, including indicators for reliability of the source across four different dimensions:[23] (a) competence; (b) truthfulness; (c) authenticity; and (d) pragmatic performance.

Competence is considered as a pre-condition for truthfulness, and aims to assess whether the source is capable of acquiring truthful knowledge in the respective domain, to be evaluated through criteria of language skills (could the

---

17 Xavier Agirre Aranburu, "The Contribution of Analysis to the Quality Control in Criminal Investigation", in Agirre, Bergsmo, De Smet and Stahn (eds.), 2020, p. 134, see *supra* note 2.

18 *Ibid.*, p. 136. For an example of this approach, see Article 5.6. of OLAF's GIP, see *supra* note 6, providing that in "evaluating whether the information is sufficient to justify the opening of an investigation or coordination case, consideration shall be given to the reliability of the source and the credibility of the allegations".

19 For a different approach, distinguishing nine criteria for the 'credibility of a witness' and eleven for 'the reliability of information, see Gabriele Chlevickaitė and Barbora Holá, "Empirical Study of Insider Witnesses' Assessments at the International Criminal Court", in *International Criminal Law Review*, 2016, vol. 16, no. 4, pp. 687–688.)

20 UN Office on Drugs and Crime, *Criminal Intelligence Manual for Analysts*, Vienna, 2011, p. 25.

21 Carl Hovland, Irving Janis and Harold Kelley, *Communication and Persuasion: Psychology Studies in Opinion Change*, Yale University Press, New Haven, 1953.

22 Agirre Aranburu, 2020, p. 192, see *supra* note 17.

23 *Ibid.*, p. 182.

source understand?), knowledge (was the source in a position to know?), and physical and mental condition.

Truthfulness probes whether the information is fundamentally true, if it corresponds with tangible, positive facts. This is to be addressed mainly through internal consistency, external verification and detail.

Authenticity involves whether the knowledge is authentic and not caused by undue self-serving design or external influence. To be evaluated through motive, independence, contamination and immediacy (direct relation to the information).

Finally, the ICC considers whether the witness is able to communicate effectively during the investigation, and also potentially to the judges after adversarial cross-examination. This evaluation of 'pragmatic performance' concerns a practical consideration and is subordinate to the substantive issues above.

Credibility is often used to refer to a single item of information or allegation at a given point in time. The credibility of information relies on internal consistency and external corroboration and can be measured against criteria of:[24] (a) comprehensiveness; (b) independent security; and (c) supportiveness.

Comprehensiveness answers the question 'how much of the relevant information is provided?'. Beyond a general standard of the completeness of information, this assessment also entails a reflection on what the source could have been expected to know, and so could have reported. When, for instance, a complaint by a competitor concerns possible corruption in a tender file, the examiner should assess what information the complainant should be able to provide (for example, description of competitors, procedure, and publication of results).

Independent security regards how solid each of the elements put forward in the initial allegation is, independent of the conclusion. This assessment relies on external verification, and indicates, for example, that a single witness statement (for example, 'he wanted them to win') does not have the same credibility as a (confirmed) bank statement indicating a financial transaction between a competitor and a member of the tender evaluation committee.

Finally, *supportiveness* involves the strength of the connection between the information and the conclusion. For example, the payment in the section above can be independent of the allegedly corrupt procurement, but would gain credibility in support of this allegation, when internally consistent with the timing of the tender and the discovery of collusive correspondence.

[24] Simon De Smet, "Justified Belief in the Unbelievable", in Agirre, Bergsmo, De Smet and Stahn (eds.), 2020, p. 143, see *supra* note 2; Susan Haack, "Warrant, Causation, and the Atomism of Evidence Law", in *Episteme*, 2008, vol. 5, no. 3, pp. 253–266.

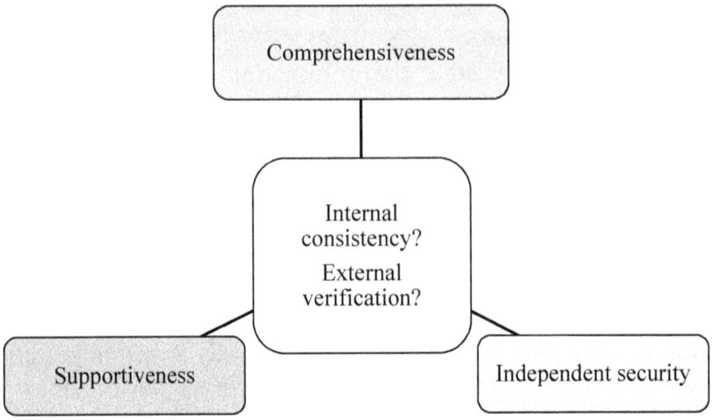

Illustration 6.1.: Criteria for credibility.

The weighing of information here is different from the evaluation of initial reporting duties.[25] Whereas, in the initial reporting, information should not consist of a fully unsubstantiated claim, the preliminary examination will take the assessment one step further in examining whether it contains the necessary information (comprehensiveness), solid elements (independent security), and supports the claim of irregularity or fraud.

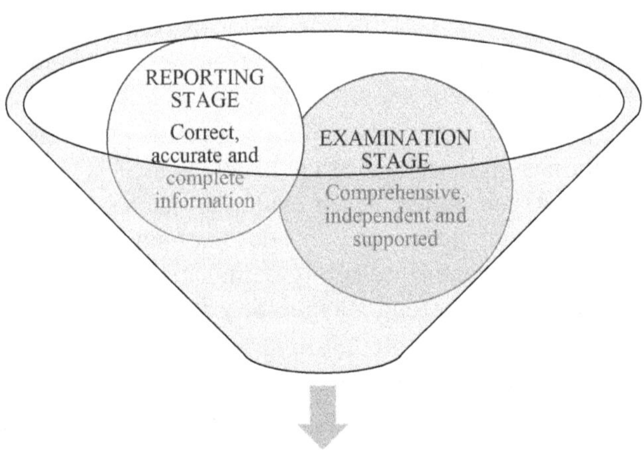

Illustration 6.2.: Quality of information parameters at reporting and examination stage.

[25] See Chapter 5.

6.4.2.2. Gravity

Gravity involves whether the (possible impact of) potential case is serious enough[26] to justify further action. It builds on the assessment of jurisdiction and veracity[27] and informs a subsequent assessment of opportunity.

6.4.2.3. Complementarity

Complementarity asks whether other proceedings are, have been, or should be conducted in relation to the same (group(s) of) person(s) and reported offence(s). It is generally based on the principle of '*ne bis in idem*'[28] and can involve a legal analysis of the exact nature (for example, criminal, disciplinary, or administrative) of possible parallel investigative processes and the sanctions they might entail.

A consistent criterion to assess possible overlap of investigation into the 'same facts'[29] is the existence of a set of concrete circumstances which are

---

[26] The Opinion of OLAF's Selection Unit is based on whether "the information [...] is sufficient to justify the opening of an investigation" (see Article 5.5. GIP, *supra* note 6). The EPPO Regulation typically refers to the damage caused or likely to be caused to the Union's financial interests. See for example Article 25(2) of said Regulation, *supra* note 5.

[27] From another perspective, the process of assessing the veracity of sources and information can be viewed as inherent to the preliminary examination process, and as such, embedded throughout all its different stages.

[28] In general, the objective of the '*ne bis in idem*' principle is to ensure that no one is prosecuted for the same facts on several accounts. The principle is included as a refusal ground in a large number of European Union ('EU') instruments on judicial co-operation in criminal matters, and included in Article 4 of Protocol 7 to the European Convention on Human Rights, 4 November 1950 (https://www.legal-tools.org/doc/8267cb/). The principle grounds the non-duplication rule between EPPO and OLAF investigations (see Article 101(2) of the EPPO Regulation, *supra* note 5, and Articles 1(4)(a), 12c(5) and 12d of the OLAF Regulation, *supra* note 7). For more non-duplication rules, see also: Article 27(2) of the EPPO Regulation for the non-duplication of criminal investigations by EPPO and the judiciary of the Member State, Article 5(3) of the OLAF Regulation for the restriction of institutions, bodies, offices and agencies of the EU to open a parallel investigation when OLAF investigates and Article 3(1) of the Eurojust Regulation (Regulation (EU) 2018/1727 of the European Parliament and of the Council of 14 November 2018 on the European Union Agency for Criminal Justice Cooperation (Eurojust), and replacing and repealing Council Decision 2002/187/JHA (https://www.legal-tools.org/doc/lreoiuo8/)) for the latter's abstinence when EPPO deals with a PIF investigation.

[29] Article 5.5. of OLAF's GIP, see *supra* note 6, provide that OLAF can exercise its competence "in compliance with its obligations of non-duplication and of reporting to the EPPO". In practice, this means that upon receipt of initial information, OLAF's selection unit systematically verifies via the EPPO's case management system whether the EPPO is conducting an investigation into the same facts (Article 5.2. GIP).

inextricably linked together in time and space.[30] Other criteria include that it should concern the same (natural or legal) person, who has been subject of a final decision.[31]

The fact that one criminal offence requires an additional constitutive subjective element as compared to an administrative punitive penalty is irrelevant for assessing the identity of the material facts.[32] On the other hand, the prohibition of duplication is not absolute, and the CJEU has clarified conditions for a justified duplication of proceedings and penalties.[33]

6.4.3. Opportunity

Confirmed jurisdiction and admissibility do not always lead to the opening of an investigation. Unless a legality principle applies,[34] the preliminary examination may take into account considerations of *opportunity to open* an investigation or not. The question here is: 'Should we give priority to other cases and treat this allegation later or not at all for that reason?'.

In assessing opportunity, the preliminary examination might want to consider whether the resources requirements for an investigation are proportionate (to the potential outcome), particularly taking into account the *gravity* of the case. A formalized set of criteria can enhance consistency and transparency in the assessment of such proportionality, for instance, by taking into account:

- the available investigative resources;
- the estimated time to complete the investigation;
- the prospected availability and accessibility of evidence;

---

30 See Court of Justice of the European Union ('CJEU'), *van Straaten v. the Netherlands and Italy*, First Chamber, Judgment, 29 September 2006, C-150/05 (https://www.legal-tools.org/doc/mh015nn0/).

31 See, for an update of the CJEU case law on the *ne bis in idem* principle in criminal matters, Eurojust, "Case-law by the Court of Justice of the European Union on the Principle of *ne bis in idem* in Criminal Matters", February 2024.

32 See CJEU, *Menci case*, Grand Chamber, Judgment, 20 March 2018, C-524/15 (https://www.legal-tools.org/doc/x8k0v50s/); CJEU, *Garlsson Real Estate SA et al. v. Commissione Nazionale per le Società e la Borsa*, Grand Chamber, Judgment, 20 March 2018, C-537/16 (https://www.legal-tools.org/doc/8nwi8q2m/).

33 See Eurojust, 2024, p. 62, *supra* note 31.

34 The legality principle establishes an obligation to prosecute where there are grounds for suspicion that an individual prosecutable criminal offence has been committed. EPPO works under this legality principle (see Recitals 66 and 81 of the EPPO Regulation, *supra* note 5, for EPPO's duty to apply "strictly the rules laid down in this Regulation relating in particular to […] the initiation of investigations" which "should as a rule lead to prosecution". Internal guidelines however introduce an element of ponderation, providing in the possibility of not pursuing the case if the damage is under a certain threshold.

- the extent to which the alleged offence(s) connect(s) to (an) already ongoing investigation(s) and/or fit(s) in the overall investigation policy of the investigative body.

Such opportunity criteria can be tactical and/or strategic.[35] The decision not to open an investigation is of a tactical nature when, after reviewing the quantity and quality of the available evidential information, the examiner finds there are no reasonable prospects of securing a sufficiently effective investigative outcome or a conviction. The decision to open an investigation is considered to be strategic when, regardless of an insufficiently supported complaint, the case might represent elements of a new type or method of fraud (for example, with RFF funds).[36]

6.5. Powers of Examination

During the preliminary evaluation, the examiners may conduct verifications with the aim of determining whether 'reasonable grounds' or another standard requirement has been met.[37] Typically, such verifications cannot entail investigative measures,[38] but the exact definition of an investigative measure in this context is not always clearly established.[39] It may be understood as 'taking active measures to obtain primary source information in order to assess whether there is criminal responsibility'.[40] A '*primary source*' is then any kind of source that conveys direct, immediate knowledge of the facts, like a direct witness or an original record.[41]

Without 'investigating', the examiner can seek additional information and attempt to contextualize the information. Above all, he or she will look for

---

35 ICC-OTP, "Policy Paper on Case Selection and Prioritisation", 15 September 2016 ('OTP Policy Paper') (https://legal-tools.org/doc/182205/).

36 The Recovery and Resilience Facility ('RFF') of the NextGenerationEU programme is a close to an EUR 8 billion financing package of grants and loans to allow the EU Member States to recover from the Covid-19 pandemic.

37 Runar Torgersen, "The Concern for Quality Control and Norwegian Preliminary Examination Practice", in Bergsmo and Stahn (eds.), 2018, p. 66, see *supra* note 1.

38 Cross, 2018, p. 247, see *supra* note 8.

39 The definition of investigative measures is sometimes fluid. According to Article 5 of its GIP, see *supra* note 6, OLAF's Selection Unit can for instance, *inter alia*, "contact the [...] EU institution, body, office or agency concerned in order to obtain clarification and further documentation concerning the initial information [...] consult relevant sources available to OLAF. [...] Collect information in the framework of operational meetings and take statements from any person able to provide relevant information".

40 Cross, 2018, p. 247, see *supra* note 8.

41 Agirre Aranburu, 2020, pp. 216–217, see *supra* note 17.

validation of the initial information.[42] *Validation* refers to a positive test of consistency of the initial information with separate independent (internal and external) sources.[43] For example, when verifications on an official website with tender data show an atypical course of the tender procedure, and the result has not been published, this might seem to validate an allegation of favouritism. Such validation can usefully take, as a starting point, the initial information that has been evaluated as sufficiently credible.[44] In practice, examiners will often rely on desktop research and try to have access to secondary sources without jeopardizing a possible investigation. Importantly, when such access to secondary sources is legally permitted (for example, collecting a statement from an expert), legal duties to co-operate with the preliminary examining authorities may be non-applicable.

That said, the general argument about the absence of investigative powers at the preliminary stage should be viewed with caution, especially when it comes to prosecutorial authorities like the EPPO, which may already be empowered to carry out intrusive measures during the initial assessment of available information. In such cases, early investigative steps may take place as part of a formally opened investigation under national law, with the corresponding safeguards, even if they are functionally similar to a preliminary examination or verification.

6.6. Standard of Proof

Initiating a formal investigation typically results in significant repercussions of varying likelihood and severity, particularly in the criminal domain but not exclusively, with primary consideration given to the position of the person under investigation. The mere information that a criminal investigation has been launched can ruin the suspect's social life. Specifically for the offences falling within the competence of the EPPO, political or high-profile economic actors may be involved.[45]

It is important to keep in mind that criminal and administrative (or non-criminal) investigations follow fundamentally different standards of proof, which reflect their distinct purposes, consequences and legal safeguards. This

---

42 OLAF's selection unit should, in ideal circumstances, provide within a timeframe of two months an opinion, which should be based on a number of verifications and analytical steps, including -contacting the source, operational meetings and even, if required, fact-finding missions (see Article 5.1. GIP, *supra* note 6).

43 Agirre Aranburu, 2020, p. 224, see *supra* note 17.

44 *Ibid.*, p. 225.

45 Hans-Holger Hernfeld, Dominik Brodowski and Christoph Buchard, *European Public Prosecutor's Office, Article-by-Article Commentary*, Nomos, Beck and Hart, Baden-Baden, München and Oxford, 2021, Article 111, p. 645.

difference has clear implications for how decisions to initiate proceedings are made and the level of certainty required at different stages.

From Chapter 5 of this volume, we recall that a standard of proof dictates what level of certainty or assurance a decision-maker should have to make his decision. In the present context, the question becomes: How 'sure' should the examiner be to recommend the opening of an investigation (or to transfer a case for further processing)?

Concerning the admissibility criterion as set out above, there is no exact cut-off point (a rule) to let the examiner decide either to start or to refrain from investigating.[46] A criterion often used is that there should be "reasonable grounds"[47] to justify the opening of an investigation. Other standards used are "reasonable basis" (to proceed or believe)'[48] or "sufficient suspicion".[49] These standards are characterized as the "likelihood that a [criminal] offence has been committed",[50] but this does not seem to add much to the criteria of veracity and gravity described above. Another proposed formulation, that the opening of an investigation is "commonly understood to involve the existence of information that satisfies an objective observer that the suspect may have committed the crime(s)",[51] presumes the identification of a suspect at this early stage of the process.

In any case, 'reasonable grounds' does not entail that a fixed threshold of probability must be met, but that the decision to investigate must be based as much as possible on objective grounds.[52] If the information available to the decision maker at the pre-investigative stage allows for reasonable inferences that at least one offence within the jurisdiction of the organization has been

[46] Adapted (the authors speak of prosecuting) from Moa Lidén, Minna Gräns and Peter Juslin, "From Devil's Advocate to Crime Fighter: Confirmation Bias and Debiasing Techniques in Prosecutorial Decision Making", in *Psychology Crime & Law*, 2018, vol. 15, no. 12, p. 5.

[47] See, for example, Articles 24(7) and 26(1) of the EPPO Regulation, *supra* note 5, and Article 40(1) of the Internal Rules of Procedure of the European Public Prosecutor's Office, consolidated version of College Decision 003/2020, 2022 (https://www.legal-tools.org/doc/yhuues8e/).

[48] The ICC refers to a "reasonable basis to proceed with an investigation" (Article 15(3) of the Rome Statute, 17 July 1998 (https://www.legal-tools.org/doc/7b9af9/) for the proposal of the prosecutor to open an investigation, and to a "reasonable basis to believe" (Article 53(1) of the Rome Statute) to initiate an investigation. The latter standard is considered to be a lower standard than 'reasonable grounds' (Cross, 2018, p. 225, see *supra* note 8).

[49] See, for example, Article 5 of the OLAF Regulation, *supra* note 7.

[50] Torgersen, 2018, p. 66, see *supra* note 37.

[51] Eleni Chaitidou, "The Judiciary and Enhancement of the Classification of Alleged Conduct", in Agirre, Bergsmo, De Smet and Stahn (eds.), 2020, p. 964, fn. 85, see *supra* note 2.

[52] Torgersen, 2018, p. 66, see *supra* note 37.

committed and that the case would be admissible, the investigative body can decide to open an investigation.[53] However, like any other fact-finding exercise, it requires that the standard be satisfied by (factual) information and not by pure conjecture or assertion.[54]

Again, one should not disregard the fact that, at the preliminary examination stage, the examiners typically have limited powers, which are not comparable to those provided at the investigative stage.[55] Consequently, the information available at such an early stage is "neither expected to be 'comprehensive' nor 'conclusive'",[56] "clear, univocal or not contradictory".[57] The CJEU has ruled that the criteria for the opening of an OLAF investigation do not require an in-depth assessment of that information, as this can only take place in the context of the investigation itself.[58]

6.7. Outcome of the Preliminary Examination

The outcome of the preliminary examination is usually a written report, collecting all the findings of the examination process. This includes an initial legal characterization of the alleged shortcomings[59] and a statement of facts indicating, at a minimum, the place(s) of the alleged commission of the potential offences, the time or time period of the alleged commission of the offences, the detrimental financial impact, if available, and the person(s) involved (if

[53] Chaitidou, 2020, p. 948, see *supra* note 51.

[54] Cross, 2018, p. 252, see *supra* note 8.

[55] Mind, however, the important caveat previously noted (see the conclusion of Section 6.5. above).

[56] ICC, *Situation in the Republic of Kenya*, Decision Pursuant to Article 15 of the Rome Statute on the Authorization of an Investigation into the Situation in the Republic of Kenya, ICC-01/09-19-Corr, 31 March 201, para. 27 (https://www.legal-tools.org/doc/f0caaf/), as quoted in ICC-OTP, "Report on Preliminary Examination Activities 2016", 14 November 2016, para. 11, p. 4 (https://www.legal-tools.org/doc/f30a53/).

[57] ICC, *Situation on Registered Vessels of the Union of Comoros, the Hellenic Republic and the Kingdom of Cambodia*, Pre-Trial Chamber I, Decision on the request of the Union of the Comoros to review the Prosecutor's decision not to initiate an investigation, 16 July 2015, ICC-01/13-34, para. 13 (https://www.legal-tools.org/doc/2f876c/).

[58] CJEU, *John Dalli v. European Commission*, General Court (Sixth Chamber), Judgment, 6 June 2019, T-399/17, para. 70 (https://www.legal-tools.org/doc/s7na9fdd/)

[59] Since 2017, the UN system uses the term 'presumptive fraud' for allegations that have been deemed to warrant an investigation and, if substantiated, would establish the existence of fraud resulting in the loss of resources to the Organization (Conclusions of the High-Level Committee on Management at Its Thirty-Third Session, UN Doc. CEB/2017/3, 26 April 2017, para. 98(c) (https://www.legal-tools.org/doc/x42dxbjg/)

identified).[60] Such a report should not be the reflection of an opinion,[61] but a statement of what the available information reasonably suggests, without conducting an investigation.[62] It should allow the director of the investigative body or a prosecutor to determine whether or not to initiate an investigation. This person decides either that there is a reasonable basis to proceed with an investigation or that the information provided does not constitute a reasonable basis to commence an investigation.[63] Depending on the legal framework or organization policies, the verification or preliminary examination may be conducted directly by the latter authority itself, rendering such a distinction moot.

Whereas some preliminary examinations are conceived as a mere analytical filter to decide on the opening of investigations (gateway model), others include proposals on the collection of material and evidence, investigative strategy, and a potential case hypothesis (preparatory model).[64]

---

60 When OLAF receives initial information indicating criminal conduct under EPPO competence, it has to report this to the EPPO, including a description of the facts, an assessment of the damage caused or likely to be caused, the possible legal qualification and any available information about potential victims, suspects and any other involved persons (Articles 24§1 and §4 of the EPPO Regulation, *supra* note 5, and Article 12c(1) and (2) of the OLAF Regulation, *supra* note 7). In such case, the sections of the selection document ('opinion') will be slightly different, when a new case is reported (by OLAF) to the EPPO and when OLAF decides not to start an own investigation (see Article 5.7. GIP, *supra* note 6).

61 The term opinion can be taken to refer here to "feelings or thoughts about something, rather than a fact" (see "Opinion", in *Oxford Learner's Dictionaries*). When OLAF refers to an 'opinion' as the outcome of its selection process (see Article 1.1. GIP, *supra* note 6), it does not reflect such ephemeral opinion, but refers to an informed recommendation, based on a systematic analytical process. The evaluation document by the ICC is called a 'Source Evaluation Report' ('SER').

62 Cross, 2018, p. 233, see *supra* note 8.

63 Chaitidou, 2020, p. 950, see *supra* note 51.

64 Presentation by Professor Carsten Stahn during the OLAF conference on "Judgment and Decision-Making in Investigations" on 8 December 2022.

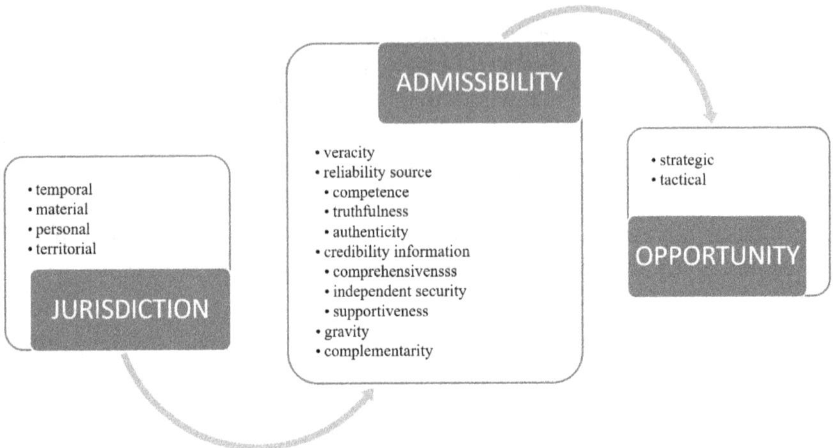

Illustration 6.3.: Overview of the preliminary examination.

6.8. The Judgment Processes

6.8.1. Challenges

The uniqueness of the preliminary examination lies in its flexible nature and broad range of decision-making choices. The examiner has to test hypotheses,[65] assess probabilities (for example, reliability of the source), and predict a possible outcome of the investigation when considering whether or not to open an investigation. In short, he or she will have to make a number of decisions and judgement calls,[66] possibly affected by bias and/or noise.[67]

As mentioned in a previous contribution on 'noise', one of the decision-making safeguards to minimize noise is applying consistent rules of measurement and attribution. This is no different during the preliminary examination, in particular when working with a '*reasonable basis*' or '*sufficient suspicion*' standard. By carefully testing the credibility of the available information, the reliability of the source(s) that produced it, and checking for noise and bias that may impact the quality of these assessments, the examiner should strive to be as objective, sound, and conclusive as possible.[68]

A fundamental principle of the preliminary examination is that the evaluation of the reliability of the source and the credibility of the information should not be influenced by personal feelings and opinions, but based (merely) on

[65] See Chapter 1.

[66] Stahn, Bergsmo and Chan, 2018, p. 8, see *supra* note 3.

[67] See Chapters 3 and 4.

[68] Policy Paper on Preliminary Examinations, paras. 31–32, p. 8, see *supra* note 6.

professional judgment.[69] However, absolute objectivity seems beyond the scope of human judgment, and individual preferences and views will likely affect any preliminary examination. Legal decision-making seems to inevitably involve some subjective interpretation of the evidence,[70] but unwanted variability or 'noise' should be avoided. We present below some approaches to this end.

6.8.2. Noise

6.8.2.1. Risks

Level noise, or the variability of the average judgments made by different individuals, explains why some examiners will, for instance, *systematically* identify intellectual falsehoods in a tendering procedure (and hence opt for the criminal investigation track), while others tend to see only possible irregularities within the same allegation.

Even when level noise is absent, and both examiners agree that a falsehood occurred, different evaluations might still persist. One examiner could for instance consider that such falsehood is sufficient to trigger an investigation or a reporting duty, while the other considers this is insufficient to warrant a full-blown investigation with any chance of success. This relates to individual differences or '*stable pattern noise*'.

Furthermore, when the *same* examiner advocates the opening of an investigation (at the start of) one day, but dismisses a similar case (at the end of a long) other day, this can be due to '*occasional pattern noise*'.

As mentioned in Chapter 3, good practices for reducing unwanted variability include:[71] (a) using the same scales and interpreting them in the same way; (b) applying individual 'decision hygiene'; and (c) installing and implementing organizational measures to avoid noise (for example, the 'four- (or multiple) eyes' principle, where more than one person goes over the examination (report)).

6.8.2.2. The Consistent Use of Scales

Sometimes, reliability of a source and credibility of information are scored on a pre-established scale (matrix), known as a '4 x 4' or other. The available information is captured in a structured evaluation grid, working with alphanumeric codes to rank the allegation by two scales related to the source and the information.

---

[69] UNODC, 2011, p. 25, see *supra* note 20.

[70] Christoph Engel, "Preponderance of the Evidence Versus Intime Conviction: A Behavioural Perspective on a Conflict Between American and Continental European Law", in *Vermont Law Review*, 2009, vol. 33, p. 441.

[71] See Section 3.3. of Chapter 3 for more details on measures to mitigate noise.

		Evaluation of information			
		1 Accuracy is not in doubt	2 Personal experience by the source	3 Indirect source but corroborated by other information	4 Indirect and not corroborated
Evaluation of the source	A No doubt.	**A1**	**A2**	**A3**	**A4**
	B Source proved to be reliable in most instances.	**B1**	**B2**	**B3**	**B4**
	C Source proved to be unreliable in most instances	C1	C2	C3	C4
	X Reliability cannot be assessed.	X1	X2	X4	X4

Illustration 6.4.: Example of a '4 x 4' matrix.[72]

Some manuals attribute default ratings and apply exclusion rules. For example, the '4 x 4' model used by Europol[73] assumes that all information from the contributing agencies, EU Member States, and EU institutions (Eurojust, Frontex, and so on) shall be rated 'A1' and that only information with a 'B3' score or higher should be used for further processing.

Using such grids adds to consistency, but carries some concerns of its own. For one, it invites 'matching', a 'System 1' heuristic that proposes quick

[72] Pierre Aepli, Olivier Ribaux and Everett Summerfield, *Decision Making in Policing: Operations and Management*, EPFL Press, Lausanne, 2011, p. 31.

[73] See Europol's "Serious and Organised Crime Threat Assessment (SOCTA) – Methodology", 4 July 2012, adopted in 2012.

associative solutions to problems as they arise, which must be endorsed by the more reflective 'System 2' in favour of more complex responses.[74] Moreover, evaluation of the initial information as a whole seems to conflict with a fundamental principle for the evaluation of sources and information, which emphasizes the importance of separately evaluating the source's reliability and the informational credibility.[75]

Research in neuroscience suggests that an approach where judges have to rate or assess each piece of evidence separately before assessing the total evidence (rather than just conducting one total assessment) improves decision quality.[76] The same could be considered applicable to initial assessments of new information.

The ambiguity of judgment scales (for example, 'likely' or 'very likely', or 'on a scale of zero to six') is one of the main sources of level noise, because matching is crude. Individuals may differ in the interpretation of labels even when they agree on the substance of the judgment.

Other criticisms on evaluation grids include that:[77]

- merely assigning a code is insufficient to address the complexity of the relevant issues, usually requiring more detailed assessment;
- they are sometimes based on the experience with the source, assuming a series of previous or ongoing engagements (for example, informant-handling), and less applicable for an investigation when the source is assessed in relation to a single event;
- assumptions of the highest validity – merely because of the formal status of the source (like in the above-mentioned Europol model) – are not necessarily appropriate and can affect the weighing of the true value of the information.

6.8.2.3. Applying Individual 'Decision Hygiene'

Measures of individual 'decision hygiene',[78] beneficial for preliminary examiners, include:

- thinking statistically and taking an outside view of the case;
  - Instead of focusing firmly on the case at hand and embedding it in a causal story, it is better to consider the case as part of a reference class

[74] Daniel Kahneman, Olivier Sibony and Cas Sunstein, *Noise: A Flaw in Human Judgment*, William Collins, London, 2021, p. 182.

[75] UNODC, 2011, p. 25, see *supra* note 20.

[76] Nils Kolling and Laurence T. Hunt, "Divide and Conquer: Strategic Decision Areas", in *Nature Neuroscience*, 2015, vol. 18, no. 5, pp. 616–618.

[77] Agirre Aranburu, 2020, pp. 173–174, see *supra* note 17.

[78] See Section 3.2.2.2. of Chapter 3.

of similar cases rather than as a unique problem. An individual report of abuse of personal assistance allowances by a Member of the European Parliament can for instance be set off against a series of similar allegations and press releases, to better assess the merits of the allegation and the strategic interests in opening an investigation.

- resisting premature intuitions;
- structuring complex judgments (for example, veracity) by decomposing them into their component parts and delaying the holistic discussion and the final judgment until all inputs have been collected;
- reducing occasional noise by making a first judgment and revisiting the issue later for a subsequent look.

6.8.2.4. Reducing Noise by Organizational Measures

Research on better judgement and good decision-making suggests that the accuracy and consistency of preliminary examination might be improved by:[79]

- involving different persons ('four-eyes principle');
- sequencing information, and avoiding premature exposure to irrelevant information early in the judgment;
- enabling comparative evaluations (see the example above);
- organizing conditions for an adequate discussion (for example, diversity of the participants, sufficient time for debate and conversation rules allowing every participant to express his or her view independently);[80]
- being aware that group deliberations often create greater confidence and unity in judgment, but also lead to greater polarization;
- documenting of the examination efforts and reasoning.

The sometimes heavy reliance on open source information (including social media) during the preliminary examination may further enhance the need to document and assess the quantity and quality of the information used (for example, the base rate of relevant websites consulted). Clarifying such (minimum) standards would make any submitted or collected information stronger for analytical purposes.

[79] See Section 3.3.2. of Chapter 3.

[80] See, for an elaborated process of noise reduction, the 'Mediating Assessments Protocol' of Kahneman, Sibony and Sunstein, 2021, pp. 63–73, see *supra* note 74.

In anticipation of the 'BREXIT' vote, the BBC broadcasted a programme in 2016, where the opinion of one expert who feared BREXIT was contrasted with that of an expert who embraced it. What it did not report was that it took the producers of the programme 5 minutes to find 60 experts who were willing to express their concern, whilst they had to call for 5 hours to find a single defender. This unequal effort was not presented to the audience under guise of the 'bothsidesism', which talks to the way it reaches a superficial balance whilst obscuring a deeper truth.[81]

Illustration 6.5.: The risk of 'bothsidesism'.

6.8.3. Heuristics and Bias

In addition to 'noise,' the reasoning and decisions of the examiner will also be affected by heuristic thinking.[82] Scholars debate whether, and in what contexts, this is deleterious, but the argument often boils down to whether a holistic (intuitive) or rather atomic (structured, rational) approach should prevail. Specific risks associated with the 'System 1' based approach are that it leads to cognitive biases, including tunnel vision and story-construction, among others.

6.8.3.1. Holistic Versus Atomistic Assessment

Some scholars[83] propose that the evaluation of information in (criminal) proceedings should involve holistic, 'System 1'-thinking, where intuition informs the preferred course of action with an aura of conviction of righteousness or plausibility, but without clearly articulated reasons or justifications. This 'knowing but without knowing why' is the internal signal of judgment completion, in which the information considered and the judgment reached simply *feel right*. All the pieces of the jigsaw puzzle seem to fit (often by ignoring pieces of evidence that do not fit). This holistic, intuitive, and firm evaluation (for example, 'this is a case of bribery, surely') has the advantage of flexibility to address multiple factors and scenarios, but its validity seems to depend on the specificities of the 'skilled intuition' involved.[84] In a recent article, neuroscientists have praised the utility and advocated the use of the 'police hunch' as an 'indispensable tool for investigators.[85] A 'hunch' is defined therein as "an often unbidden,

---

[81] See speech of former Newsnight reporter Emily Maitlis on 22 August 2022, in Sky News, "In Full: Emily Maitlis Delivers the MacTaggart Lecture at the Edinburgh International TV Festival", *YouTube*, 24 August 2022, starting at 30:40 (available on *YouTube*).

[82] See Chapter 4.

[83] See, for example, Gerd Gigerenzer and Christian Engel (eds.), *Heuristics and the Law*, MIT Press, Cambridge, 2006.

[84] See Section 2.4.3 of Chapter 2.

[85] Gareth Stubbs and Karl Friston, "The Police Hunch: The Bayesian Brain, Active Inference, and the Free Energy Principle in Action", *Frontiers in Psychology*, 2024, vol. 15, pp. 1–11.

salient intuition experienced by a police officer that subsequently influences their actions".[86]

On the contrary, the 'atomistic' school defends a purely abstract, formal and logical approach to decision-making.[87] On this view, only rigorous reasoning and pure analytical thinking (that is: 'System 2' deliberative thinking) should inform the judgment process.[88]

Yet, other scholars advocate a combination of both, with a multi-level approach addressing both the whole at the macro level, the atoms at the micro level, and various intermediate levels.[89] Intuition should not be banned, but it should be informed, disciplined, and delayed until after structured analysis.[90] Thus, the evaluation of a 'reasonable basis' or other standard would always contain a subjective, holistic component.[91] Despite the segmented and sequenced outlook of the examination, as a matter of practice, they would always be followed in a holistic manner.[92] Consequently, the examiner should not consider whether or not particular pieces of information are themselves 'reasonable' (for example, suspicion of intent). Rather, he or she should apply the standard of 'reasonable' or 'sufficiency' to the factual findings that are indispensable to the determination and weigh the available information as a whole.[93]

---

86 *Ibid.*, p. 3.

87 See, for instance De Smet, 2020, see *supra* note 24.

88 For a comment that this analytical dissecting of all elements of an argument is typical of Western culture, while the rest of the world relies more on holistic, collective and contextual thinking, see Joseph Henrich, Steven J. Heine and Ara Norenzayan, "Most People Are Not WEIRD", in *Nature*, 2010, vol. 466, no. 29, pp. 71–73.

89 Agirre Aranburu, 2020, p. 234, see *supra* note 17.

90 Kahneman, Sibony and Sunstein., 2021, p. 373, see *supra* note 74.

91 OLAF's preliminary examination process invites for a holistic approach when it holds that all information collected during the selection process shall be taken into account in justifying the opening (or not) of an investigation (see Article 5.6. GIP, *supra* note 6) and that the 'opinion' should take into account "the information and elements provided by the source *as a whole*" (emphasis added).

92 Policy Paper on Preliminary Examinations, para. 77, p. 18, see *supra* note 6.

93 Cross, 2018, p. 245, see *supra* note 8.

Individualistic atomistic	Holistic intuitive
Focused on individual item, case-by-case	Based on skilled intuition, depends on professionalism and objectivity of the evaluator
Logical dissecting	More in line with contextual thinking
Useful for building structured analysis	Problem: Cognitive limits in complex cases?
	Should not be excluded but applied with caution, for example, after structured analysis?

Illustration 6.6.: Atomistic versus holistic evaluation.

Whereas the absence of (expected) information informs a judgment of comprehensiveness of the initial information (see above), information gaps at the end of the preliminary examination should, in principle, not be taken into account for the final proposal or decision of whether or not to open an investigation. The decision makers should make their decision based on the information available, and avoid 'it is possible' or 'one cannot exclude' reasoning.

6.8.3.2. Tunnel Vision

The preliminary examination stage is particularly vulnerable for confirmation bias and related phenomena of tunnel vision.[94] Pre-programmed to build stories, the examiners might be tempted to only look for and interpret information in line with the initial allegation or their impression of it, and ignore or discard information providing alternative accounts. To avoid this, scholars have proposed distinguishing between the necessary steps of *verification* of initial information and *corroboration*. 'Verification' is a neutral term, and it signifies aiming at a determination about the truth. This makes for an impartial parameter, different from the term 'corroboration,' which means positive confirmation. The evaluation during the preliminary examination must aim at impartially verifying the validity of the evidence, with no prejudice towards confirming or dismissing it. It should impartially consider points of confirmation and contradiction.[95]

During verifications, the examiner should also be aware of *asymmetrical scepticism*. This refers to how decision makers tend to uncritically approve of

[94] See Chapter 4.

[95] See Moa Lidén, "Confirmation Bias in Investigations of Core International Crimes: Risk Factors and Quality Control Techniques", in Agirre, Bergsmo, De Smet and Stahn (eds.), 2020, pp. 461–562, see *supra* note 2.

hypothesis-consistent information (for example, the suspect was quoted in a previous investigation), whereas they more critically scrutinize hypothesis-inconsistent information (for example, no mention of the person in a previous, similar investigation).[96] This poses a risk that criteria used for reliability and credibility assessments might be applied differently depending on whether the information is consistent or inconsistent with a case hypothesis.[97] Such asymmetrical scepticism is more pronounced in relation to so-called *elastic evidence*, that is, evidence in relation to which there is a wide range of possible subjective interpretations that can be justified.[98] For instance, witness evidence is typically considered more elastic than DNA evidence.

6.8.3.3. Availability Effect

A large body of studies has demonstrated that when individuals need to make assessments about uncertain events, they tend to base these estimates on the ease with which similar events come to mind. The common human tendency to judge the probability (for example, chance to be prosecuted) or frequency (for example, the number of convictions of white-collar criminals) of an event by the ease with which one can remember or imagine the number of relevant instances of similar events is called the *availability heuristic*.[99] It is a thinking shortcut in people make judgments about the likelihood of an event based on how easily a similar example, instance, or case comes to mind. What is easily remembered or imagined is estimated to be more frequent or likely than what is not.

In relation to preliminary examination, this means that a reported case could be more readily considered to indicate fraud or an offence, if it bears resemblance to another fraud case that recently appeared in the media and is thus salient in the mind of the selector.

6.8.3.4. The Representativeness Heuristic

The representativeness (also: resemblance) heuristic is a mental shortcut that produces judgments about a person, object, or event based on its perceived

96 *Ibid.*, p. 483.

97 *Ibid.*, p. 485.

98 Karl Ask, Anna Rebelius and Pär Anders Granhag, "The 'Elasticity' of Criminal Evidence: A Moderator of Investigator Bias", in *Applied Cognitive Psychology*, 2008, vol. 22, no. 9, pp. 1245–1259.

99 Amos Tversky and Daniel Kahneman, "Judgment Under Uncertainty: Heuristics and Biases", in *Science*, 1974, vol. 185, pp. 1124–1131; Richard J. Heuer, *Psychology of Intelligence Analysis*, Central Intelligence Agency, Langley, 1999, p. 147.

similarity to a typical member of that category of person, object, or event.[100] When asked about the probability that something belongs to a certain category, one might substitute this question for a simpler one: 'How similar is it to a typical member of that category?'. The subjective probability judgment rests on how representative (resembling) object 'A' is of class 'B'.[101] System 1 often automatically replaces the difficult estimation question with a judgment of resemblance to the class at hand, often related to a stereotype.

In relation to preliminary examination, selectors or evaluators might mentally compare the alleged suspect to their perception of a prototypical offender and base their probability judgment of fraud on the extent to which the reported suspect's behaviour is representative of guilty suspects.

6.8.3.5. Story-Construction

Research suggests that story construction is at the core of cognitive process people use to make sense of criminal evidence[102] and determine facts in adjudication.[103] A *story* is the representation of an event or a series of events.[104] It entails the actions and experiences of one or more protagonists and a plot line with certain schematic elements (for example, setting, event, attempt, reaction and consequence).[105] The organization of a story is based on relations which imply causes and intentions of actions, according to the judge's general knowledge concerning action sequences.[106] People are indeed by far the most talented species at spotting causal relationships; that is, situations where one event is seen

---

[100] Rüdiger Pohl "Introduction: Cognitive Illusions", in *id.* (ed.), *Cognitive Illusions: A Handbook on Fallacies and Biases in Thinking, Judgment and Memory*, Psychology Press, Hove, 2004, p. 6.

[101] Richard H. Thaler and Cas R. Sunstein, *Nudge: Improving Decisions About Health, Wealth and Happiness*, Penguin books, London, 2009, p. 30.

[102] Eva-Catherine Hillemann *et al.*, *Psychological Factors in Criminal Intelligence Analysis: What They Are, Why They Are Important, and How to Deal With Them*, VALCRI White Paper Series, 1 January 2017, submitted in the framework of the European Research Project "Visual Analytics for Sense-Making in Criminal Intelligence Analysis" (VALCRI).

[103] Nancy Pennington and Reid Hastie, "A Cognitive Theory of Juror Decision Making: The Story Model", in *Cardozo Law Review*, 1991, vol. 13, nos. 2–3, pp. 519–557.

[104] H. Porter Abbott, *The Cambridge Introduction to Narrative*, Cambridge University Press, 2002, p. 12.

[105] David E. Rumelhart, "Notes on a Schema for Stories", in Daniel G. Bobrow and Allan Collins (eds.) *Representation and Understanding: Studies in Cognitive Science*, Academic Press, New York, 1975, pp. 211–236.

[106] Enide Maegherman, "Tunnel Vision and Falsification in Legal Decision-Making", in Sara Landström, Pär Anders Granhag and Peter J. van Koppen (eds.), *The Future of Forensic Psychology*, Routledge, 2022, p. 148.

as a cause, and another event as the effect linked to the cause.[107] The same mechanisms of story construction might affect the preliminary examination.

In this view, evaluators and investigators form initial impressions quickly, interpret them as coherent, and assume causal relations and individual responsibility as the key agents. The evidence considered can consequently be distorted, at least to some extent, to fit initial snap judgments[108] and to make the judge feel confident in his assessment. This is not different from reading an allegation for the first time. Some people may automatically make it a 'really serious fraud case' or rather a case of someone making false allegations out of an 'act of revenge'. When the constructed story is comprehensively coherent, contains vivid details, and there are no attractive alternatives,[109] the examiner is liable to find any allegation very credible. This might come at the expense of neglecting missing information that is relevant for a balanced judgment.

The risk of scenario building is exacerbated because of the saliency of some information. The term refers to information that catches the attention and receives more weight (or more attention) than it objectively deserves because of its vividness. For example, consider the case in which the corporate address of an organization, suspected of fraud, is located at the same address of the consulate of some offshore paradise (without any further indication of relevance).

The point was made before that, persons involved in investigations (here: the examiner) should not stick to a single story but practice falsification and consider alternative hypotheses, reflecting on whether another reasonable reading of the information is possible.[110] This includes also considering the consequences of the analysis, that is, what if the information is wrong, misleading, or subject to a different interpretation?

The openness for, and practice of, such alternative hypothesis-testing may depend on the system of preliminary examination. Story-building or considering a lead hypothesis can be an integral part of a more preparatory-oriented preliminary examination, where the examiners already suggest venues for investigation, based on a prioritization of information to increase the plausibility of a story. When the preliminary examination is conceived of primarily as a mere filtering of information (gateway model), such story-building will be less prevalent.

---

107 Christer Sturmark, *The Flame of Reason: Clear Thinking for the Twenty-First Century*, Head of Zeus, London, 2022, p. 117.

108 Kahneman, Sibony and Sunstein, 2021, p. 173, see *supra* note 74.

109 *Ibid*., p. 202.

110 See Chapters 1 and 2.

Finally, the question of how a previous complaint or conviction of the reported wrongdoer should be taken into account is much debated. Studies suggest that knowledge of a prior conviction increases judgments of the defendant's criminal propensity and the perceived chance of guilt. Like ethnicity or socio-economic background, it is considered to be irrelevant context information that is legally not supposed to have an impact on charging decisions or verdicts but probably facilitates the incriminating story construction process. This would seem to be particularly the case when the prior conviction(s) is (are) similar to the present offense and when there is not much other evidence available.[111]

6.8.3.6. The Conjunction Fallacy

Another relevant type of judgment bias relates to how people judge the probability of events based on the detail with which these events are described. In particular, it has been found that more detailed descriptions of an event can give rise to higher judged probabilities (here: that a criminal offence took place). This bias has been termed 'the conjunction fallacy'[112] because it shows that people erroneously believe that events described in more detail are more probable than those that are described in less detail. People tend to prefer and feel better in assessing the credibility of a story (a 'S1' informed perception mainly based on the coherence of a story), rather than judging the probability (a 'S2' based statistical deduction) it actually took place. Combining both simultaneously – the logic (coherence) of an assertion and its probability – seems outside the scope of our fallible brain.[113]

> Any prediction can be made more believable, even as it becomes less likely, if filled with internally consistent details. In defiance of logic, the prediction that "A massive flood somewhere in North America next year, in which more than 1,000 people drown" was found less likely to occur than "An earthquake in California sometime next year, causing a flood in which more than 1,000 people drown".[114]
>
> Likewise, auditors assessed the risk of misstatements in detailed accounts (for example, 'investing', 'payroll', 'insurance', *et cetera*) higher than when the accounts were described in larger categories of bookkeeping (for example, 'commercial

---

111 See Susanne M. Schmittat, Birte Englich, Lyane Sautner and Petra Velten, "Alternative Stories and the Decision to Prosecute: An Applied Approach Against Confirmation Bias in Criminal Prosecution", in *Psychology, Crime & Law*, 2022, vol. 28, no. 6, pp. 608–635, and research quoted there.

112 Amos Tversky and Daniel Kahneman, "A Heuristic for Judging Frequency and Probability", in *Cognitive Psychology*, 1973, vol. 5, pp. 207–232; Tversky and Kahneman, 1974, see *supra* note 99.

113 Maria Konnikova, *Mastermind: How to Think Like Sherlock Holmes*, Viking Penguin, New York, 2012, p. 250.

114 Daniel Kahneman, *Thinking, Fast and Slow*, Farrar, Straus and Giroux, New York, 2011.

activities'). Unpacking the large category into several sub-labels lead to a higher probability assessment of finding misstatements there.[115]

Illustration 6.7.: The conjunction fallacy.

6.8.3.7. Anchoring

The anchoring bias is the tendency to base final judgements on information obtained early in the decision-making process. Typically, initial exposure to a number serves as a reference point, influencing subsequent judgments about value, but the effect has also been described for non-numerical information. The process usually occurs outside of the decision maker's awareness[116] and consists of incremental adjustments from the first implicit or explicit reference point (the 'anchor') until reaching the cognitive 'comfort zone'. Research suggests that these adjustments are often not sufficient.[117]

The anchoring bias is closely related to confirmation bias and story-building and considered particularly problematic when selectors or investigators must assess initial case information. Psycho-legal researchers have demonstrated that agents who form theories early in an investigation are more likely to dismiss information that disconfirms their beliefs as less reliable.[118]

As PIF investigations pertain to numeric quantities, they are also affected by numeric anchors, for instance minimal sentences that the law presents or sentences demanded or recommended by prosecutors.[119] Likewise, the amounts mentioned in a complaint (for example, reported damage) or in a preliminary examination report (for example, estimated financial damage) may receive disproportionate weight compared to their real merits and continue to be used throughout the process.

6.9. Concluding Remarks

The preliminary examination is a crucial step in the (pre-) investigative cycle where an organization decides whether or not it should open an investigation. As such, this phase primarily involves a legal and factual analytical process

[115] Richard G. Brody, John M. Coulter and Alireza Daneshhar, "Auditor Probability Judgments: Discounting Unspecified Possibilities", in *Theory and Decision*, 2003, vol. 54, pp. 85–104.

[116] Tversky and Kahneman, 1974, see *supra* note 99.

[117] *Ibid.*

[118] Ask, Rebelius and Granhag, 2008, see *supra* note 98.

[119] For anchoring effects in adjudication, see Birte Englich and Thomas Mussweiler, "Sentencing Under Uncertainty: Anchoring Effects in the Courtroom", in *Journal of Applied Social Psychology*, 2001, vol. 31, no. 7, p. 1535; Birte Englich, Thomas Mussweiler and Fritz Strack, "Playing Dice with Criminal Sentences: The Influence of Irrelevant Anchors on Experts' Judicial Decision Making", in *Personality and Social Psychology Bulletin*, 2006, vol. 32, no. 2, p. 188.

aimed at determining whether an investigation should be initiated. Depending on the applicable legal framework and organizational practices, common features of this stage generally include:

- *Absence of investigative powers*: verifications are conducted to establish whether the available information reaches the requisite level of seriousness and satisfies specific statutory criteria, without involving the authority to carry out investigative measures, especially intrusive ones. However, as noted above, depending on the legal framework, criminal investigative authorities may already dispose of intrusive powers even during the verification of incoming information, as is the case for the EPPO.
- *Competence and gravity assessment*: determining the organization's competence to adjudicate the matter and assessing the severity of the allegations to establish their admissibility. This evaluation is often accompanied by an assessment of the opportunity to investigate, with the caveat already laid out regarding criminal frameworks governed by the principles of legality.
- *Seriousness of allegations*: The seriousness of the allegation is gauged, based on the reliability of the source and the credibility of the information, generally necessitating a distinct assessment.
- *Source reliability and information credibility*: The reliability of the source typically involves examining their expertise, honesty and authenticity. The credibility of information can be tested against criteria like completeness, independent corroboration and whether it supports the conclusions drawn.
- *Objective standards*: Although a preliminary examination cannot be entirely objective, using standardized scales and organizational protocols that incorporate multiple perspectives can help reduce inconsistencies.
- *Final evaluation*: The concluding evaluation often entails a detailed, analytical review of each piece of information followed by an overarching assessment in the final phases.
- *Bias vigilance*: Examiners must remain vigilant against inherent biases, including the tendency to form narratives, overemphasize striking details, and succumb to confirmation bias.

7

Investigation Plans

Antonio Angotti, Kris Vandenberk and Julius Dirma*

7.1. Introduction

When an investigation is opened, its course is planned, set and steered by the investigators. They will have to acquire sufficient in-depth knowledge of the case, understand what is required to confirm or discard the allegations, and develop a strategy and tactics to investigate. The planning and subsequent management of the investigation is as critical to a fair and effective outcome as much as it is to the investigative work-process. Questions that will be addressed in this chapter include: To what depth should the investigation be planned? What is the role and importance of an investigation plan? What are the different functions of an investigation plan? And what are the precautions and good practices relevant to the correct deployment of investigation plans?

7.2. The Investigation Plan

In a previous chapter of this volume, the authors proposed that a preliminary examination should define the contours of the situation that may eventually be investigated, in particular in terms of its geographical and temporal scope, but this should not be binding on any future investigation that may derive from it.[1] The investigative process evolves with its own findings and, after the investigation is opened, it is in the hands of the investigators.

When an investigation is opened, the first key questions concern how comprehensive and all-embracing the investigation should be, what and how much evidence should be sought and collected, and how to choose and prioritize the necessary investigative steps to obtain such evidence. In institutional contexts,

---

* **Antonio Angotti** is a Fellow of the Centre for International Law Research and Policy ('CILRAP') and an attorney at the Bar Association of Florence. **Kris Vandenberk** is a senior case analyst at the European Public Prosecutor's office ('EPPO'). **Julius Dirma** is a deputy head of unit at the European Anti-Fraud Office ('OLAF'). This chapter is authored in the contributors' personal capacity and does not necessarily reflect the views of EPPO, OLAF, CILRAP or other institutions mentioned therein.

1 See Chapter 6, referring to Matilde E. Gawronski, "The Legalistic Function of Preliminary Examinations: Quality Control as a Two-Way Street", in Morten Bergsmo and Carsten Stahn (eds.), *Quality Control in Preliminary Examination: Volume 1*, Torkel Opsahl Academic EPublisher ('TOAEP'), Brussels, 2018, p. 182 (https://www.toaep.org/ps-pdf/32-bergsmo-stahn/).

there also may be questions of budget, staffing and organizational policy, which should be addressed at this early stage.[2] The answer to these and other relevant questions at the start of the investigation can be integrated into an 'investigation plan' or 'investigation work plan'.

Investigation plans are strategic documents that spell out the objectives of an investigation and the means to attain them, often adopted at the investigation's very beginning and focusing on *case assessment*, *planning*, *management* and *reporting* (or *monitoring*). These functions are performed by means of a written outline of factual hypotheses and legal requirements relevant to what the investigation aims to prove,[3] a list of the main investigative steps that must be taken in order to reach the goals of the investigation, and a schedule that assigns the responsibility for the implementation of each step within the investigative team, to ensure the goals of the investigation are met efficiently.

Investigation plans are an important tool to enhance the quality of the investigation. They provide a structured approach to conducting an effective investigation and are hence recognized as a best practice,[4] in particular for fact-rich cases.[5] They allow stakeholders to:

- focus the work of the investigation team and management on meeting the agreed objectives;[6]
- set a reasonable timeframe, and assess whether the direction of an investigation has changed;
- ensure that an investigation meets the principles and standards of independence and objectivity;[7] and

2 For instance, the risk of waste of resources can be greatly mitigated by adopting an investigation plan, see European Court of Auditors, Special Report No. 1/2005 concerning the management of the European Anti-Fraud Office ('OLAF'), together with the European Commission's replies, 18 August 2005, para. 22.

3 See National Police Directorate of Norway, "Guidelines for Investigation Plans Version 1.0", 2017, quoted in Alf Butenschøn Skre, "Investigation Plans as a Tool for Managing Investigations in Norway", in Xabier Agirre Aranburu, Morten Bergsmo, Simon De Smet and Carsten Stahn (eds.), *Quality Control in Criminal Investigation*, TOAEP, Brussels, 2020, p. 888 (https://www.toaep.org/ps-pdf/38-qcci/).

4 Markus Eikel, "Investigation Plans in International Criminal Investigations: The Example of the ICC Office of the Prosecutor", in Agirre, Bergsmo, De Smet and Stahn (eds.), 2020, p. 801, see *supra* note 3.

5 Antonio Angotti, "Investigation Plans in the Draft Regulations of the ICC Office of the Prosecutor: An Italian Perspective", in Agirre, Bergsmo, De Smet and Stahn (eds.), 2020, p. 832, see *supra* note 3.

6 OLAF Supervisory Committee, "Analysis of OLAF Investigations Lasting More Than 36 Months in 2019", Opinion 5/2021, December 2021, p. 19 ('SC Opinion 5/2021').

7 Conference of International Investigators, "General Principles for Scoping and Planning", May 2021 ('CII 2021').

- give due consideration to the foreseeable costs and risks entailed by the investigation, as applicable to the situation and the institutional priorities.

More generally, investigation plans help with some of the typical challenges of an investigation, such as the lack of overview of information, unclear formulation of responsibilities or liabilities,[8] or the haphazard collection of (too much) evidence.[9]

A marked advantage of adopting investigation plans is that they are tailored to the needs and reality of an individual investigation. Solutions which are applicable office-wide, or even throughout an institution (such as directives, circulars or protocols) may make for more uniform investigative approaches and enable better monitoring, but they cannot replace the tailored functions that investigation plans perform.[10] Moreover, the preparation of an investigation plan pushes the investigative team to reflect upon and agree on the implementation of a formulated plan *ex ante*, which has been argued to be a more efficient approach compared to scrutinize *ex post* whether the ideal investigative avenues have been pursued.[11] However, one should not exclude the latter approach, which often yields useful insights for organizations and investigators.

Investigation plans are not specific to one type of investigative work. They are an essential tool for all types of evidence-, fact- and law-based investigations, but can be particularly important in specific cases. For example, this is true for fact-rich, trans-national cases involving international investigative teams,[12] regardless of whether they investigate a crime or an administrative irregularity.

7.3. Functions of the Investigation Plan

7.3.1. Overview

In order to be efficient, an investigation plan should be comprehensive and thorough enough to provide clear direction, but also flexible and able to respond to evolving, and sometimes unanticipated, demands. The general purpose of an

---

[8] This chapter uses the terms 'responsibility' and 'liability' interchangeably, as the investigations relevant to this publication may be concerned with both the wider meaning of responsibility and the narrower notion of legal liability (that is, the obligation to account for one's own actions, including accepting a possible sanction, see "Legal Liability", *Cambridge English Dictionary*).

[9] See the discussion on investigative bottlenecks in Morten Bergsmo, "Towards a Culture of Quality Control in Criminal Investigation", Policy Brief Series No. 94 (2019), TOAEP, Brussels, 2019, pp. 2–3 (http://www.toaep.org/pbs-pdf/94-bergsmo/).

[10] Angotti, 2020, p. 840, see *supra* note 5.

[11] *Ibid.*, 2020, p. 849.

[12] *Ibid.*, 2020, p. 847.

investigation plan is to help advance the investigative process in a methodical, efficient and expeditious manner.

Key elements that should be developed, discussed and agreed upon prior to the start of any substantive investigative activity include:

- *fundamental questions*, that is, questions that the investigation will hopefully be able to answer through the collection of credible and reliable evidence;
- the *legal framework*, including theories of liability, possible irregularities and crimes alleged to have been committed and their legal constitutive elements or requirements;
- primary *investigative avenues*, such as summaries of what is presently known, people whose activities will be examined, potential witnesses and evidence, including documentary;
- a summary of investigative *tasks* to be undertaken;
- the *resources* to be deployed to conduct the investigative activities (including their roles, responsibilities and reporting lines), details on specialized staff members, language or interpretation requirements, service providers, information to external stakeholders, involvement of other offices and institutions and equipment;
- potential risks and obstacles; and
- a *timeline*, keeping track of the duration of a case.[13]

This combination of separate but interlinked objectives of oversight, strategy and monitoring[14] can be broken down into four major functions of the investigation plan:[15]

a) case *assessment*, to demonstrate a thorough understanding of the investigative setting and content, to acknowledge the challenges and to clarify the objectives of the investigation;
b) *planning*, to propose an approach to evidence collection and investigative avenues;
c) investigation *management* (for example, leading and associated roles, resources, support internal or external experts); and
d) *reporting* and *monitoring*.

The investigation plan best complies with its role as a quality-control tool if all functions are adequately addressed.[16] The plan should strive to strike a

---

[13] See Carsten Stahn, "From Preliminary Examination to Investigation", in Agirre, Bergsmo, De Smet and Stahn (eds.), 2020, p. 61, see *supra* note 3.

[14] Angotti, 2020, p. 821, see *supra* note 5.

[15] Eikel, 2020, pp. 801–808, see *supra* note 4.

[16] *Ibid.*, pp. 819–820.

balance between serving more managerial concerns (such as the duration of cases) and quality enhancement.[17]

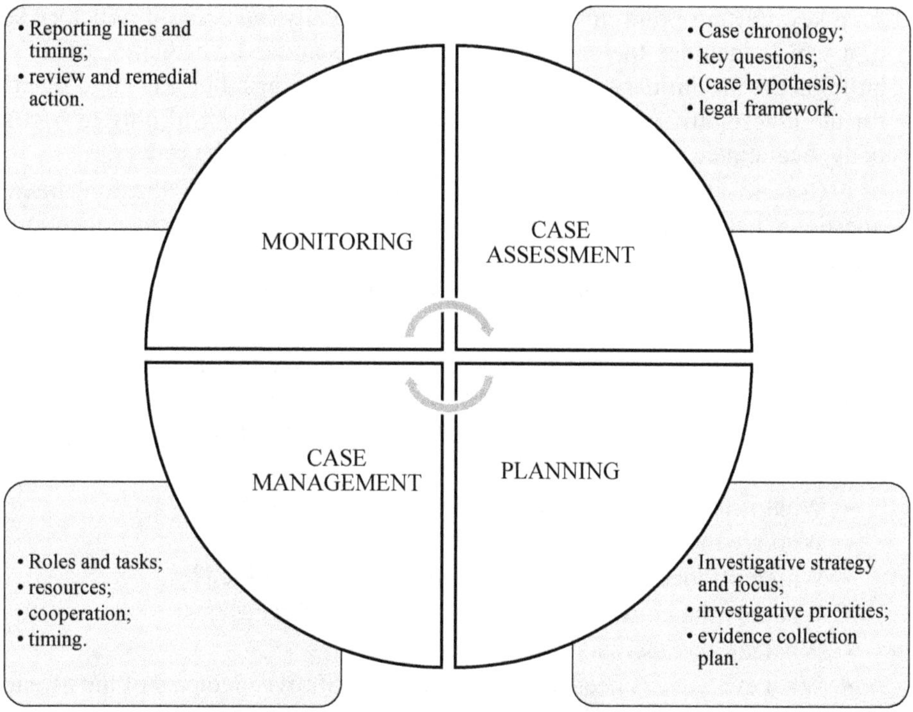

Illustration 7.1.: Functions and sections of the investigation plan.

---

[17] OLAF's investigation plans ('initial work plans') are mainly a tool to monitor and control the duration of cases. Stemming from the legal obligation to "conduct its investigations continuously over a period which must be proportionate to the circumstances and complexity of the case" (Article 7(5) 'OLAF Regulation', Consolidated text of Regulation (EU, EURATOM) No. 883/2013 of the European Parliament and of the Council of 11 September 2013 concerning investigations conducted by the European Anti-Fraud Office (OLAF) and repealing Regulation (EC) No. 1073/1999 of the European Parliament and of the Council and Council Regulation (Euratom) No. 1074/1999 (https://www.legal-tools.org/doc/6f0ede/)), the established practices during the past years and spurred by opinions of its Supervisory Committee, OLAF readopted the principle of 'work plans' in its internal investigative guidelines in October 2021 (Guidelines on Investigation Procedures for OLAF Staff, 11 October 2021 ('GIP') (https://www.legal-tools.org/doc/tgfdldc7/)). According to the Supervisory Committee, the purpose of these work plans is to: (i) focus the work of the investigation team and management on meeting the agreed objectives; (ii) set a reasonable timeframe for the investigation and allocate appropriate resources to this end; and (iii) ensure there is a framework for managers to identify any undue delays that need to be addressed, to assess whether the direction of the investigation has changed from the initial assessment and whether the investigation should be discontinued (see SC Opinion 5/2021, *supra* note 6).

7.3.2. Case Assessment

7.3.2.1. Fundamental Questions

As a key starting point, investigation plans typically have an introductory section which includes the assessment of the case under investigation. This can build on the preliminary examination in the proceedings, but it is good practice for the investigative team to perform its own analysis, even if only to become better acquainted with the allegations and background of the case.

Case assessment can help identifying, from the outset, the fundamental questions that the investigation will hopefully answer through the collection of credible and reliable evidence. Without such guidance, there is a risk that investigative efforts will lack the necessary focus to identify and collect the required evidence effectively and efficiently.

In a criminal case, the investigation must prove that a certain event or a certain state of affairs, which is forbidden by the law, has been caused by the suspected person's conduct, and that this conduct was accompanied by a prescribed mental state. Fundamental questions include:

- What is the relevant background or context of the case?
- Who are the suspects and (possible) accomplices?
- Which offences are suspected to have been committed?
- What are the constitutive elements of these offences?
- What are the ancillary offences, if any?
- What evidence is needed to prove the constitutive elements of the offences (including, in a criminal case, evidence needed to establish *mens rea*) and their responsibility?

Answering these fundamental questions helps to define the exact scope of the case and establishes clear objectives, within the parameters set by the allegations under investigation.

7.3.2.2. Legal Framework

Investigation plans are most effective when aligned with the legal case assessment, which ensures the investigative strategy, objectives and activities directly fulfil the identified legal requirements and enable targeted and properly prioritized collection of evidence.[18] This entails a legal preview of substantial and procedural issues.

Through *offence recognition*, the investigators will consider the different possible legal qualifications for the reported facts, and begin to assemble an (mental) inventory of the evidence that will be required to support the claim that the recognized offence(s) have been committed. For example, can the

[18] Eikel, 2020, pp. 819–820, see *supra* note 15.

information available at the beginning indicate corruption, price fixing, bid rigging or (just) market division?[19] The investigators should ask themselves whether the reported facts might be indicative of a bribery, kickbacks or a conflict of interest, and if so, whether such facts, if true, constitute a sanctionable case of corruption.[20] The investigators will have to consider all these hypotheses, reflect on what the actual constitutive elements are for the suspected criminal offences and on what evidence is required.

Comprehending the specific legal requirements and maintaining an overview of information, facts and evidence already at the start of an investigation is an important requirement, as insufficient understanding of such complexity can affect the quality of justice delivered further down the line.

In criminal investigations, offence recognition can entail an early reflection about possible charges, closely related to the evidence that must be sought.[21] Offence recognition can guide an investigation while being shaped by its results. As evidence is progressively collected and reviewed, it may also point the investigation towards different or more refined avenues. An investigation plan needs to clearly set out the requirements to be proven for each charge or accusation, as defined in the relevant legal or regulatory framework: "The process of

---

[19] For example, see United Nations ('UN'), Department of Management Strategy, Policy and Compliance, *Fraud and Corruption Awareness: A Handbook for Staff*, 2022, pp. 28–29 and 32, which distinguishes three types of collusive agreements, described as occurrences when there is a secret combination, conspiracy or concert of action between two or more persons for fraudulent or deceitful purposes:

- price-fixing: involving an agreement among competitors to manipulate prices;
- bid-rigging: involving an agreement among competitors on which firm will submit the winning bid;
- market division: agreements whereby competitors divide markets among themselves.

[20] For example, the same 2022 UN handbook on *Fraud and Corruption Awareness* (*ibid.*, pp. 3 and 33), makes three distinctions:

- corruption: any act or omission that misuses official authority or that seeks to influence the misuse of official authority in order to obtain an undue benefit for oneself or a third party;
- bribery: the offering, giving, receiving or soliciting of anything of value to influence action as an official or in the discharge of legal or public duty;
- kickbacks: the exchange of something of value for preferential treatment.

Interestingly, the set of indicators for the aforementioned shortcomings and for conflict of interest are the same.

[21] A charge is considered here as the decision (of the prosecutor) to formally notify to a (where applicable, natural or legal) person a statement of facts and circumstances (*including* the time and place of the alleged crimes) and a legal characterization of these facts, against which the accused persons will have to defend themselves. See Gilbert Bitti, "Quality Control in Case Preparation and the Role of the International Criminal Court", in Agirre, Bergsmo, De Smet and Stahn (eds.), 2020, p. 927, see *supra* note 3.

articulating and discussing possible charges guides fact-finders and reviewers towards constantly asking questions that are relevant to formulating tentative charging hypotheses".[22] Formulating tentative *discharging* hypotheses also helps preventing tunnel vision (see Section 7.3.2.3. below).

This reflection should include recognizing the evidence and fact patterns that constitute *ancillary offences* (for example, forgery)[23] and forms of sanctionable behaviour other than commission (such as membership of a criminal organization, complicity, conspiracy, attempt, aiding and counselling).

The question of to what extent the preliminary examination is binding or guiding for the first investigation plan is likewise relevant. Preliminary examination is – even in its 'gateway' conception[24] – not simply an account of suspicions or allegations of crime, but a selective assessment of those allegations which meet the standards applicable to the preliminary examination. Accordingly, a preliminary examination will not necessarily be a reliable guide to the contours of the subsequent investigation. Frequently, there may be alleged (or even unknown) crimes which cannot be substantiated to the required standard in the preliminary examination stage, but which can be established by further investigative activities.[25] This can require a modification of the scope of the investigation, in addition to updating the investigation plan as new avenues and possibilities are uncovered by the team's work (see also Section 7.4.4.).

Depending on the legal setting, the purpose of an investigation may not be finding 'the one truth' (that is, what happened), but rather to (only) find out whether the alleged offences have been committed.

From a procedural standpoint, some methods for obtaining evidence, such as wiretapping, may be available only in the case of certain suspected offences, while others may require meeting proportionality, necessity, or subsidiarity standards. This reinforces the need to perform a legal assessment early in the process and is related to the management function (see Section 7.3.4.).

---

22 Angotti, 2020, p. 830, see *supra* note 5.

23 See 'inextricably linked offences' in Article 22(3) and Recital 54 of the 'EPPO Regulation' (Council Regulation (EU) No. 2017/1939 of 12 October 2017 implementing enhanced cooperation on the establishment of the European Public Prosecutor's Office ('the EPPO') (https://www.legal-tools.org/doc/plfszr14/)).

24 See Section 6.7. of Chapter 6.

25 Matthew Cross, "The Standard of Proof in Preliminary Examinations", in Morten Bergsmo and Carsten Stahn (eds.), *Quality Control in Preliminary Examination: Volume 2*, TOAEP, Brussels, 2018, pp. 216–217 (https://www.toaep.org/ps-pdf/33-bergsmo-stahn/).

7.3.2.3. Case Hypothesis

Various manuals and articles on investigations propose that investigators develop a case hypothesis, or case theory,[26] at the start of any investigation.[27] In this view, the investigation plan should contain hypotheses that are coherent with the available information and facts collected thus far which appear relevant to the investigation.[28] Some go as far as proposing that refusing to have hypotheses guide the investigation would be accepting coincidence as a master.[29]

Investigation theorists propose that an investigation starts in a state of *entropy*,[30] in which all hypotheses and options are open, and that investigators should advance the investigation by,[31]

a) first, developing hypotheses about what happened based on their findings, without considering possibility or probability at this stage[32] (this is called *abduction*: searching for the causes of the observed effects);
b) subsequently, testing such hypotheses with validation and further inquiries (the process of *deduction*: 'if this hypothesis is true, than we should find X' (from cause to expected effects));

---

26 A hypothesis (a Greek word meaning 'guess') is an uncertain claim presented on its own. It differs from a theory, a term used to describe a set of inter-related ideas that explain a specific event or a general set of phenomena. See Christer Sturmark, *The Flame of Reason: Clear Thinking for the Twenty-First Century*, Head of Zeus, London, 2022, p. 67.

27 See, for example, Simon Baechler *et al.*, "Un modèle continu, non linéaire et collaboratif de l'enquête", in *Criminologie*, 2020, vol. 53, no. 2, pp. 43–76; Guillaume Louis, "Enquête policière et techniques d'enquête: un regard scientifique", in *Criminologie*, 2021, vol. 53, no. 2, p. 6 ; Kim Rossmo, "Anatomie d'une enquête criminelle", in *Criminologie*, 2020, vol. 53, no. 2, pp. 17–42; Ivar Fahsing, "Beyond Reasonable Doubt: How to Think Like an Expert Detective", in Paulo Barbosa Marques and Mauro Paulino (eds.), *Police Psychology*, Elsevier Academic Press, 2022, p. 270.

28 For guidelines to create hypotheses in investigation plans, see Eivind Kolflaath, quoted in Butenschøn Skre, 2020, p. 898, see *supra* note 3.

29 In the original version: "Refuser de prendre l'hypothèse pour guide est se condamner à prendre le hasard pour maître", Gustave Le Bon, *Hier et demain. Pensées brèves*, Ernest Flammarion, Paris, 1918.

30 Scientific term historically most used in physics, applied to the field of investigations by Baechler *et al.*, 2020, p. 48, see *supra* note 27, and referring to a state of disorder, chaos and uncertainty.

31 See *ibid.*, p. 49; Carol E. Cleland, "Methodological and Epistemic Differences Between Historical and Experimental Science", in *Philosophy of Science*, 2002, vol. 69, no. 3, pp. 474–496; Louis, 2021, see *supra* note 27.

32 In practice, the number of working hypotheses can be reduced by eliminating those below a certain threshold of probability, to avoid cognitive load. See the technique of 'Analysis of Competing Hypotheses' developed by Richard J. Heuer, *Psychology of Intelligence Analysis*, Central Intelligence Agency, Langley, 1999.

c) finally, to reconstruct the past and propose a working *narrative*, to be pursued by the prosecutor and consolidated by the judge at a later stage.

Such hypothetical-deductive reasoning would operate in a format of dual processing of information, as the abductive selection of hypotheses (the best hypothesis) would occur almost automatically (System 1), to be complemented by a retroactive reasoning phase to select the most probable theory.[33] Depending on the results of the investigation and the available evidence, the theory's believability will be either strengthened or weakened.

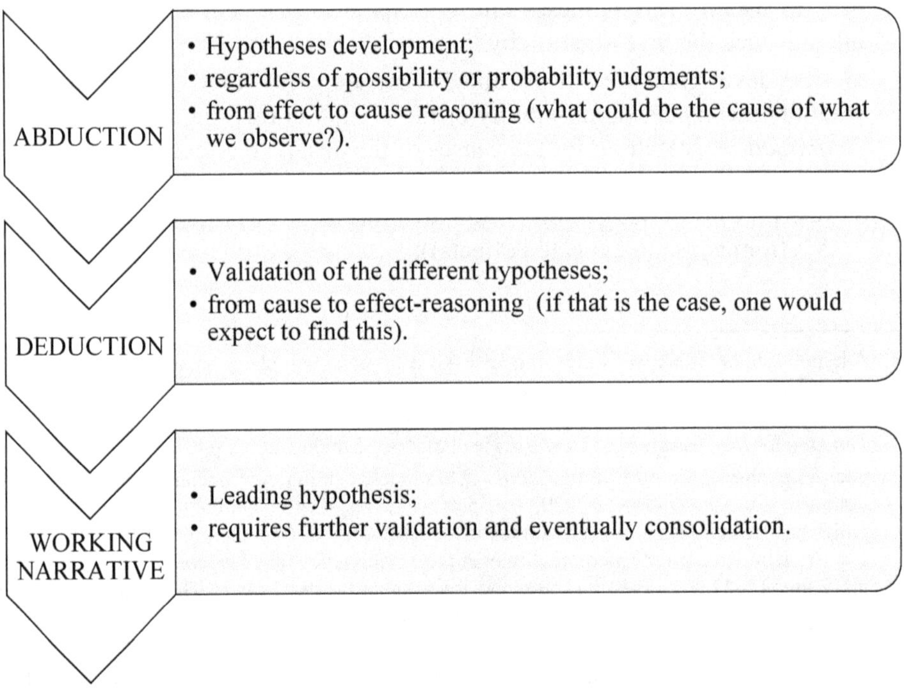

Illustration 7.2.: From abduction to deduction.

It can be argued that theory-development and the identification of (competing) hypotheses are less important for PIF investigations[34] compared to other kinds of investigations, which typically identify the potential offences at the start and develop different theories and hypotheses to identify and validate

[33] Louis refers to an operation of 'rational instinct'. See Louis, 2021, p. 5, and references quoted there, *supra* note 27.

[34] The notion of 'PIF crimes' refers to crimes against the financial interests of the European Union ('*protection des intérêts financiers*'), pursuant to its Directive (EU) No. 2017/1371 of the European Parliament and of the Council of 5 July 2017 on the fight against fraud to the Union's financial interests by means of criminal law (https://www.legal-tools.org/doc/3lsm7y4u/).

information indicating specific perpetrators. By contrast, PIF investigations typically start with a known (alleged) perpetrator, but face the challenge of proving an offence and demonstrating guilty intent.

Moreover, hypothesis-building carries a risk of tunnel vision.[35] More than a century ago, forensic scientists already warned about the risks of confirmation bias and tunnel vision when they wrote that "[t]here must be no hypothesis at the commencement, and the examiner must depend wholly on what is seen, leaving out of consideration all suggestions or hints from interested parties".[36]

Whilst avoiding tunnel vision, PIF investigators should not only consider alternative hypotheses and scenarios, but also endeavour to falsify the most salient theories.[37] An investigation plan can, for example, envisage as a testable hypothesis that the reported events are either an irregularity or a fraud, and thus identify investigative steps that would indicate or counter-indicate both options.

7.3.3. Planning

7.3.3.1. Principles

Arguably, the most important function of the investigation plan is to strategically plan and prepare for the foreseeable needs and steps of the investigation.

This starts with defining the objectives of the investigation, that is, the question 'what are we trying to prove?'. Having an offence in mind, the investigators should focus on the desired *results* to guide their thinking and investigative actions. If we know where we are going (for example, proving fraud or, rather, irregularity) and the results we are aiming for, we will know how to *prioritize* our actions in order to reach those results. This mental mapping includes the range of *powers* and authorities to be used, and provides a reasonable and justifiable *explanation* of how and why a certain course of action was chosen. This is not an easy task. As humans, we tend to fail to see our errors of omission in comprehension and classification because we lack the knowledge base that is necessary to recognize things outside our ken.[38]

---

[35] See Sections 1.4. of Chapter 1 and 4.6. of Chapter 4.

[36] William E. Hagan, *A Treatise on Disputed Handwriting and the Determination of Genuine From Forged Signatures*, Banks & Brothers, New York, 1894, p. 82.

[37] See, for example, Moa Lidén, "Confirmation Bias in Investigations of Core International Crimes: Risk Factors and Quality Control Techniques", in Agirre, Bergsmo, De Smet and Stahn (eds.), 2020, p. 524, see *supra* note 3.

[38] Kaidi Wu and David Dunning, "Hypocognition: Making Sense of the Landscape Beyond One's Conceptual Reach", in *Research of General Psychology*, 2018, vol. 22, no. 1, p. 28. See also Nederlands Financieel Forensich Instituut (Dutch Financial Forensic Institute), *Hypocognition van accountants en andere professionals* (*Hypocognition of Accountants and Other Professionals*), 2018.

Planning for the investigation phase normally considers the following broad work-categories, as part of the drafting of the investigation plan:[39]

- collection and preservation of evidence;
- prioritization and approach to investigative avenues (including time frame, relevant actions and planned tasks);
- witness interviews;
- collection and archival of non-evidentiary documents and information;
- access to records;
- resources and support needed (for example, digital forensics, interpretation, co-operation in logistics);
- critical or essential deadlines (including statute of limitations, where applicable, or notifications to stakeholders);
- potential risks and obstacles.

These categories are not exhaustive: the workplan must be tailored to the specific circumstances of each investigation and kept *flexible*, so that adjustments can be made as changes arise and any new information is discovered.[40] The investigation plan is, therefore, a collection of assessments that attempt to anticipate the investigative process.

7.3.3.2. Investigative Strategy

Based on the assessment of the case and the available investigative options, the team should develop an overall *investigative strategy*, built on objectives defined for the case and the legal elements requiring further evidence. This strategy and contingent action should match the scope of the investigative mandate.

Following this strategy, the investigation plan will identify concrete investigative and analytical *priorities*. For each of the identified priorities, the plan will provide specific information on the investigative activities the team intends to undertake, including the types of evidence to collect (such as interviews of certain witnesses or the collection of specific documents).

Important points to consider include to:[41]

- conduct a comprehensive investigation from the outset and identify the exact *factual* contours of the case;

[39] United Nations Office of Internal Oversight Services, *OIOS Investigations Manual*, p. 42 ('OIOS').

[40] See below Section 7.4.4. on dynamic investigation plans.

[41] Eleni Chaitidou, "The Judiciary and Enhancement of the Classification of Alleged Conduct", in Agirre, Bergsmo, De Smet and Stahn (eds.), 2020, p. 992, see *supra* note 3.

- collect *relevant evidence* of sufficient probative value during the investigation, with a view to providing a solid basis for a future judicial assessment against the applicable evidentiary thresholds;
- be aware that pursuing "narrower but stronger cases" may increase the "speed, efficiency and effectiveness of investigations and prosecution";
- assess whether the investigation satisfies the requirements to bring the case forward, or if it should be prolonged until they are met;
- commence to build up the analysis of the evidence on a continuous basis already at the investigation stage, applying exacting standards;
- prefer the use of law-driven analysis tools over fact-driven ones. Of essence is not whether a particular factual allegation has been proven by a high number of pieces of evidence, but rather if the particular factual allegation, as proven by the available evidence, fulfils the legal elements of the crimes and the required forms of criminal responsibility;
- critically *review* the classification of alleged conduct and pursue the classification of crimes or forms of criminal responsibility that are squarely supported by the evidence;
- remember that *quality beats quantity*: for example, criminal proceedings involving the prosecution of PIF crimes might generate voluminous evidence which is difficult to handle – sometimes, 'less is more'.

In complex, cross-border investigations, identifying the custodians of relevant documents and data, anticipating and avoiding deletion tactics, and gathering the evidence in due form, are substantial and crucial undertakings in themselves. Having in mind that the investigative team can be held accountable for its strategic and tactical choices at the start of the investigation, this should encourage exploratory reasoning and better decision-making.[42] Good strategic and tactical decisions can be tested against parameters of:[43]

a) *utility*: a determination to what extent the envisaged results are preferable in terms of the investigation's objectives and expected additional information yield. This assessment should take into account all possible consequences and impact of the decision, including considerations of (financial and human) resources, risks and irreversibility;

[42] Jennifer S. Lerner and Philip E. Tetlock, "Bridging Individual, Interpersonal, and Institutional Approaches to Judgment and Decision-Making: The Impact of Accountability on Cognitive Bias", in Sandra L. Schneider and James Shanteau (eds.), *Emerging Perspectives on Judgment and Decision Research*, Cambridge Series on Judgment and Decision Making, Cambridge University Press, 2003, pp. 431–457.

[43] Baechler *et al.*, 2020, p. 55–58, see *supra* note 27.

b) *credibility*: an assessment of the ability to reduce false positives (for example, reducing the selection of suspects to avoid diluting suspicions of fraud and avoiding 'fishing expeditions');
c) *integrity*:[44] the professionalism and ethical standards of the investigators, such as performance of their duties without personal biases, which in turn influences *evidentiary integrity* (the ability to reduce false negatives, for example, copying entire email correspondence to enable full view of the responsibilities, rather than being too selective upfront);
d) *timing*; and
e) *flexibility*.

Experienced criminals can be masterful at coming up with alternate explanations of their involvement in events, so it is sometimes helpful for investigators to consider if the fabrication of an alternate explanation is possible. If an alternate explanation or other counter-strategies can be anticipated, this can also be considered in the investigative plan.[45] Additional investigation can sometimes confirm or challenge the (un)true aspects of the alternate possibilities.

7.3.3.3. Collection Plans

The investigation plan should preliminarily indicate the main categories and the amount of evidence that is likely to be required to prove the possible charges. Knowing in advance which kind of evidence is needed can greatly facilitate meeting evidentiary thresholds, and fosters co-ordination among analysts, investigators, prosecutors, and (where applicable) investigative judges.

Effective collection management will identify[46] (a) what precisely needs to be collected; (b) how these needs might best be met in a timely manner; (c) the remaining evidentiary gaps as they appear during the course of an investigation; and (d) the filling of these gaps.

In realizing these objectives, effective evidence collection management will concomitantly ensure the avoidance of over-collection.[47]

An *evidence collection plan* can be integrated in, or be an addition to, the investigation plan. The undertaking of evidence collection activities on the basis

---

44 'Integrity' in the international criminal law discourse is normally understood as referring to personal integrity (see, for example, Morten Bergsmo and Viviane E. Dittrich (eds.), *Integrity in International Justice*, Torkel Opsahl Academic EPublisher, 2020 (https://www.toaep.org/nas-pdf/4-bergsmo-dittrich/). We use the term here in relation to its evidence-related dimension.

45 The investigation plan of the ICC includes an anticipation of exonerating information and likely defence theories (see Eikel, 2000, p. 814).

46 Ewan Brown and William H. Wiley, "International Criminal Investigative Collection Planning, Collection Management and Evidence Review", in Agirre, Bergsmo, De Smet and Stahn (eds.), 2020, p. 553, see *supra* note 3.

47 *Ibid.*, p. 553; see also Bergsmo, 2019, p. 3, point 3.6, *supra* note 9.

of such plan can avoid the diversion of finite investigative resources from more pressing evidentiary requirements and burying the investigative team in superfluous information.[48] There is no fixed format for a crime base collection plan; such documents are organic in nature in that they are subject to ongoing amendment in accordance with the findings of the investigation as the latter evolves.[49] There are, however, three distinct components of collection management:[50] (a) requirement management; (b) mission management; and (c) asset management.

Requirement management is the most essential of the three subfields of collection management and, arguably, the most relevant to PIF investigations. In particular, requirement management determines which information needs to be acquired and its deadlines.

Mission management sets out plans for the direct tasking of sources.

Asset management deals with the execution of specific collection and exploitation tasks. For financial investigations, for instance, the collection plan should consider both obtaining evidence on the predicate crimes and tracing and freezing the assets of identified suspects.[51]

Collection management should not be confused with *data* (or *evidence*) *management*, which refers to (software) systems to collect and preserve evidence in respect to the chain of evidence.

Whereas adopting a collection plan pushes the investigative team to contemplate and develop a road map to secure the required evidence, it does not by itself guarantee sufficient evidence gathering. Limitations may stem from critical internal and external factors, including co-operation with external partners, security, protection, available resources and available investigative tools. It should also be noted that, whereas the alleged crimes themselves are sometimes compelling and visible, they can often be the easiest part of evidentiary work. Securing evidence of personal liability typically requires the most challenging of collection plans.[52]

Another great challenge for fact-finders is to know the full extent of the theoretically relevant evidence. Compiling a comprehensive evidential dataset requires careful surveying of the theoretical totality of the evidence in light of all plausible hypotheses of the case. This is an *iterative process*: as more

48 Brown and Wiley, 2020, pp. 536–537, see *supra* note 46.

49 *Ibid.*, p. 537.

50 *Ibid.*, p. 555.

51 See, for example, Bitti, 2020, pp. 917–918, *supra* note 21.

52 Andrew T. Caley, "Constraints and Quality Control in Preliminary Examination: Critical Lessons Learned from the ICTY, the ICC, the ECCC and the United Kingdom", in Bergsmo and Stahn (eds.), 2018, p. 62, see *supra* note 1. See also Chapter 10 of this volume for an exploration on how to best prove guilty intent.

evidence is found, new hypotheses may become plausible and old ones may be abandoned. In many cases, predicting the existence of evidence is speculative. Much depends on the details of the propositions under consideration. For example, if the proposition to be proven is that two persons entered into a common plan to do a certain deed (as is the case for corruption), they may have reached this agreement in many different ways. For example, there may or may not be a document containing the plan; the two persons may have met or they may have negotiated through intermediaries; any meeting during which the plan was discussed may have been attended by other individuals (potential witnesses) or not, *et cetera*, in each case outlining what evidence can be expected to exist.

If fact-finders have no idea about how the plan came into existence, they cannot make a reasonable estimation about the relevant evidential dataset. If the correct explanation of how the plan came into being involves a scenario that the fact-finders do not even contemplate, they may not even realize that there is a gap in the evidential dataset. Thus, it is far from difficult to imagine situations where fact-finders do not know about the existence of evidence, without being aware of their own ignorance. These are the infamous 'facts we don't know we don't know'.

Instead of starting to investigate in all directions, without any planning or priorities, it is better practice to think about what you want to (dis)prove in your case from the start, and identify where and how the relevant evidence could be found.

This prevents you from – like the Texas sharpshooter – collecting your widespread and incoherent findings (bullet holes) to come to some investigative conclusion (target zone) *ex post*, ultimately by coincidence.

Illustration 7.3: The Texas sharpshooter fallacy.

7.3.4. Investigation Management

7.3.4.1. Overview

An investigation plan is an important tool to guide the teams and manage investigations, in particular "to focus the work of the investigation team and management on meeting the agreed objectives" and employ the investigation plan "as a framework for managers to identify any undue delays that need to be addressed, to assess whether the direction of the investigation has changed from the initial assessment and whether the investigation should be discontinued".[53] Among

[53] SC Opinion No 5/2021, para. 61, see *supra* note 6.

other matters, the management function of investigation plans is concerned with:[54]

- the establishment of the overall direction of a case;
- the tasking of investigators;
- the work of team analysts, language and support staff;
- the general monitoring and direction of the collection effort;
- mission planning and execution;
- security and witness-protection issues, including whistle-blower protection where applicable;
- the interactions between the investigation and the wider institutional priorities;
- personnel-management and logistics issues;
- co-operation of and collaboration with other institutions or bodies, when required; and
- matters of policy.

Other matters that concern investigation management are the *potential risks or obstacles* that may negatively impact the investigation, such as conflicts of interest, security concerns, privileges and immunities, travel restrictions, potential evidence destruction, confidentiality arrangements, and cross-border investigations, to mention a few.[55]

7.3.4.2. Allocating Resources and Staff

An initial management function of the investigation plan is the definition of the resource requirements for the team. For example, what are the projected needs in terms of investigators and their required competencies to conduct online or financial investigations? What other internal staff are necessary? These questions necessarily imply previous assessments of the work that needs to be done, which is itself beneficial for planning logistics and staffing. Having the right resources prepared and on notice beforehand can save significant time, compared to reacting when the needs arise. If the need to understand an uncommon language arises, for instance, hiring or seconding an interpreter might take weeks or months.

Investigative bodies with a limited budget must plan beforehand in order to prioritize what to expend and, if they manage more than one case at a time, in which investigation. There can also be budgetary requirements that demand more or less detailed authorizations, which further warrant planning ahead. Strategically planning helps ensure efficient use of the allocated budget.

[54] Brown and Wiley, 2020, p. 553, see *supra* note 46.

[55] See CII 2021, *supra* note 7.

7.3.4.3. Co-operation and Co-ordination

A second major aspect of management is the identification of the support that is required from other institutions or bodies, where co-operation and co-ordination are relevant. Some investigative bodies must follow regulatory or hierarchical requirements on matters of co-operation, which take more time if the procedures are not initiated early. For example, sharing evidence secured by a national jurisdiction often has specific legal requirements that must be met. This is also the case when staff must be seconded by other institutions.

7.3.4.4. Common Understanding and Knowledge Sharing

A third management function of the investigation plan is establishing a shared framework. The process of drafting an investigation plan provides an opportunity for the whole case team to take stock and develop a common understanding of where the investigation stands and what the required next steps are. This practice offers the concerned teams a space to exchange their views and agree with the other teams working on the investigation. Furthermore, the process creates a knowledge base which facilitates the inclusion of new team members or external co-operators.

7.3.5. Reporting and Monitoring

While the investigation plan fulfils an important role within the investigation cycle, it does not stand in isolation. It also serves as the overarching umbrella to bring together the individual investigative activities that have been initiated and ensures that they comply with the overall investigative strategy and objectives. In the investigation plan, the team will *justify* its decisions and allow for (possibly external) review[56] of the proper implementation of the plan.[57] Investigation plans[58] are thus an important contribution to maintain an *overview* of information, primarily in terms of capturing investigative strategies and decisions, but also for creating a historical record for the investigation.[59]

---

[56] The review can involve office members tasked with other aspects of the case, for example the prosecuting team charged with the trials subsequent to the investigation. For a proposal to involve the defence counsel in the preparation of an investigation plan to ensure that early preservation of exonerating evidence is thoroughly pursued, see Bitti, 2020, p. 920, *supra* note 21.

[57] *Ibid.*, pp. 917–919.

[58] In addition to dedicated investigation plans, the statutory reporting duties to OLAF's Supervisory Committee (see Article 7(8) of the OLAF Regulation, see *supra* note 17) may also be considered as a supervision tool covering every investigative step envisaged and where possible, a timetable for each step, thus, forming an integral part of investigation planning.

[59] Eikel, 2020, pp. 819–820, see *supra* note 4. See also the 'overview of information' issue discussed in Bergsmo, 2019, p. 2, *supra* note 9.

The reporting via investigation plans is normally addressed to the senior staff responsible for the management of the investigation, and takes place on two levels, answering the subsequent questions: (i) has the case team done what it intended to do and, (ii) in doing so, what knowledge has the case team acquired (in relation to the case hypothesis or case theory)?

As for the first question, the investigation plan (and its updates) allows senior management to assess the pace of the investigation and keep duration in check. Such an assessment puts the speed of the investigation into context, which implies also looking at the framework in which the investigation is conducted. Therefore, an investigation plan *may* include a table indicating the timeline of the investigation to date and the impact of main factors, such as co-operation, security and resources over time.

The reporting function also includes an explanation as to why certain investigative activities or lines of inquiry were not pursued.

The investigation plan also has merit because it provides a knowledge base for the entire investigation. When updated with the incoming information and collected evidence, it is the best resource to prepare operational activities and reporting, including briefings, interviews and intermediate reporting. However, this requires an investigation plan to be detailed and include different hypotheses.

7.4. Good Practice

7.4.1. Authors, Validators and Format

In organizations where 'intake and evaluation' is a separate function allocated to a dedicated department dealing with the assessment of initial information, planning activities may be already part of the preliminary examination.[60] However, investigation planning is typically the responsibility of the investigative team once it is assigned a case.

The investigation plan is typically prepared by the investigative team, but requires review and validation by supervisors or management.[61] It is important that high-level decisions are taken by staff of an adequate hierarchical level: in the example of an international criminal tribunal, the chief prosecutor would

[60] See Chapter 6.

[61] CII 2021, paras. 2 and 6, see *supra* note 7. The investigation plan of the ICC is adopted in various steps, with sequence (See Eikel, 2020):

a) agreement by the case team internally;
b) peer-review at investigation division management level in order to benefit from ideas that have worked in other cases and to ensure compliance with the investigative standards, policies and rules as developed by the Office; and
c) finally discussed with and approved by senior management.

decide whether to open an investigation, but the deputy prosecutors immediately below in the hierarchy should be responsible for the major planning and management decisions. The drafting of the investigation plan should definitely not be left to the most recent hires merely because they might have more time to spare.

The structure of the investigation plan can usefully follow the different functions it has, and it can be recorded in a semi-structured standard template.[62]

62 Until recently, the preparation of a work plan was "a good practice followed by investigative units on a case-by-case approach" (SC Opinion 5/2021, para. 66, see *supra* note 6). Different versions of a work plan were used, but in practice, the investigation planning was set out in various documents registered in the case, such as notes, email, or minutes of management meetings (*ibid.*, para. 65).

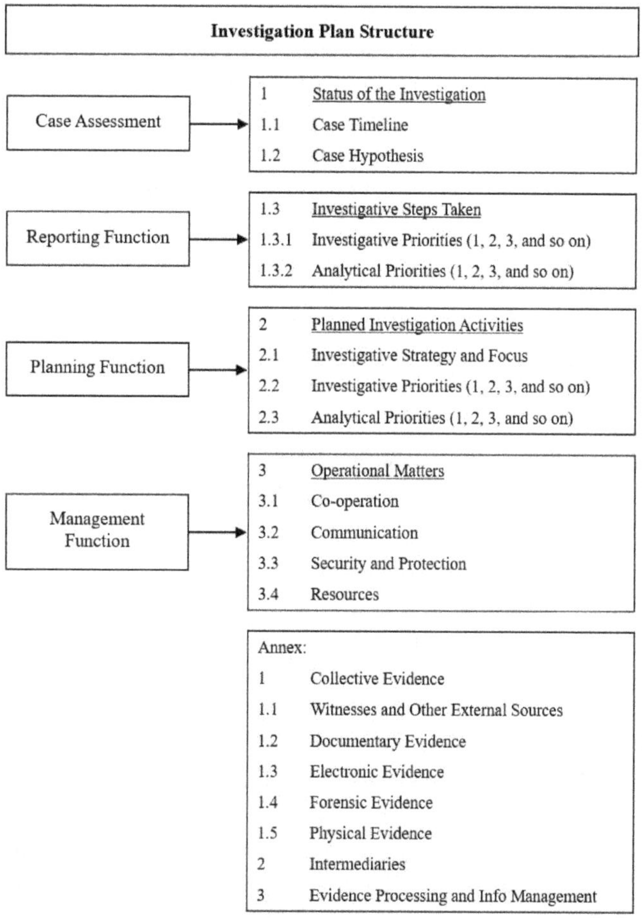

Illustration 7.4: Template of an international criminal justice investigation plan.[63]

7.4.2. Avoiding Inefficiency

The preparation and monitoring of investigation plans can be time-consuming and add to the considerable red-tape with which the investigators are already confronted. If its function is reduced to reporting to the management when the investigation can be expected to be closed, it can lead to a mindset in which investigators doubt the usefulness of such plans. Drafting an investigation plan then becomes another mechanical step in the investigation process, risking neglect of its crucial potential for quality assurance and enhancement through solid

[63] Based on key international criminal justice documents and ICC practice, from Eikel, 2020, p. 809, see *supra* note 4.

case assessment, adequate planning and focused investigation management. Excessively focusing on reporting and progress control would detract from the more strategic functions of the investigation plan.

The purpose of an investigation plan is to decrease the administrative burden on investigators and their management, rather than increase it.[64] It may be the case that not all investigations across all investigative bodies of the world need to employ an investigation plan. For example, prosecutors dealing with familiar (and small scale) crimes, suspects and contexts with the help of well-established teams that have worked with the very same crimes, suspects and contexts for decades can certainly manage some cases without adopting a written investigation plan. Investigation plans seem less necessary when:

- teams composed by investigators with similar legal and cultural backgrounds (they might have studied in the same institutions, as is the case in many national police bodies) are more predictable to one another, which reduces the need to plan common approaches;
- some domestic organized crime investigations are led by what the evidence progressively reveals so much that it is difficult to determine their direction beforehand. This is the case with criminal networks involved in an ever-evolving criminal reality. For example, a gambling operation can be found to be part of a money-laundering scheme in the framework of a corruption case, so the goals of the investigation will evolve as the information is collected and reviewed, which makes planning more difficult;
- in many national contexts, investigative bodies can count on decades of precedents and jurisprudence, in addition to the nuanced legal framework provided by domestic law, *ipso facto* tailored to its own context and often ready to use. Codes of criminal procedure, for example, often provide detailed procedures in the form of requirements, resulting in a basic plan that is required to be followed;
- many investigative bodies are constrained by issues of budget which increase the need for planning: on the contrary, offices of the prosecutors in jurisdictions where prosecution is mandatory can often employ what resources are needed to pursue their mandate (at least for reasonable pursuits).[65]

---

64 SC Opinion 5/2021, para. 68, see *supra* note 6.

65 The examples are discussed in Angotti, 2020, pp. 845 ff., see *supra* note 5. The author points to the differences between criminal investigations in Italy and at the International Criminal Court ('ICC') to elaborate on the possible reasons for the absence of mandatory investigation plans in the Italian criminal legal system. He concludes by arguing that the same reasons indicate that international bodies working on fact-rich cases should employ investigation plans.

7.4.3. Preventing Tunnel Vision

The investigation plan can significantly improve the management, planning and allocation of investigative and prosecutorial efforts and resources. Conversely, the adoption of investigation plans at the beginning of the investigative process, when they are more effective, also brings concerns over tunnel vision and confirmation bias, in particular when combined with the foregrounding of investigative hypotheses and theories.

In order to avoid tunnel vision, it is essential that "investigative results and accusatory hypotheses can inform each other",[66] and thus the investigation plan must provide for and task the team with the necessary 'moments of reflection' for the relevant assignments. Target-driven investigations[67] are, in this regard, more at risk than open-ended investigations.[68]

Specific risks for confirmation bias and tunnel vision in the preparation and use of an investigation plan include:

- focusing on a single hypothesis or theory of events,[69] causing asymmetrical scepticism[70] in relation to hypothesis-inconsistent evidence, which, in turn, can result in case hypotheses not being challenged enough;[71]
- drafting a collection plan aimed only to obtain evidence confirming the allegations (whereas falsifying lines of defence would considerably strengthen the case); or
- a lack of awareness of missing evidence.[72]

We already discussed how, in order to avoid tunnel vision, the investigation team should consider alternative scenarios and engage in falsification efforts of the leading hypotheses. Discharging hypotheses should also be considered and

66 Angotti, 2020, p. 830, see *supra* note 5.

67 See Chapters 2 and 4 for more detail on the concept and risks of target-driven investigations.

68 Morten Bergsmo and William H. Wiley, "Human Rights Professionals and the Criminal Investigation and Prosecution of Core International Crimes", in Siri Skåre, Ingvild Burkey and Hege Mørk (eds.), *Manual on Human Rights Monitoring: An Introduction for Human Rights Field Officers*, Norwegian Centre for Human Rights, Oslo, 2008, p. 8 (https://www.legal-tools.org/doc/8362d5/).

69 The ICC institutionalized the use of investigation plans in 2010. These plans are meant to include "the investigative focus as determined in the case hypothesis" (see Eikel, 2020, p. 184, *supra* note 4). Differently, the investigation plan of the Norwegian police should include *factual hypotheses* that are coherent with the available facts collected thus far, and that appear relevant to the investigation (see Butenschøn Skre, 2020, pp. 896–902, *supra* note 3).

70 See Chapter 4.

71 Lidén, 2020, p. 523–524, see *supra* note 37; Joshua Klayman and Young-won Ha, "Confirmation, Disconfirmation, and Information in Hypothesis Testing", in *Psychological Review*, 1987, vol. 94, no. 2, pp. 211–228; Rossmo, 2020, p. 27, see *supra* note 27.

72 Rossmo, 2020, p. 31, see *supra* note 27.

assessed, to the same end of not ignoring potentially relevant investigative results.

As changing the decision maker between different situations or stages triggers more of a critical stance, the new case assessment by the investigators appointed after the preliminary examination is, as such, a good start and helps prevent confirmation bias. Investigators should, however, avoid to "seize and freeze"[73] their mind on the basis of decisions about who should be investigated and for what,[74] as described in the preliminary examination. Arguing against an already formed story is difficult,[75] but investigators should avoid replacing one fixated story with their own.

In addition, investigators should not ground the investigation plan merely on the information available, but explore what information and evidence might be missing or should exist and be sought. The presence of instances such as the allegations and the information in support of them has more influence on our judgments than their absence, and we tend to disregard the possibility of missing information.[76]

Good practice is to outline one's own analysis, assumptions and deductions, and invite team members to challenge them.[77] This will indicate when evidence might be misinterpreted or if a single suspect or theory is being exclusively pursued to the point where other viable suspects and theories are being excluded or ignored. Even if a case hypothesis was not made explicit, the drive for cognitive coherence would nevertheless likely make investigators formulate such a

[73] Arie W. Kruglanski and Donna M. Webster, "Motivated Closing of the Mind: 'Seizing' and 'Freezing'", in *Psychological Review*, 1996, vol. 103, no. 2, pp. 263–283.

[74] Ivar Fahsing and Karl Ask, "Decision Making and Decisional Tipping Points in Homicide Investigations: An Interview Study of British and Norwegian Detectives", in *Journal of Investigative Psychology and Offender Profiling*, 2013, vol. 10, no. 2, pp. 155–165; Moa Lidén, Minna Gräns and Peter Juslin, "The Presumption of Guilt in Suspect Interrogations: Apprehension as a Trigger of Confirmation Bias and Debiasing Techniques", in *Law and Human Behavior*, 2018, vol. 42, no. 4, pp. 336–354.

[75] See, for example, Eric Rassin, Anita Eerland and Ilse Kujpers, "Let's Find the Evidence: An Analogue Study of Confirmation Bias in Criminal Investigations", in *Journal of Investigative Psychology and Offender Profiling*, 2010, vol. 7, no. 3, pp. 231–246

[76] Gary L. Wells and R.C. Lindsay, "On Estimating the Diagnosticity of Eyewitness Nonidentifications", in *Psychological Bulletin*, 1980, vol. 88, no. 3, pp. 776–784.

[77] Studies found that the willingness and preparedness to explain a decision-making process (process accountability) upfront, encourages exploratory reasoning and has a more positive effect than post-decisional accountability informed by confirmatory and self-justifying reasoning (outcome accountability). See, for example, Lerner and Tetlock, 2003, *supra* note 42.

hypothesis in their minds. Yet, an explicit formulation of a case hypothesis will make the hypothesis more open to important critical scrutiny.[78]

The risk of confirmation bias will also depend on how open or closed the investigation plan is.[79] If, for example, the investigation plan is a dynamic, online knowledge-base for the investigation team (see Section 7.4.4. below), it may evolve on a daily basis and not be a one-off, rigid document, finalized early in the investigation.[80]

Finally, when assessing whether an investigation plan needs to be updated in the light of new evidence, it is likely that an individual who has not been part of formulating the initial case hypothesis is more capable of reasoning independently about it. Therefore, such a person or groups of persons, such as evidence review panels are less likely to be asymmetrically sceptical in relation to the new evidence and, consequently, more likely to update the investigation plan when this is mandated by the evidence.[81] As reported earlier, self-generated hypotheses are 'stickier' than hypotheses generated by others.

7.4.4. Dynamic Investigation Plans and Updates

As soon as an investigation is opened, the ageing process commences. The awareness of such ageing should enable the investigators to identify and anticipate potential problems in the management of a case. However, to be efficient, any work plan must be flexible and able to respond to evolving and sometimes unanticipated demands.[82] It must be comprehensive and thorough enough to provide clear direction to advance the investigation process in a methodical but expeditious manner,[83] but not designed to be static.

The investigation plan should hence follow the case from intake to closure, and be updated in accordance with the results of completed steps[84] or to accommodate external factors that may change the framework of the investigation

---

[78] Lidén, 2020, p. 524, *supra* note 37.

[79] *Ibid.*, p. 470.

[80] *Ibid.*, p. 471.

[81] *Ibid.*, p. 521.

[82] In its 2021 opinion, OLAF's Supervisory Committee held that "[i]n order to carry out effective investigations, it is essential to draw up investigation plans at the outset and update them whenever necessary". It had found that, for 2019, only in very few cases did the case file include an initial working plan and regular updates, and recommended a consistent and uniform approach to strategic case planning across all investigative units, coming with a "detailed investigation plan drawn up for every opened investigation, regularly updated and annexed to the case file of each investigation" (see SC Opinion 5/2021, pp. 19–20, supra note 6).

[83] OIOS, p. 42, see *supra* note 39.

[84] Angotti, 2020, p. 824, see *supra* note 5.

beyond the investigator's will.[85] When, for instance, an action anticipated by the investigation plan is not completed in a timely manner, the failure to satisfy the planned requirements must be documented for the record[86] and a re-evaluation of the investigation plan or its execution may be warranted.

Such dynamic investigation plans are specifically designed to be continuously updated as the investigation progresses. More than mere reporting of the progress of the investigation to management,[87] they fit in a circular approach to investigations, with periodic review in light of the different phases of the investigation, changing hypotheses, and evolving collective knowledge of a particular event. Planning, implementation and evaluation are the lifeline of the investigation, and the investigation plan should be the monitor.

A dynamic investigation plan is particularly useful to identify the areas of the case where the evidence is assessed as weak, and the areas where potentially exonerating material exists. A *gap analysis* can lead to indications as to what legal elements would require the collection of additional evidence as a priority and, therefore, further deserve investigative and analytical attention. It can come in the form of a written narrative, but is also possible as an evaluation matrix or evaluation table, integrated in the investigation plan.

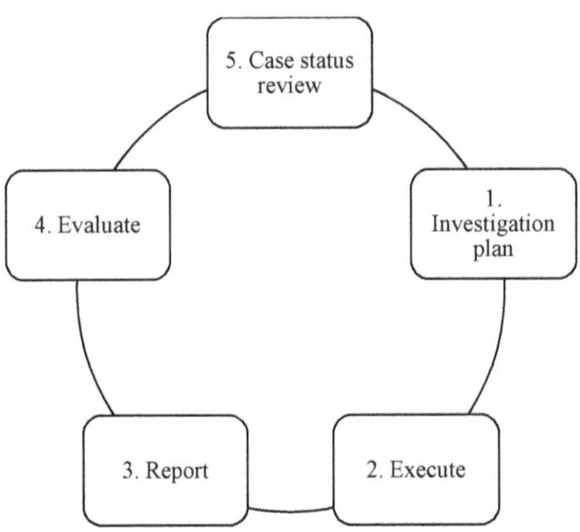

Illustration 7.5: A Dynamic Investigation Plan

85 Eikel, 2020, pp. 801–820, see *supra* note 4.

86 In the setting of UN investigations, the common practice is that all versions of the investigation plan are kept. Though the revised plan leads the investigation from the moment of its adoption, a record of all previous versions of the plan should be archived as part of the record of the investigation and be kept available (see OIOS, p. 42, see *supra* note 39, and CII Guidelines, para. 18).

87 See *supra* note 58 for the statutory reporting duties to OLAF's Supervisory Committee.

7.4.5. An Integrated and Living Document

In practice, what an investigation plan looks like necessarily depends on its institutional context. This section provides two examples of (i) how investigation plans do not exist in a vacuum, but are rather a part of a complex process; and (ii) bridging the gap between designing dynamic, 'living' investigation plans and concretely updating, often by technical means.

First, regarding the *integration* of investigation plans into the wider investigative process, a meaningful example is the 2003 Draft Regulations for the ICC Office of the Prosecutor ('OTP'), which were not adopted as legally binding standards but informed part of subsequent OTP practice and policy.[88] In the system designed in the Draft Regulations, the investigation plan is one of three essential quality assurance instruments, the others being a *proof chart*, providing an overview of the available evidence, and the *draft charges document*, which draws on the results of the preliminary examination, the investigation plan, and the ongoing investigation to ensure that the investigative results match the charges that must be proven.[89] Evidence should be sought based on what is needed, which is in turn defined by the crimes that are charged and their legal requirements. As such, the three documents work if properly integrated, and allowed to inform one another. As new evidence is collected, the charges may need to be amended, and the investigation plan must surely be updated to reflect it. More evidence will, in turn, be needed and secured, and thus the proof chart will consequently expand. Considering the ICC's scope of work, often involving large-scale and atrocious crimes ordered by power structures distant from the actual crime scenes, it seems adequate that the formulation of charges, available evidence, and investigative planning advance together as the case takes shape, forming part of an integrated, 'living' and permanently updated powerbase of the in-depth, open-ended ICC investigations.[90]

---

[88] The first ICC Prosecutor adopted, *ad interim*, parts of the 2003 Draft Regulations, see Angotti, 2020, pp. 821–822 and 826, see *supra* note 5; other elements became parts of ICC-OTP practice and the model investigation plan, see Chapter 15 of the same volume, by Markus Eikel, see *supra* note 4. The text of the ICC-OTP Draft Regulations is available in the annex to Carlos Vasconcelos, "Draft Regulations of the Office of the Prosecutor", in Morten Bergsmo, Klaus Rackwitz and Song Tianying (eds.), *Historical Origins of International Criminal Law: Volume 5*, TOAEP, Brussels, 2017, pp. 834–93 ('Draft Regulations') (https://www.legal-tools.org/doc/09c8b8/).

[89] Angotti, 2020, p. 824, see *supra* note 5.

[90] As the ICC-OTP, "Strategic Plan June 2012–2015" of 11 October 2013 (https://www.legal-tools.org/doc/954beb/) "changed the overall directions of OTP investigations to the principle of in-depth, open-ended investigations", a new approach which "included a change in investigative strategy and planning; and the development of a new investigation plan template", see Eikel, 2020, p. 814, *supra* note 4.

Second, *updating* dynamic investigation plans, thus making them 'living' documents, must be implemented in the workflow of an office. As is the case in Norway's prosecution service, an alternative way to conceptualize an investigation plan is to make them available in a knowledge-based format which, as a single inter-linked document, has a continuous existence and is designed as a living and growing instrument that follows the entire investigation and case preparation stage. Such investigation plans are handled through web-based electronic templates to facilitate sharing among the investigative team and updating as necessary.[91] They should be prepared immediately after the report of an alleged crime, and be developed as a 'living' document throughout the investigation, in response to results of the investigative steps that are taken.[92] This approach allows organizing evidence so as to have an up-to-date overview of the case at all times.[93] The document is a shared resource for the team, which has direct access to it, and it thus requires a reliable mechanism to *log changes* made to the investigation plan. This is particularly important in order to reconstruct decisions made during an investigation, as would be the case, for example, in an evaluation that goes back to the start of the process.[94]

7.5. Concluding Remarks

Investigation plans are an important quality tool in investigations. Their role should not be reduced to mere enumeration of routine steps of any investigation and the prognosis and monitoring of deadlines for completion. They should be specific and cover four main functions:

- *Assessment*: the formulation of an in-depth understanding of the case and its evidentiary requirements, building on (a review of) the preliminary examination, when applicable;
- *Planning*: anticipating investigative steps, defining how the investigators will try to obtain the required evidence in the most strategic way (objectives and priorities);
- *Management*: an analysis of the capacity, powers and skills required to bring the investigation forward, and the contingent measures to implement;
- *Reporting*: allowing review, monitoring, and recording of the course of the investigation, in particular in terms of time and resource management.

---

91 Butenschøn Skre, 2020, p. 887–902, see *supra* note 3.

92 *Ibid.*, p. 894.

93 Olympia Bekou, "Enhancing the Quality of Investigations: What Role Can the In-Depth Analysis Charts Play?", in Agirre, Bergsmo, De Smet and Stahn (eds.), 2020, p. 590, see *supra* note 3.

94 Butenschøn Skre, 2020, p. 895, see *supra* note 3.

Investigation plans are particularly useful in transnational or international fact-rich and complex investigations, involving investigators from diverse backgrounds, often having different level of expertise, as is the case in PIF investigations.

The investigation plan should be detailed enough to cover the specifics of the investigation at hand (demonstrating knowledge of the field and careful strategic and tactical thinking), without becoming too rigid. Rather, it should be a flexible document, anticipating, adapting to, and recording (substantial) changes in the investigative planning.

The investigative plan can articulate a main investigative hypothesis (likely stemming from the legal evaluation in the preliminary examination), but should entertain other hypotheses and take methodological precautions to avoid tunnel vision. A good strategy to avoid dysfunctional focus on a single story and suspect is to have several people involved in the drafting and review of the plan.

A *collection plan* can be part of the investigation plan and is very useful to consider what evidence is required and might be missing to prove, for example, guilty intent. Likewise, a *gap analysis* of (missing) evidence is another useful component of the investigation plan. The latter should best combine standard and open-ended sections for completion, to accommodate each case separately, without losing consistency.

In an ideal scenario, the investigation plan is a 'living' document that records and 'feeds' the investigation at all times, because it contains a knowledge-base that is continuously updated and often sustained by suitable technologies, including web-based versioning and knowledge management tools.

8

Fact-Finding, at the Core of the Investigation Process

Anna Sagana, Judit Tátrai and Olivier Coene[*]

8.1. Introduction

When an investigation is opened, and the investigation plan is in place, the investigative team can begin its work. This phase is essentially about establishing what actually happened or, in other words, fact-finding. This is a progressive process, involving exploratory and active stages, during which the investigators use their legitimate powers to collect, organize and analyse evidence. Eventually, they will have to consider whether and when they have a good enough case to present it to the decision maker. The primary questions we address here include: What kind of evidence is needed? Do we need to prove every single element of the alleged offence, and when do we have enough evidence?

8.2. Fact-Finding

In essence, the investigative process comprises a series of activities or steps that move from the preliminary examination to evidence gathering tasks and information analysis – as outlined and recorded in an investigation plan – to formulating investigative conclusions. At its core, it is about the (often tedious) process of fact-finding,[1] the crucial endeavour to establish a 'fact-base'. That is, to establish, as accurately as possible, what actually happened.[2]

---

* **Anna Sagana** is an Assistant Professor of Legal Psychology at Maastricht University. **Judit Tátrai** is a senior legal support officer in the European Public Prosecutor's Office ('EPPO'), with experience in prosecuting before the courts of Hungary and the internationalized appellate courts of Kosovo. Formerly, she led the legal team of the Trial Chamber of the Special Tribunal for Lebanon. **Olivier Coene** is case reviewer at the European Anti-Fraud Office ('OLAF'). Formerly, he was senior prosecutor for financial-economic crime at the Belgian Prosecution Office. This chapter is authored in the contributors' personal capacity and does not necessarily reflect the views of EPPO, OLAF or other institutions mentioned therein.

1 Rod Gehl and Darryl Plecas, *Introduction to Criminal Investigation: Processes, Practices and Thinking*, Justice Institute of British Columbia, New Westminster, 2016, p. 7.

2 Dermot Groome, "Evidence in Cases of Mass Criminality", in Ilias Bantekas and Emmanouela (eds.), *Criminological Approaches to International Criminal Law*, Cambridge University Press, 2014, pp. 117, 121–122.

Fact-finding is understood here as the different methods of ascertaining facts, based on evidence.[3] These methods include several types of work on facts or alleged facts, including work processes to identify, locate, obtain, verify, analyse, summarize, structure and present these facts, along with their supporting evidence, to the trier of facts.[4] Fact-finding in 'PIF' investigations involves a systematic series of steps designed to detect, prevent and address financial misconduct, irregularities and fraud. The overarching goal is to uncover the truth and – so doing – to protect the financial interests of the European Union (that is, 'PIF').

Fact-finding can be broken down into three main elements, namely[5] (a) a hypothesis (the allegation); (b) evidence; and (c) a theory (the prosecution or defence case).

Hypotheses are propositional claims about reality that can be tested empirically. In practice, such hypotheses initially appear in the form of an allegation of a criminal offence, which triggers a criminal investigation and must be verified. Moreover, the investigators should formulate and consider other hypotheses, based on past experiences (for example, known criminal phenomena) or emerging evidence.[6]

Evidence consists of all forms of information (for example, observations, data) that may either support or refute the hypotheses.

A *theory* (for example, the prosecution's case theory) at the end of the investigation is a coherent and logical explanation consistent with the evidence that ties together the relevant facts, which constitute the elements of a criminal offence, and attributes the offence to an identified perpetrator or group of perpetrators. A good prosecution case theory shows that the evidence excludes alternative explanations of the facts. Conversely, a good defence case casts reasonable doubt on the prosecution's theory, supporting the presumption of innocence.

In this conception, fact-finding is inherently iterative, representing a dynamic cycle of investigative inquiry. It begins with the formulation of

---

3 See Illustration 5.2. in Chapter 5 for a proposed distinction between information and evidence.

4 Adapted from Marina Aksenova, Morten Bergsmo and Carsten Stahn, "Non-Criminal Justice Fact-Work in the Age of Accountability", in *id.* (eds.), *Quality Control in Fact-Finding*, Second Edition, Torkel Opsahl Academic EPublisher ('TOAEP'), Brussels, 2020, p. 2 (https://www.toaep.org/ps-pdf/19-bergsmo-stahn-second/).

5 Simon De Smet, "Justified Belief in the Unbelievable", in Xabier Agirre, Morten Bergsmo, Simon De Smet and Carsten Stahn (eds.) *Quality Control in Criminal Investigation*, TOAEP, Brussels, 2020, pp. 81 and 83 (https://www.toaep.org/ps-pdf/38-qcci/).

6 See the investigation as an abductive process in Section 1.4.3. of Chapter 1 and the initial situation of entropy in Section 7.3.2.3. of Chapter 7.

hypotheses rooted in existing background knowledge. As evidence is systematically collected and analysed, it serves to either validate or challenge these hypotheses. This, in turn, guides the refinement of the initial theories or propositions. This process drives investigative progress. Ideally, over time, the fact-finder's comprehension of the case matures and the theory becomes refined, enabling increasingly more substantial and precise conclusions.

Importantly, fact-finding occurs within contexts of uncertainty. The investigation process entails collecting evidence, which is, *prima facie*, relevant to reconstructing the historical facts as certainly as possible, but it offers no *absolute* truth, only a *legal* one. When fact-finders make a 'finding', they claim knowledge about the past but only truly offer their perspective on what the evidence demonstrates.[7]

8.3. Evidence

8.3.1. General Remarks

Evidence refers to a wide range of information that may ultimately be found by the trier of facts to prove, to the applicable standard of proof (see hereafter), that a suspected individual has (or has not) committed an offence.[8] It should be brought forward by the prosecuting office. The defence may also present evidence, though as beneficiary of the presumption of innocence, the defendant is not obliged to do so.

The main conditions and qualities of evidence are that it is (in a logical sequence of evaluation): (a) relevant; (b) reliable; (c) probative; (d) admissible; and (e) persuasive.

Evidence is *relevant* if it relates to the facts reported to the trier of facts. For example, the evidence is relevant if it relates to a recommendation to recover funding, to the criminal indictment, or to any other substantive issue that comes up at trial. In criminal investigations, it covers the power of the evidence to demonstrate the identity, illegal act(s) and guilt of a suspect. However, evidence cannot be selected in function of a single theory, and should include anything relevant to any of the different hypotheses that are being considered, including those brought forward by the defence or that are ultimately rejected. All evidence should be documented and its origin traceable. Rules of transparency and access to the file should enable reasonable control of evidence selection.[9]

---

7 De Smet, 2020, p. 83, see *supra* note 5.

8 Gehl and Plecas, 2016, p. 33, see *supra* note 1.

9 See the glossary of OLAF's Guidelines on Investigation Procedures for OLAF Staff, 11 October 2021 ('GIP') (https://www.legal-tools.org/doc/tgfdldc7/), defining evidence as "anything that is relevant to the facts under investigation"; and Article 45(1) of the Council Regulation (EU) No. 2017/1939 of 12 October 2017 implementing enhanced cooperation on the

Reliability[10] refers to the accuracy or veracity of the evidence. Evidence can only serve as proof if it is safe for the fact-finder to rely on the information contained in it. Therefore, evidence only adds weight to a given claim when it is considered reliable. False or misleading information, no matter how it is collected, will lead to inaccurate outcomes.

The '*probative value*' of evidence is the weight or persuasive value of evidence that enables the decision maker to reach a decision of proof. To be probative, the evidence must be relevant and *prima facie* reliable, at least at the phase of its admission by the court. Evidence is 'strong' when it makes a particular proposition much more probable or is an important factor in favouring a particular explanation. However, each piece of evidence is characterized by some degree of uncertainty and often does not form a coherent and cohesive picture taken together.[11]

Admissibility refers to compliance with the legal framework for collecting evidence. Evidence may not be admitted when its probative value is substantially outweighed by its prejudicial effect to ensure a fair trial. This is the case, for example, if it is obtained by methods that cast substantial doubt on its reliability or if its admission is antithetical to, or would seriously damage, the integrity of the proceedings.[12] Evidence obtained in violation of the defendant's rights, for instance, cannot be used in court and can sometimes even lead to a complete failure of the investigation and prosecution.

The relevance, reliability, probative value and admissibility of evidence are important factors, but do not necessarily account for whether or not the evidence is persuasive. The latter depends in part on[13] (a) how much relevant evidence the evidence includes (comprehensiveness); (b) how solid each of the elements of the evidence is, independent of the conclusion (independent security); (c) how

establishment of the European Public Prosecutor's Office ('the EPPO') ('EPPO Regulation') (https://www.legal-tools.org/doc/plfszr14/) for the rule that "the case file shall contain all the information and evidence available to the EDP that relates to the investigation or prosecution by the EPPO".

10 In Chapter 6, reliability was explained in relation to the trustworthiness of a source of initial information, and credibility as a quality of the information. The term reliability used here in relation to evidence encompasses both aspects of information quality.

11 Peter J. van Koppen, *Overtuigend bewijs: Indammen van rechterlijke dwalingen* [*Convincing Evidence: Reducing the Number of Miscarriages of Justice*], Nieuw Amsterdam, Amsterdam, 2011.

12 See, for example, International Criminal Court ('ICC') Rules of Procedure and Evidence, 9 September 2002, Rule 63 (https://www.legal-tools.org/doc/8bcf6f/), and Rome Statute of the ICC, 17 July 1998, Article 69 (https://www.legal-tools.org/doc/7b9af9/).

13 See Section 6.4.2.1. of Chapter 6 for reference to the same three first criteria to evaluate the *credibility* of information.

strong the connection is between the evidence and the conclusion (supportiveness); and (d) the degree to which the evidence favours a suspect's guilt versus the plausibility of alternative interpretations for the evidence (significance).[14]

It is important to note that the weight of an evidence data set and the accuracy of any findings that are based on it are correlated. Exceptionally, a fact-finder may – by sheer coincidence – get everything right on the basis of very thin evidence, just like a fact-finder may draw the wrong conclusions from an optimal evidential dataset. In general, having a great number of strong evidence increases the chances of an accurate outcome.

To be complete, it is worth noting that some have argued that – with the necessary caveats – evidence of uncertain reliability might be maintained in the evidential dataset,[15] for instance when it corroborates a proposition.[16] This is, however, not without risks, as research indicates that people often give greater weight to 'significant' (vivid) evidence, even when its credibility is questionable.[17] Although professional judges and prosecutors might be expected to surpass lay people in appropriately evaluating evidence with tainted reliability and credibility, research indicates they are not free from noise and bias.[18]

8.3.2. Categories of Evidence

8.3.2.1. Major Distinctions

Evidence can be categorized into different types and subgroups, depending on the perspective taken. The most commonly used distinction is between *direct* and *indirect* evidence (see the next section).

Another way of categorizing evidence is based on the nature of the evidence. Familiar categories here include 'documentary evidence', 'physical' or 'real' evidence, and 'testimonial' evidence. Within these broad categories, further categorization is possible. For example, testimonial evidence may be categorized according to whether it is first-hand (or perceptual), derivative (hearsay), or opinion evidence,[19] and stemming from a whistle-blower, witness or suspect.

A final distinction to make is between *inculpatory* and *exculpatory* evidence. Inculpatory evidence is any evidence that will directly or indirectly link an accused person to the offence being investigated. Conversely, exculpatory

---

[14] John E. Eck and Kim Rossmo, "The New Detective: Rethinking Criminal Investigations", in *Criminology & Public Policy*, 2019, vol. *18, no.* 3, p. 610.

[15] De Smet, 2020, p. 119, see *supra* note 5.

[16] *Ibid.*, p. 111.

[17] Dale Griffin and Amos Tversky, "The Weighing of Evidence and the Determinants of Confidence", in *Cognitive Psychology*, 1992, vol. 24, no. 3, pp. 411–435.

[18] See Chapters 3 and 4.

[19] De Smet, 2020, p. 120, see *supra* note 5.

evidence operates in the opposite direction by indicating that the accused person or suspect did not engage in the criminal act. For an investigator, it is imperative not only to seek out inculpatory evidence but also to contemplate evidence from an exculpatory standpoint.[20] Considering evidence from the exculpatory perspective demonstrates that an investigator is being objective and is not falling into the trap of tunnel vision.[21]

8.3.2.2. Direct Evidence

Direct evidence proves a point of fact without need for further interpretation.[22] It is any evidence that can show that something occurred without the need to make inferences or assumptions to reach a conclusion. Examples include the testimony of an eyewitness who saw the accused shoot a victim; a security camera showing the suspect entering a building; or a confession from the person concerned.

A related but not identical concept to direct evidence is a *primary source*, referring to direct witness testimony, original records, or any other kind of source that conveys direct, immediate knowledge of the facts. These notions relate to a distinction made between *primary* evidence, which cannot be surpassed, and *secondary* evidence, a form of evidence implying some better evidence exists.

8.3.2.3. Indirect Evidence

Indirect evidence, also called *circumstantial evidence*, is all other evidence. It does not by itself prove the offence, but through interpretation of the circumstances and in conjunction with other evidence may contribute to a body of evidence that could prove that an offence has been committed or guilt.[23] The video-recording mentioned above can prove that a suspect entered an office, for example, but it does not explain what he or she did there. It adds to the investigation in that the person went to his office outside working hours (which might have been denied in the past, something new in this way) but is not sufficient to show that the suspect is, for instance, engaged in corruption.

Circumstantial evidence requires contextual reasoning to prove a fact. It builds on assumptions and logical inferences. The latter are conclusions reached

---

20 Gehl and Plecas, 2016, pp. 35 and 36, see *supra* note 1.

21 Tunnel vision is the tendency to focus on a single goal or point of view. It is a form of cognitive bias and it can lead to finding what one expects rather than to what is true (see Keith A. Findley and Michael S. Scott, "The Multiple Dimensions of Tunnel Vision in Criminal Cases", in *Wisconsin Law Review*, 2006, vol. 2, p. 291).

22 Gehl and Plecas, 2016, p. 35, see *supra* note 1.

23 *Ibid.*, p. 35.

on the basis of evidence and reasoning, mainly generalizations.[24] Examples include the fingerprint of an accused found at the crime scene; the finding that a special code was used for additives in meat production in a case of food fraud; or the testimony from a co-evaluator that the chair of the evaluation committee was acting very agitated the day before the final meeting.

Apart from the materiality of the acts, circumstantial evidence can also demonstrate that a person concerned had a combination of intent,[25] motive (for example, financial problems), opportunity (for example, monopoly position by unique expertise), or the means (for example, technical abilities) to commit the offence, all of which are meaningful features of criminal conduct.

8.3.2.4. Missing Evidence

Although not evidence *per se*, missing evidence is relevant because of its contribution to the overall weight of the evidential dataset (see the notion of comprehensiveness above). This is because it is the totality of the theoretically relevant evidence, rather than the sheer quantity of obtainable evidence, that determines the weight of the evidence.[26] Consequently, the absence of evidence or gaps in the evidentiary dataset are significant because they diminish the overall weight of the evidentiary framework.

Even if the existing evidence includes all available information, it may lack maximum weight.[27] This could compromise the robustness of the evidence framework, making it insufficient to support substantive conclusions. It is therefore imperative to consider both the presence and absence of evidence to ensure a comprehensive assessment of the true weight and implications of the underlying evidence base.

---

24 Terence Anderson, David Schum and William Twining, *Analysis of Evidence*, Cambridge University Press, 2005, p. 82.

25 See Chapter 10 for the crucial role of circumstantial evidence in demonstrating guilty intent ('*mens rea*'). For now, it suffices to highlight the importance of establishing facts, as the Directive (EU) No. 2017/1371 of the European Parliament and of the Council of 5 July 2017 on the fight against fraud to the Union's financial interests by means of criminal law ('PIF Directive') (https://www.legal-tools.org/doc/3lsm7y4u/), Recital 11, holds that "[t]he intentional nature of an act or omission may [only] be inferred from objective, factual circumstances".

26 L. Jonathan Cohen, "Twelve Questions About Keynes's Concept of Weight", in *British Journal for the Philosophy of Science*, 1985, vol. 37, no. 3, p. 264

27 De Smet, 2020, p. 111, see *supra* note 5.

8.4. Progression of the Investigation

8.4.1. The Different Stages of the Investigation Process

Investigating is inevitably a dynamic process of critical thinking and action.[28] It requires investigators to anticipate, balance and respond to a wide range of challenges, often exacerbated in cross-border cases like most PIF investigations. There can be no 'one-size-fits-all' approach and conducting and handling an investigation was labelled "an art rather than a science".[29]

Nevertheless, every investigation will arguably encompass similar phases, ranging from a more exploratory initial stage to building the case. Groome, for instance, distinguishes three main stages, starting with a collection phase, followed by building phase, including a gap analysis, and ending with a final phase, aimed at providing a solid conclusion of the investigation.[30]

Alternatively, the '6 Cs' 'Generic Investigative Cycle'-model[31] covers the collection and build-up phase of a (homicide) investigation in the form of six steps. These steps make it possible to identify categories of investigative questions ('what?', 'where?', *et cetera*) that every fact-finder needs to address in the course of the investigation.

Models of investigation do not always take into account the specificities of PIF investigations. When, for instance, Rossmo[32] refers to a 'suspect selection phase' after the gathering of evidence, this does not necessarily reflect the reality of PIF investigations, in which the actor of the material facts is usually known. Additionally, the range of (competing) hypotheses seems to be reduced in PIF investigations compared to common offences. Typically, the suspect or perpetrator is known from (or toward) the start of the investigation and the main competing hypothesis is whether the misinformation was the result of an error or mistake, or rather a deliberate violation of the rules.

This chapter will stay in line with the '6 Cs-model' hereafter, to present different phases of the (PIF) investigation.

---

28 See Chapters 1 and 2.

29 Judith Seddon *et al.* (eds.), *The Practitioner's Guide to Global Investigations*, Global Investigations Review, 2020, p. 21.

30 Groome, 2014, pp. 117, pp. 121–122, see *supra* note 2.

31 See Section 1.4.4. of Chapter 1, referring to Ivar Fahsing and Karl Ask, "Decision Making and Decisional Tipping Points in Homicide Investigations: An Interview Study of British and Norwegian Detectives", in *Journal of Investigative Psychology and Offender Profiling*, 2013, vol. 10, pp. 155–165.

32 Kim Rossmo, "Anatomie d'une enquête criminelle" [Anatomy of a Criminal Investigation], in *Criminologie*, 2020, vol. 53, no. 2, p. 18.

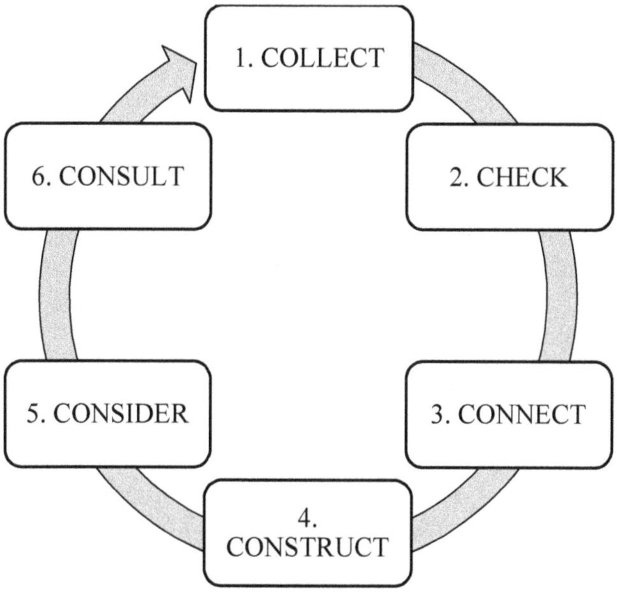

Illustration 8.1.: Case progression according to the '6 Cs' Investigative Cycle model.

8.4.2. The Collection Phase

During the collection phase, the investigation focuses on identifying, locating and gathering the evidence in pursuit of the first lines of enquiry, or to eliminate doubt in relation to certain hypotheses, as set out in the investigation work plan. A logical and typical order in which the investigators can proceed includes:

- gathering evidence by using the powers of investigation (for example, searches of premises), including digital forensics;
- preserving (for example, by posing seals) or safeguarding (for example, by notifying restriction or production orders) records and other evidence;
- accurately documenting the seizures with sound evidence management;
- freezing assets, where possible;
- taking witness statements.

The nature and scope of the activities during the investigation and the outcome of the investigation are crucial to what will be asserted in the charging and adjudication stages, and for the basis of the decision made by the trier of facts.[33] Captured in the metaphor 'garbage in, garbage out', ultimately the quality of the

[33] Frank J. Erkens, "'Checks and balances' in het proces van waarheids- en rechtsvinding" ['Checks and Balances' in the Process of Finding the Truth and Justice], in *Tijdschrift voor sanctierecht & Onderneming*, 2021, vol. 1, no. 2, p. 20.

evidence at the end of the process is determined by what happens at the beginning.[34]

Many investigators adhere to the principle of being exhaustive when determining what evidence to collect.[35] From this point of view, more is always better than less, because once the investigative step has been completed (for example, a search), returning to collect forgotten evidence is often not possible. It is therefore better to collect everything that is, or may become, relevant.[36] However, the investigator should remain within the boundaries of the mandate and scope of the investigation and strike a balance between the aforementioned criteria of credibility and integrity[37] to avoid 'fishing expeditions'.

8.4.3. Building of the Case

In the next stage, the investigation considers how to build its case, step by step, to prove that a criminal offence has (or has not) been committed and who is legally responsible for it. This is a team effort, entailing (a) the analysis of collected evidence (including the aspects of Checking and Connecting the information and Constructing hypotheses); (b) the identification of evidence gaps and the Consideration of contingent further investigative steps, possibly after Consultation and review; and (c) a legal case build-up.

By *checking* what information is correct, accurate and complete, the investigative team can distinguish non-validated information from evidence; get an overview of possible and available evidence; set the right parameters for further collection; consider specialist support.

Then it is time to *connect* the dots and to refine, structure, and possibly visualize the relevant information and evidence, to address questions like: What is known and not known about the investigation? How can the available information and evidence be understood? How well do the different pieces of information and evidence correspond with each other?

Checking and connecting information allow one to (*re*)*construct* the event under scrutiny. Such construction can often be a meticulous and painstaking process that entails considering all competing explanations of available information and evidence by preparing a timeline or thematic overview; identifying all plausible and competing explanations; including innocence (falsification).

This construction of events should allow one to identify the best (so far) and alternative explanations, and to *consider* how these could be tested by filling

34 *Ibid.*

35 Gehl and Plecas, 2016, p. 113, see *supra* note 1.

36 *Ibid.*

37 See Section 7.3.3.2. of Chapter 7.

in information gaps. Good practice is to 'think' in terms of proving and disproving claims (see earlier discussion of confirming and disconfirming evidence); set lines of enquiry; make a plan and set priorities; explore the law and determine what to prove; identify resources needed; and record all critical decisions.

8.4.4. Team-Work

The different stages of fact-finding require the commitment and continuous effort of a diverse team of experts who share the same investigative objectives. Case building in a PIF investigation typically covers a range of specializations within the field of financial investigation[38] and forensic accounting.[39] These include the analysis of accounts, financial data, and bank records, as well as tracing and recovering assets. In addition, with the proliferation of electronic data, digital forensic experts play an increasingly important role in the analysis of such data. They can process the data to present investigators with exploitable evidence or perform further data mining themselves.

A seamless co-operation between the investigators and the operational analysts is key, but this is not always easy to achieve. Whether the forensic expert should limit his or her role to the position of an *ad hoc* 'evaluator' confined to a particular field of expertise or whether he or she should contribute as an assistant to the investigation is open for debate.[40] Beyond merely discussing roles, the debate also includes the different ways investigators and forensic scientists reason and evaluate information.[41] Arguably, both roles and thinking styles should be applied in conjunction to successfully understand a criminal problem or solve a case.

8.4.5. Consultation

The *Consult* step of the '6 Cs' model refers to the invitation of a trusted person to validate your starting hypothesis (which will dictate initial direction) and subsequent adaptations that narrow down your investigation in iterative cycles. It is good practice to always get a second opinion; consider whether further expertise is necessary (and available); identify any blind-spots; make sure all plausible

---

[38] For an overview of three methods of financial investigation to investigate an allegation of corruption, see Organisation for Economic Co-operation and Development, "Investigation and Prosecution of Corruption Offences: Materials for the Training Course", 2012, p. 25.

[39] For an overview and description of forensic accounting skills, see, for example, Seddon *et al.* (eds.), 2020, pp. 375–395.

[40] Simon Baechler *et al.*, "Breaking the Barriers Between Intelligence, Investigation and Evaluation: A Continuous Approach to Define the Contribution and Scope of Forensic Science", in *Forensic Science International*, 2020, vol. 309.

[41] Graham Jackson *et al.*, "The Nature of Forensic Science Opinion – A Possible Framework to Guide Thinking and Practice in Investigation and in Court Proceedings", in *Science & Justice*, 2006, vol. 46, no. 1, pp. 33–44.

explanations are investigated; and assess whether the findings meet the burden of proof.

8.4.6. Quality Concerns

The collection and analysis of evidence enables one to assess the strength of the case and serves to identify or remedy evidentiary gaps. This is done by planning and executing subsequent investigative steps, which requires objectivity. For instance, it is crucial that the process of adding new evidence is not biased by systematically collecting or selecting evidence that favours a particular proposition. A biased collection process will add little to the available evidence. Even an insufficient investigation of mitigating circumstances might give the impression of a biased investigation. This applies to circumstances such as finding (but not reporting) that:[42]

- the offender has prevented, reversed, or limited the harm or loss of welfare caused by the offence, or sought to do so;
- the offence was to a significant degree occasioned by the circumstances of the aggrieved party; or
- the offender had, at the time of the act, reduced capacity to realistically assess his or her relationship to the outside world due to mental illness, mental disability, impairment of consciousness or a state of severe mental agitation.

Building an optimal evidentiary dataset is therefore not simply a matter of increasing the volume of evidence. The additions must, to the greatest extent possible, fairly reflect all of the available evidence and contain all of the "information (that is) practically derivable from all extant sources that can reasonably be made available to and considered by the decision-maker".[43] If certain evidence is missing (that is, evidence known to exist but not obtainable), this gap in the evidential dataset should be flagged in the evidential dataset.

8.5. Concluding the Fact-Finding

The question as to when an evidential dataset is optimal or what and how much evidence is needed to conclude the fact-finding can be answered from different, interrelated perspectives. The evidence should (a) meet the required standard of proof, which entails a quantitative and qualitative aspect; (b) support the factual allegations and allow the application of the law to them (*subsumption*); (c)

---

42 Tor-Geir Myhrer, "The Importance of Successful Co-operation Between Police Investigators and the Prosecution Service to Secure Efficient and Fair Court Proceedings and Verdicts", in Agirre, Bergsmo, De Smet and Stahn (eds.), 2020, p. 1025, see *supra* note 5.

43 Cohen, 1985, p. 264, see *supra* note 26.

enable the individual attribution of guilt; and (d) enable the sanctioning of perpetrators and the recovery of the undue payments.

8.5.1. Standard of Proof

The 'standard of proof' varies at different stages of the criminal proceedings.[44] The term is used here to indicate the threshold of sufficient evidence and persuasiveness that the investigation has to produce to convince the prosecutor,[45] and eventually the trier of facts, of the righteousness of the claim.[46]

In adjudication, guilt must be typically proved '*beyond a reasonable doubt*'.[47] Proof beyond a reasonable doubt does not mean proof to an absolute certainty: it is more than proof that the accused is probably guilty, but not proof beyond any doubt. This means that the evidence must be considered almost certain to be true or at least that the prosecution should convince the judge that there is no other reasonable explanation that can be derived from the evidence presented at trial.

Most (inquisitorial) continental legal systems embed this judgment in the concept of '*intime conviction*' of the judge.[48] This should be understood as meaning that the assessment of whether guilt is established beyond reasonable doubt concerns a strictly subjective impression in the judge's mind. From this perspective, it is sufficient that the judge is personally convinced that the

44 See Chapters 5 ("Initial Reporting") and 6 ("Preliminary Examination of Information") for the standards proposed at those stages of the investigative process.

45 For a study demonstrating that the threshold to charge somebody seems to be lower and one does not need to be completely convinced of the suspect's guilt, see Susanne M. Schmittat, Birte Englich, Lyane Sautner and Petra Velten, "Alternative Stories and the Decision to Prosecute: An Applied Approach Against Confirmation Bias in Criminal Prosecution", in *Psychology, Crime & Law*, 2022, vol. 28, no. 6, pp. 608–635.

46 More technically: "The burden of proof is a party's obligation in legal proceedings to establish an assertion or charge, encompassing the burden of production (provision of sufficient evidence) and the burden of persuasion (preponderance of evidence)", in Fundamental Rights Agency, *Presumption of Innocence and Related Rights: Professional Perspectives*, 2021, p. 5.

47 See, for example, *ibid.*, p. 66; United Nations Human Rights Committee, General Comment No. 32, Article 14: Right to equality before courts and tribunals and to a fair trial, UN Doc. CCPR/C/GC/32, 23 August 2007, p. 9, para. 30 (https://www.legal-tools.org/doc/17c458/).

48 See, for example, Mirjan Damaška, "Epistemic Foundations", in *id.* (ed.), *Evaluation of Evidence: Pre-Modern and Modern Approaches*, American Society of Comparative Law Studies, Cambridge University Press, 2018, pp. 27-46.

evidence presented weighs in favour of his or her subjective conclusion that the defendant is guilty.[49] However, the duty of motivation does apply.[50]

Other standards of proof are '*clear and convincing*' evidence and the '*balance of probabilities*'.[51] These are typically applicable in civil cases and administrative inquiries. In the latter case, a claimant (for example, the European Commission in recovery procedures for irregularity) is required to prove the case against the defendant on the aggregate (the 51 per cent test) of probabilities.[52] It is important for an investigator to understand that, even though there may not be enough evidence to meet the requirement for a criminal prosecution or to establish proof beyond a reasonable doubt, the evidence may still be sufficient to establish civil liability within a balance of probabilities standard. In case there is a possibility of civil action, investigators should thus remain diligent in collecting and preserving evidence, even if they believe there will be no criminal prosecution.

'Proof beyond a reasonable doubt' is a different test from the one investigators are required to meet when considering the value of evidence *during* their investigation (for instance to justify a search).[53] '*Reasonable grounds to believe*' is a typical standard here, which is a lower level of belief, because it requires investigators to articulate only a subjective belief in light of the evidence available to them at the time of their investigation. It allows them to act, for instance, on physical evidence they have seen, records they have reviewed, and hearsay information acquired from witnesses.

Although 'proof beyond reasonable doubt' is a superior level standard that is not imposed here, it could usefully inform the investigative results. The investigative team may wish to 'over-deliver': that is, strive to meet the

---

49 For a comparison between instructions for German and Dutch judges to respectively explain or justify their decisions, see Enide Maegherman, Karl Ask, Robert Horselenberg and Peter J. van Koppen, "Accountability in Legal Decision-Making", in *Psychiatry, Psychology and Law*, 2021, pp. 1-19.

50 The German judge has, for instance, an extensive duty to motivate the decision: the written decision not only needs to include the proven fact and the evidence used, but also needs to explain the selection and evaluation of evidence. In addition, he or she has to pay attention to facts that indicate an alternative, but not accepted, version of events. See Paul A.M. Mevis, "Modernisering van het strafprocesrecht op z'n Duits" [Modernization of Criminal Procedural Law in the German Way], in *Delikt en Delinkwent*, 2019, vol. 7, pp. 40–47.

51 The 'balance of probabilities' is defined as "sufficient evidence – more evidence supports the finding than contradicts it (51%)", see Stephen Wilkinson, *Standards of Proof in International Humanitarian and Human Rights Fact-Finding and Inquiry Missions*, Geneva Academy of International Humanitarian Law and Human Rights Law, 2012.

52 Gehl and Plecas, 2016, pp. 14, 16, see *supra* note 1.

53 *Ibid*., p. 15.

evidentiary threshold required for the next, higher stage (for example, the prosecutor's decision to indict), already before entering a new procedural stage.[54]

8.5.2. Subsumption

The role of the investigator is not only to establish the facts and circumstances underlying PIF offences, but also to provide a provisional – or at least enable – a legal characterization of the facts. Therefore, 'case building' cannot be limited merely to finding facts, but also involves framing and qualifying them.

The facts to prove will vary depending on the offence being alleged or discovered during the investigation. The prosecutor's task of obtaining a conviction requires proof beyond a reasonable doubt of each element of the offences charged and the accused person's individual criminal liability. The investigator's ability to identify and present evidence, and to determine its relevance and importance in relation to the legal aspects of the case, is critical to the success of the case.[55]

A key organizing principle is that one must ensure that the criminal law applies to the facts. This is called 'subsumption'. Put differently, investigators should ensure that their factual findings cover all the constituent parts of the incrimination put forward. Such a correspondence between (possible) incrimination and fact-finding builds on a focused planning of the investigation and a targeted collection of evidence. It requires that the investigative team maintain evidence oversight at all times.[56] Regarding PIF offences, the investigators must follow national law, as EPPO is competent to investigate and prosecute PIF offences as implemented by national law, regardless of whether the same criminal conduct could be classified as another type of offence under national law.[57]

To recognize the types of evidence that need to be collected with respect to various (PIF) offences, an investigator must become intimately familiar with the concept of *actus reus*. This is a Latin term definable as "the guilty act" or "the criminal act", and the concept of *mens rea*, another Latin term meaning "guilty mind" or "the intent to commit an offence".[58] As a general rule, someone who acted without mental fault is not liable in criminal law. It is necessary to

---

[54] Matthias Neuner, "Investigations of Criminal Responsibility by the ICC Office of the Prosecutor", in Agirre, Bergsmo, De Smet and Stahn (eds.), 2020, p. 702, see *supra* note 5.

[55] Olympia Bekou, "Enhancing the Quality of Investigations: What Role Can the In-Depth Analysis Charts Play?", in *ibid.*, p. 590.

[56] We refer to the 'bottlenecks' of too much or not enough evidence, stemming from the finding that in practice the knowledge-base of the investigation frequently ends up being broken up, resulting in efforts ending up being duplicated or precious information being lost (see *ibid.*, p. 588).

[57] Article 22(1) of the EPPO Regulation, see *supra* note 9.

[58] Gehl and Plecas, 2016, p. 21, see *supra* note 1.

prove a subjective mental element to establish liability. This is expressed by the Latin expression: '*actus reus non facit reum nisi mens sit rea*', that is, 'the act is not culpable unless the mind is guilty'.[59] The *actus reus* represents the objective component of the crime, while the *mens rea* is the perpetrator's subjective relation to the crime. In addition to proving the punishable material act or omission described in the criminal code or other legislation, an investigator must therefore prove this "guilty mind".[60]

For certain types of crimes, the law may impose additional conditions for a sanctioned *mens rea*, such as the intent to cause harm or premeditation. The crimes under the jurisdiction of the EPPO encompass diverse constitutive elements and various legal requirements, including different forms of guilty intent. To secure a conviction, evidence must be presented to support each of these elements.[61]

Proceeding to a more detailed identification of the crime-base and modes of liability may exceed the capacities of the investigators. While the 'review' function traditionally intervenes later in the process, investigative teams may benefit from relying on 'legal direction' throughout the investigation phase, including the 'case-building' stage.

8.5.3. Individualization of Guilt

The centrepiece of any investigation, prosecution, trial and judgment is the attribution of guilt to an individual or legal person and a determination of their individual criminal responsibility. The role of the investigator is not only to establish the facts and circumstances underlying PIF offences, but also to explore possible avenues of responsibility of the (legal) persons involved. The main questions to answer here are: What is the correct mode of responsibility that most accurately describes the wrongdoing? And how does this translate into a liability?[62]

Sometimes scholars refer to the *principal* as the person who '(c)ommits' the sanctionable act(s) by directly perpetrating the culpable act or acting as direct or indirect co-perpetrator. By contrast, an *accomplice* orders, solicits or induces, aids or abets in any other way contributing to the occurrence of the offence.[63]

---

[59] David Lanius, *Strategic Indeterminacy in the Law*, Oxford University Press, 2019, p. 113.

[60] Gehl and Plecas, 2016, p. 21, see *supra* note 1.

[61] See Chapter 10 for a specific approach to proving guilty intent.

[62] See Section 7.2. of Chapter 7.

[63] See, for example, Article 25(3) of the ICC Statute, *supra* note 12, and Article 5 of the PIF Directive, *supra* note 25, for the punishable acts of complicity and attempt to fraud.

For 'crimes of omission', it is only necessary to find evidence that the accused failed to meet the standard of care that is expected by law. This omission can be intentional (for example, omitting to submit a tax statement) or the result of negligence (for example, not registering a lost invoice in the accounts). When, for instance, a public official delegates his signature to his assistant, who subsequently signs off on his own claims for non-work related costs, the public official could be considered a co-perpetrator, a wilfully blind accomplice, or just a negligent person depending on whether there is evidence to suggest that he allowed the assistant to use his signature (negligence); unlike a reasonable person, he did not actually foresee the particular consequences which could flow from his trust (wilfully blind); or he became aware of the need for some inquiry but declined to make the inquiry because he does not wish to know the truth (omission).

8.6. Quality Control

8.6.1. The Concern

The process of fact-finding is rich, demanding, and hence subject to many potential considerations for improving its quality. Whereas in theory investigators generally grasp the burden and standards of proof required, in practice they are often unable to consistently determine whether there is sufficient evidence to meet the requisite evidentiary standards for a conviction on a particular charge.[64]

Typical challenges include:[65]

- collecting information of *prima facie* evidentiary value which fails to transform into relevant evidence through analytical processes (for example, over-collection of more easily accessible forms of information, like social media);
- fully grasping the depth, quality and quantities of evidence required to ensure a reasonable prospect of conviction;
- understanding forensic expert reports;[66]
- improper functioning of evidence-review processes.

[64] Ewan Brown and William H. Wiley, "International Criminal Investigative Collection Planning, Collection Management and Evidence Review", in Agirre, Bergsmo, De Smet and Stahn (eds.), 2020, p. 532, see *supra* note 5.

[65] *Ibid.*, pp. 532–533.

[66] For a study indicating that the error in understanding forensic expert reports reached 90% for judges and lawyers and 60 per cent in experts, see Jan De Keijser and Henk Elffers, "Understanding of Forensic Expert Reports by Judges, Defense Lawyers and Forensic Professionals", in *Psychology, Crime & Law*, 2012, vol. 18, no. 2, pp. 191–207.

Professional literature offers various avenues for improving the quality of the investigation, ranging from adopting a right mindset and using adequate thinking skills[67] to specific review processes, as briefly discussed below.

8.6.2. The Mindset

Quality control in fact-finding is above all about nourishing a mindset that encourages constant questioning of the way fact-finding is undertaken by those who are engaged in it. It invites investigators to permanently consider how the quality of every functional aspect of fact-finding can be improved, including work processes to identify, locate, obtain, verify, analyse, corroborate, summarize, synthesise, structure, organize, present and disseminate facts. It is a state of mind characterized by a will to professionalize, and not just by the *ad hoc* development and adoption of standard procedures or universal methodologies that come so easily to lawyers.[68] The pursuit of best practice in fact-finding should not be undertaken in isolation,[69] but result from a culture of quality control, in which the will of individual fact-finders to professionalize is nurtured by example.[70]

8.6.3. Review

Professional literature distinguishes several quality assurance tools consisting of a process of review. It concerns tools or processes where others' specialized competences and expertise are actively sought to obtain comments, including dissenting opinions. Formats include classical review panels and innovative diagnostic and adversarial techniques. These review instruments aim at dissecting the content of the case after breaking them down into tangible elements that can be subject of individual examination[71] in view of possible redress. The review can for instance focus on information management (for example, loss of information overview), insufficient evidence evaluation, or inadequate formulation of responsibility.[72]

---

67 See Chapter 2.

68 Morten Bergsmo, "Foreword to the First Edition by the Editor", in Bergsmo and Stahn (eds.), 2020, p. xvi, see *supra* note 4.

69 *Ibid.*, p. xii.

70 Aksenova, Bergsmo and Stahn, 2020, p. 31, see *supra* note 4.

71 Xavier Agirre Aranburu, "The Contribution of Analysis to the Quality Control in Criminal Investigation", in Agirre, Bergsmo, De Smet and Stahn (eds.), 2020, p. 242, see *supra* note 5.

72 *Ibid.*, pp. 242–255.

Such review has proven to be an effective debiasing strategy in complex decision-making[73] and to contribute to a better quality of the investigation.

8.6.3.1. Review Panels[74]

A review panel (or board) is a fundamental quality-control mechanism for the investigation and the proposed legal case. It consists of experts from within or outside the office, who have not been involved in or exposed to the investigation, and provide an independent and unbiased assessment of the status and adequacy of the investigation.

While review procedures are usually applied at the end of an investigation, some argue that review should have a wider scope, active throughout the duration of any given investigation.[75] In this view, investigative teams may benefit from relying on 'legal direction' throughout the investigation phase, including the 'case-building' stage. Proceeding to a more detailed identification of the crime-base and modes of liability may indeed exceed the capacities of the investigators.

The main purpose of the review panel is to critically assess the case resulting from the investigation, advising on whether the available evidence is sufficient (to file charges or not).[76] The basic question is: 'do we have the evidence or not?'. Questions of fact should inform the procedure but be separated from questions of law to the largest extent possible, respecting the boundaries of the respective missions of fact-finders and reviewers.[77] This is a difficult exercise. In this respect, the review of procedural aspects is an accessory, a simpler quality-control mechanism, than the overall assessment of the strength of the investigation, and it should not replace it.

Given the seriousness of the decision at hand, the reviewers should aim for a high standard of certainty, based only on the actually available and admissible evidence. The question for the reviewers is not only about their personal certainty ('are you certain about the alleged facts and responsibilities?'). Critically, the reviewers need to assess whether the prosecution is able to communicate this certainty and successfully prove the case after an adversarial challenge based on the actual evidence. This is a complex prospective assessment. Hence, the question for the reviewers becomes: 'are you certain about the alleged facts and

---

73 See, for example, Charles R. Schwenk, "Effects of Devil's Advocacy and Dialectical Inquiry on Decision Making: A Meta-Analysis, Organizational", in *Behavior and Human Decision Processes*, 1990, vol. 47, no. 1, pp. 161–176.

74 Agirre Aranburu, 2020, pp. 259–269, see *supra* note 71.

75 Brown and Wiley, 2020, p. 557, see *supra* note 64.

76 Agirre Aranburu, 2020, p. 259, see *supra* note 71.

77 Aksenova, Bergsmo and Stahn, 2020, p. 27, see *supra* note 4.

responsibilities, and is the office able to prove this case beyond reasonable doubt with the actually available and admissible evidence?'.[78]

8.6.3.2. Key Assumptions Check

Checking key investigative assumptions is a quality-control approach that consist of identifying all factual assumptions underlying a given investigative hypothesis (for example, there is guilty intent because the suspect tried to hide another version of the contract) and verifying their factual and logical validity in detail.[79]

Such questioning of assumptions may be difficult if they follow from cultural consensus (for example, 'people from that community do not care for paperwork'), precedent in other cases, policy orientation or 'groupthink'.[80] If the team is not able to check certain assumptions, or does not consider them critical to the case, these assumptions should at least be stated clearly for the record. In this way, the investigative findings are subject to the validity of those underlying premises (for example, the control environment in country 'X' has not been adequate in excluding dubious beneficiaries from the grant system).

8.6.3.3. Analysis of Competing Hypotheses

Identifying multiple hypotheses and comparing them systematically is generally a good idea for any complex investigation.[81] The Analysis of Competing Hypotheses ('ACH')[82] takes this a step further and is essentially a table that compares these different hypotheses against the relevant evidence. The different hypotheses should be expressed in the plainest terms possible and as the most plausible factual explanation of the alleged crimes. Often this takes the form of a syllogism or chain of discrete propositions that logically ('if …, then …') leads to a conclusion of responsibility.[83] This analysis helps to identify gaps and other weaknesses in the hypotheses and the available knowledge and serves as a guide for the investigative process (in particular, the collection plan).[84]

---

78 Agirre Aranburu, 2020, p. 269, see *supra* note 71.

79 *Ibid.*, p. 243.

80 See Section 3.3.2.2. in Chapter 3.

81 See Chapter 1.

82 Richard J. Heuer, *Psychology of Intelligence Analysis*, Central Intelligence Agency, Langley, 1999.

83 Agirre Aranburu, 2020, p. 245, see *supra* note 71.

84 Patrick J. Treanor, "Research and Analysis in the Investigation, Prosecution and Adjudication of Crimes", in Morten Bergsmo, Klaus Rackwitz and Song Tianying (eds.), *Historical Origins of International Criminal Law: Volume 5*, TOAEP, Brussels, 2017, p. 138 (https://www.toaep.org/ps-pdf/24-bergsmo-rackwitz-song/).

ACH step-by-step	
1	Identify the possible hypotheses to be considered. Use a group of analysts with different perspectives to brainstorm the possibilities.
2	Make a list of significant evidence and arguments for and against each hypothesis.
3	Prepare a matrix with hypotheses across the top and evidence on the side. Analyse the 'diagnosticity' of the evidence and arguments – that is, identify which items are most helpful in judging the relative likelihood of the hypothesis.
4	Refine the matrix. Reconsider the hypotheses and delete evidence and arguments that do not have diagnostic value.
5	Draw tentative conclusions about the relative likelihood of each hypothesis. Proceed by trying to disprove the hypotheses rather than prove them.
6	Analyse how sensitive your conclusion is to a few critical items of evidence. Consider the consequences for your analysis if that evidence were wrong, misleading, or subject to a different interpretation.
7	Report conclusions. Discuss the relative likelihood of all hypotheses, not just the most likely one.
8	Identify milestones for future observation that may indicate events are taking a different course than expected.

Illustration 8.2.: Analysis of Competing Hypotheses.

It can be argued that, contrary to other sorts of investigations, in PIF investigations it is less productive to identify all possible hypotheses from the early stages of the investigation, as suspect will typically be known and material facts will often be quite clear. Moreover, in large cases, an overall 'case hypothesis' may be too complex to be subsumed under a table with a few rows. However, the method can also be used for general guidance or otherwise applied to discrete propositions within the case. Moreover, the ACH can be a very helpful tool when assessing or attempting to prove guilty intent, using it as a method to identify the '*inference to the best explanation*' (IBE).[85] Judges could then use the ACH method in their deliberations to meet a higher standard of certainty. In that case, a conviction would require not just that the alternative hypotheses are less compelling, but rather that they are not reasonable in view of the available evidence.[86]

---

[85] See Chapter 10.

[86] Agirre Aranburu, 2020, p. 251, see *supra* note 71.

8.6.3.4. Case Evaluation Table

The purpose of a case evaluation table[87] is to test the premises of the case hypothesis against specific pieces of evidence and to produce a synopsis that should help to identify investigative priorities, ultimately deciding on the sufficiency of the evidence for eventual charges. The case hypothesis is specified with one row for each of its premises, stated in precise factual terms, while the columns show the different sources of evidence that have been assessed positively as a matter of source evaluation.

	Case hypothesis	**Complaint**	**Witnesses**	**Documents**	**Forensics**	**Total**	**comments**
1	Company X was close to bankruptcy because of COVID	X	1/3	No	Yes	4	E-mail of 26 March 2021 ('it is time to be creative'), but accounts show reserve
2	Company looked for public contracts outside expertise	X	2/4	Yes	Yes	5	
3	Consultant Y claims privileged access to officials	-	-	-	Yes	4	E-mail 12 of June 2021 ('I can solve that' – 'my network')
4	Y contacted official of administration Z	-	2/2	Yes		4	*Official* letter dated 21 June 2021
. .							

Illustration 8.3.: Case evaluation table.

8.6.3.5. In-Depth Analysis Chart

The ICC introduced the idea of the In-Depth Analysis Chart ('IDAC') to streamline the disclosure of evidence, which is mandatory under the ICC rules,[88] an idea originating in the ICC Case Matrix and the preparatory team of the ICC Office of the Prosecutor. All evidence disclosed by either party must be in the form of an IDAC, where each piece of evidence is presented according to its

[87] *Ibid.*, pp. 251–254.

[88] Bekou, 2020, p. 593, see *supra* note 55.

relevance in relation to the constituent elements of the crimes presented by the Prosecutor.[89]

The prosecution's obligation to present evidence in accordance with this so-called 'analytical disclosure' does not extend to exculpatory evidence.[90] Incriminating evidence, however, should be entered in a table breaking down each confirmed charge into its constituent elements – contextual circumstances as well as material and mental elements, as prescribed by the elements of crimes. For each element, the prosecution must set out the precise factual allegations that it intends to prove at trial in order to establish the constituent element in question. For each factual allegation, the prosecution shall specify the evidence it intends to rely on at trial in order to prove the allegation.[91]

The use of IDACs compels the prosecution team to undertake fact-related work with the (draft) legal classification of the case in the forefront of their minds.

8.6.3.6. Adversarial Techniques

Adversarial techniques are designed as a 'stress test', to challenge the investigative findings in order to control for 'tunnel vision' and 'confirmation bias', and to anticipate the counterarguments of adversarial litigation.[92] Best-known are the 'consider-the-opposite',[93] the Devil's Advocate ('DA') and Red Teaming ('RT'). The latter is similar to a DA but more demanding: beyond challenging the proposed argument, a RT is expected to build an alternative argument or scenario with the same information.

Findings on the efficiency of this adversarial techniques are mixed. The success of the procedures seems to be dependent, for instance, on how 'devilish' the DA really is;[94] that is, whether the dissent is genuine or contrived.[95] For a DA to have the intended effect, rather than becoming a pointless ritual, the DA should actively research and advocate a contrary position, not just pose

---

89 *Ibid.*, p. 594.

90 *Ibid.*, p. 596.

91 *Ibid.*, p. 594.

92 Agirre Aranburu, 2020, p. 255, see *supra* note 71.

93 See, for example, Edward R. Hirt and Keith D. Markman, "Multiple Explanation: A Consider-an-Alternative Strategy for Debiasing Judgments", in *Journal of Personality and Social Psychology, 1995, vol. 69, no. 6*, pp. 1069–1086.

94 Morgan D. Jones, *The Thinker's Toolkit: 14 Powerful Techniques for Problem Solving*, Crown Currency, New York, 1995, p. 218.

95 Stefan Schulz-Hardt, Marc Jochims and Dieter Frey, "Productive Conflict in Group Decision Making: Genuine and Contrived Dissent as Strategies to Counteract Biased Information Seeking", in *Organizational Behavior and Human Decision Processes*, 2002, vol. 88, no. 2, pp. 563–586.

rhetorical questions and make insincere or unsubstantiated comments before slipping back into the mainstream of conventional thought.[96]

Moreover, research on 'consider-the-opposite' and DA as an effective approach to reducing bias in a number of different domains has shown that these tactics may ultimately strengthen the initial position. If the opposite is hard to consider or the dissent is not genuine, alternative stories may not lead to the desired results of a balanced information evaluation but may instead backfire.[97]

8.7. Concluding Remarks

The essence of investigation is fact-finding: identifying, locating, obtaining, verifying, analysing, validating, summarizing, structuring and presenting this set of information and facts to the trier of facts as evidence.

This chapter asserts that good practices in fact-finding involve the following:

- After a more exploratory phase, where the investigators will use their legitimate powers to collect evidence, they will have to build a case based on the available evidence and consider whether they have a good enough case to present to the decision maker.
- Evidence can be direct, when it does not have to rely on inferences to demonstrate a fact, or indirect or circumstantial, when the evidence does not prove the offence in itself but supports its occurrence by means of generalizations.
- Good evidence must be admissible (a legal criterion) but also relevant, reliable and probative. The more comprehensive, strong and supportive of the conclusion the evidence is, the more weight (or persuasive power) it will have in convincing the trier of facts.
- At the end of the investigation, the evidence obtained should satisfy the standard of proof, apply a correct legal description to the facts, and enable individualization of guilt.
- In most cases, the evidence will need to demonstrate beyond reasonable doubt the existence of the sanctionable act or omission and a culpable mindset.

The quality of the investigation can be ensured with reviews by experts who were not involved in the investigation, standard control procedures, and

[96] Moa Lidén, "Confirmation Bias in Investigations of Core International Crimes; Risk Factors and Quality Control Techniques", in Agirre, Bergsmo, De Smet and Stahn (eds.), 2020, p. 518, see *supra* note 5.

[97] See, for example, Charlan Nemeth, Keith Brown and John Rogers, "Devil's Advocate Versus Authentic Dissent: Stimulating Quantity and Quality", in *European Journal of Social Psychology*, 2001, vol. 31, no. 6, pp. 707–720.

adversarial challenging techniques. Above all, however, there should be a culture of quality concern.

9

Models of Rational Proof in Investigation

Daniela-Simona Tatu, Jorick Schreurs and Tom Willems*

9.1. Introduction

At the end of the fact-finding stage, the investigative team will have to prepare its 'case'. This will often come in the form of a final report comprising a statement of the facts and an analysis of the collected evidence, followed by the conclusions of the investigation. Bearing in mind that the burden of proof for establishing guilt falls on the prosecution, the investigative team is charged with seeking both inculpatory and exculpatory evidence, to be submitted to the prosecutor or trier of facts. In full respect of the applicable legal framework and defence rights, there will nevertheless exist some margin of manoeuvre in the selection and presentation of evidence. In this chapter, we inquire: what makes for the conclusions of an investigation, what are the boundaries or constraints of selection and presentation of evidence, and what are the models of rational proof used?

9.2. Basics

Fact-finders[1] should only make factual claims that they themselves believe to be true, and are expected to be able to 'justify' their beliefs in front of a trier of fact, judge or jury. Whether a belief is justified depends on a number of factors, the most important of which is the totality of evidence the fact-finder has at his or her disposal. As the evidence one has can, at least in theory, always be challenged or defeated by evidence one does not have, it follows that as long as one does not have all the evidence, one's beliefs remain *defeasible*. Therefore, apart from giving us the hypotheses and the theories that underpin them, fact-finders

* **Daniela-Simona Tatu** serves as a Senior Legal Support Officer at the European Public Prosecutor's Office, where she provides legal assistance to a permanent chamber in fulfilling its duties related to investigation monitoring and case adjudication. She possesses extensive experience in investigating and prosecuting financial crimes, having previously served as public prosecutor within the Romanian criminal justice system. **Jorick Schreurs**, a public prosecutor in the Netherlands, is currently working as National Expert at the European Anti-Fraud Office ('OLAF') where he contributes to the cooperation between OLAF and its external stakeholders, most notably EPPO. **Tom Willems** is co-ordinator for international relations at OLAF, after a long career as investigator in fraud and corruption cases at the Belgian police and OLAF. This chapter is authored in the contributors' personal capacity and does not necessarily reflect the views of EPPO, OLAF or other institutions mentioned therein.

1 See Chapter 8 for more detail on good practices in fact-finding.

should be able to express how confident they are of the accuracy, reliability and strength or solidity of their findings. This estimation should be based on more than the fact finder's intuition. Ideally, the fact-finder should be able to explain exactly what the sources of uncertainty or doubts are, and to what extent they impact the accuracy of the findings. In order to be able to convey this information, fact-finders must have a method for determining their level of confidence in the findings, ideally measuring this when possible, and communicating it.[2]

Fact presentation methods and decisions contingent on proven facts that are violations of criminal law, must be rational because of what is at stake. Rationality here is to be understood as methods and decisions based on sound reasoning, securing warranted conclusions and open for critical scrutiny. The decision-making process must also be cognitively feasible, given realistic cognitive limitations,[3] and it must comply with the relevant legal and procedural constraints.[4] Given these considerations, three approaches to rational reasoning are particularly useful:[5] (a) probabilities, (b) arguments, and (c) scenarios.

These approaches are not mutually exclusive and fact-finders are not compelled to choose between one or the other, and many may opt to combine them. They all acknowledge that evidence cannot provide watertight support for a factual claim, as there is always room for doubts and counter-claims (see *defeasibility*). Probabilistic approaches account for this by applying Bayesian probability theory, argumentative approaches emphasize the comparison of supporting and opposing arguments, and scenario-based approaches involve comparing alternative scenarios about what may have happened in a given case.[6] Although none of these schools offers ready-made reasoning models that always lead to the truth, let alone provide simple algorithms that are easy to apply in practice, it is nevertheless quite useful to be aware of them, because a better

---

2 Simon De Smet, "Justified Belief in the Unbelievable", in Xabier Agirre, Morten Bergsmo, Simon De Smet and Carsten Stahn (eds.) *Quality Control in Criminal Investigation*, Torkel Opsahl Academic EPublisher, Brussels, 2020, p. 85 (https://www.toaep.org/ps-pdf/38-qcci/).

3 See Chapters 3 (on noise) and 4 (on bias).

4 John H. Wigmore, *The Principles of Judicial Proof*, 2nd ed., Little, Brown and Company, Boston, 1931.

5 Bart Verheij *et al.*, "Arguments, Scenarios and Probabilities: Connections Between Three Normative Frameworks for Evidential Reasoning", in *Law, Probability and Risk*, 2016, vol. 15, no. 1, pp. 35–70.

6 Hendrik Prakken, Floris Bex and Anne Ruth Mackor, "Editors' Review and Introduction: Models of Rational Proof, in Criminal Law, Topics in Cognitive Science", 2020, vol. 12, no. 4, pp. 1053–1067.

understanding of the underlying concepts may improve the way in which fact-finders approach their work.

9.3. Probabilistic Approaches

9.3.1. Description

The basic idea of probability theory is that our beliefs about the world are not categorical but come in degrees.[7] By convention, a person's degree of belief is expressed on a scale from 0 (one is certain a proposition is false) to 1 (one is certain a proposition is true). When asked about whether one thinks a fair coin will land on heads, the answer should therefore be '0.5', expressing the fact that one has no basis on which to predict which of the two sides will land up.

The probabilistic method aims at establishing the probability of factual propositions based on the laws of probability. Probabilistic approaches have been central to much of the research on the assessment of evidence, particularly when the probabilities can be determined based on 'hard' data (for example, DNA and fingerprint databases).

Probabilistic accounts for fact-finding include: (a) frequency-type probability, (b) belief-type probability, and (c) Bayesian networks.

9.3.2. Frequency-Type Probability

Frequency-type probability refers to making predictions about certain types of events that are based either on logical calculations (for example, chance of rolling dice ending on number 6) or on statistical data (for example, DNA predicting a certain disease). A practical example for investigations is deciding when there is evidence of systematic or organized customs fraud. The investigative service could make some controlled purchases of certain goods to follow a money trail and establish whether these goods are sold under the market price. But how many of such purchases should one make to obtain a statistically relevant sample, enabling the fact-finder to draw appropriate probabilistic inferences about the population (here: total import) as a whole? In other words, how many examples are needed to conclude a whole traffic line is corrupted? Careful sampling is a potentially very powerful tool that can vastly improve the quality of fact-finding, but relies on solid frequency-type probability.

9.3.3. Belief-Type Probability

Belief-type probability relies on a person's individual confidence level about an uncertain event or proposition as a starting point. The classical definition of belief-type probability states that it is "a degree of belief (as actually held by someone based on his whole knowledge, experience, information) regarding the truth

[7] De Smet, 2020, p. 85, see *supra* note 2.

of a statement or event".[8] Belief-type probability will be appropriate whenever the event in question cannot be considered as part of a long sequence of repetitions under identical conditions. A typical example is the assessment of intention.[9] This cannot be empirically established and thus necessarily relies on a subjective probability assessment. Other examples include the assessment by the investigator, judge, or jury of the trustworthiness of a whistle-blower or the credibility of a document handed over by a witness.

The strength of beliefs often cannot be measured and there is no single universal method to determine subjective (or personal) probability estimates. One approach that is popular among probability theorists is to estimate a person's degree of confidence in a particular proposition by gauging how much risk the person would be willing to take when offered the bet. A likely more relevant approach in our context is to express the probability in shared verbal or numerical scales that are illustrated with examples common to all.

People can disagree about the degree of probability when perceiving certain evidence. Their judgment will, for instance,[10] depend on the level of background information in light of which the assessment is being made. Despite this 'noise', people are however usually able to distinguish between reasonable and unreasonable probability assessments.[11] One of the main constraints is that the assessor should respect the basic rules of probability. These include that:[12]

- if someone considers several possible hypotheses that completely explain a single event, the sum of the probabilities for all of these hypotheses must be 1;
- a probability estimate about the truth of a particular proposition must be inversely proportionate to the probability of the proposition being false (for example, a 0.7 probability that an irregular cost claim was made in conscious violation of the rules, implies that there is a 0.3 probability that it was made by negligence or error);
- the probability of a conjunction can never be higher than that of its individual components. For example, if you suppose that the probability that company 'A' prepared and sent false documents is 0.6, and the probability that manager 'X' is in control of this company is 0.7, your resulting probability estimate of X being the person who orchestrated the fraud must be

8 Bruno De Finetti, "Probability: The Subjectivistic Approach", in Raymond Klibansky (ed.), *La philosophie contemporaine*, Volume 2, Firenze, La Nuova Italia, 1968, p. 45.

9 See Chapter 10.

10 See Chapter 3 for more detail on scales and standards and the 'noise' that comes with their use.

11 Julia Mortera and Paszko Dawid, "Probability and Evidence", in Tamas Rudas (ed.), *Handbook of Probability: Theory and Applications*, Los Angeles, Sage, 2008, p. 404.

12 De Smet, 2020, p. 89, see *supra* note 2.

equal to or less than the conjunction of the two probability estimates; in other words, your estimate that X orchestrated the fraud must not be greater than 0.42 (0.6 x 0.7). Assigning X's probability of orchestrating the fraud a value of, say, 0.9 would be improper.

9.3.4. Bayesian Networks

A 'Bayesian network' is a tool for evaluating information and determining how a vast collection of evidence relates to one or more hypotheses.[13] It is based on Bayes' rule, which estimates the probability of an event based on prior knowledge of conditions that might be related to the event.[14] For example, when a person goes to the doctor with a rash, the doctor will base her diagnosis of the possibility of cancer not only on this evidence, but also on her general knowledge that the chance of a cancer increases with age. Likewise, when customs authorities note that the price of the imported goods on a customs declaration is significantly lower than the selling price of identical goods, and the exporting company is investigated for customs fraud in a different case, the latter finding allows the investigators to infer a probable conclusion: the exporting (and importing) company agreed to under-evaluate the goods to reduce the related customs duties.

Imagine a house was robbed and the eyewitness stated she saw the thieves escape in a white Fiat.

Given that 2 per cent of the cars in that city are Fiats and that eyewitness testimony has a 90 per cent accuracy rate on average, the Bayesian probability rule suggest that the eyewitness probably made a mistake, because it is five times more likely she misidentified another car for a Fiat. Put more explicitly:

- assuming there are 50.000 car in the city, 1000 (2 per cent) are Fiats;
- as the eyewitness is right in 90 per cent of the cases, this makes for 900 correctly identified cars;
- as she is also wrong in 10 per cent of the cases, this however also makes for 4.900 (10 per cent of 49.000) non-fiat cars she would identify as Fiat;
- Thus, out of 5.800 (900+4900) cars the witness would identify as Fiats only 900/5.800=15,5 per cent are Fiats.

Illustration 9.1.: Advanced Bayesian reasoning.

[13] Norman Fenton, Martin Neil and Daniel Berger, "Bayes and the Law", in *Annual Review of Statistics and Its Application*, 2016, vol. 3, pp. 51–77.

[14] More technically: the Bayes' rule considers the conditional probability of the evidence given the hypotheses (the likelihood ratio) and the prior probability of the hypotheses (that is, their probability before taking any evidence into account) to compute the posterior probability of the hypotheses given the available evidence (see Prakken, Bex and Mackor, 2020, p. 1055, see *supra* note 6).

Other examples of a simplified use of Bayesian probability assessment in investigations include:

- when after a burglary, the police take for questioning a person acting nervously (raising suspicion), the chance of having caught the right person is higher when he corresponds to a description as 'a man with a tattoo on his arm and dressed in a black T-shirt with an inscription', than when the description is merely 'a man in black shirt and jeans'. The logic of base rates (prior knowledge) enforced the likelihood of arresting the right suspect among people behaving nervously;
- the selection of containers to be controlled on a ship with irregular import documents, based on an analysis of big data identifying a shift in high-risk sea-routes;
- the likelihood that an informant provided correct information will be weighted taking into account that he was highly reliable and well-informed on previous occasions;
- the fact that an email was found in an encoded folder (prior probability of importance) gives weight to the inference that the ambiguous wording of the email found ('we will do business together') refers to corruption.

The main advantages of Bayesian thinking are that it allows one to integrate 'subjectivity' or 'the degree of belief' into otherwise rigid statistical models (for example, reliability of a source) and can be used to gradually update the probability of an event having occurred, as additional evidence or data is gathered.

In practice, Bayes' inferences are often used to make structured, graphical representations of probabilistic relationships between several random variables in so-called Bayesian networks. These are basically a snapshot of a given fact-finder's state of knowledge of the investigated facts at any given moment in time and a tool to express and analyse theories about what happened and who bears the responsibility for those events. The Bayesian network forces the fact-finder to analyse the evidence in much greater detail, both in terms of relevance and probative value. Arguably, this leads to greater accuracy in the overall probability assessment, as research suggests people make better probability assessments when asked to assess each of the items of evidence and hypotheses separately.[15] Other advantages of using a Bayesian network include that it:

- demands the fact-finder to think carefully about how evidence and hypotheses may be connected (or not);

[15] See Fred Luminoso, "Bayesian Belief Network Analysis of Legal Evidence", in *Stanford Undergraduate Research Journal*, 2002, vol. 1, p. 49.

- helps avoid mistakes and allows others to review and criticize the reasoning;[16]
- enables one to identify missing evidence, including evidence that might be expected to exist, but is not available;
- informs the fact-finder about the defeasibility of the available evidence, by providing an indication of the potential impact of the missing evidence on the overall probability estimate, if it were to be found;
- helps explicitly model the probabilities of various scenarios, including the best one;[17]

Moreover, Bayesian networks are state of the art in artificial intelligence, and many software packages exist for creating Bayesian networks and computing with them.

The limitations of using a Bayesian network include that:

- the required (sufficient) data set is often not available;
- fact-finders may find it to be complex and counterintuitive at first, possibly leading to more, instead of fewer errors;[18]
- it is difficult to represent the probability of the 'weight' of evidence; in that the probability of a hypothesis based on a large body of evidence is better justified than the same estimate made on a small subset of the evidence;[19]
- softer types of evidence might be 'dwarfed' in that only easily quantifiable forms of evidence will be considered;
- the mathematical form of a testimony gives the misleading impression of objectivity;[20]
- in many cases, fact-finders will have considered at least part of the evidence before any hypotheses are formulated, influencing the prior probability of the hypothesis before Bayes' rule can be applied;
- if only one hypothesis is considered, there is a risk that certain evidence will simply be overlooked because it stands in no obvious probabilistic relationship to that hypothesis.

---

[16] De Smet, 2020, p. 96, see *supra* note 2.

[17] Hendrik Prakken, presentation during the OLAF conference on "Judgement and Decision Making in Investigations", Brussels, 7 December 2022, referring to Norman Fenton, Martin Neil, Barbaros Yet and David Lagnado, "Analyzing the Simonshaven Case Using Bayesian Networks", in *Topics in Cognitive Science*, 2020, vol. 12, no. 4, pp. 1092–1114.

[18] Richard O. Lempert, "The New Evidence Scholarship: Analyzing the Process of Proof", in *Boston University Law Review*, 1986, vol. 66, pp. 439–477.

[19] Prakken et al., 2020, p. 1055, see *supra* note 6.

[20] Laurence H. Tribe, "Trial by Mathematics: Precision and Ritual in the Legal Process", in *Harvard Law Review*, 1971, vol. 84, no. 6, pp. 1329–1393.

In legal practice, practitioners have so far used the Bayesian probability account almost exclusively on parts of the evidence and at so-called source level to determine from which source a particular trace (for example, DNA, foot tracks or fingerprints) comes from. This use is limited to establishing the weight of this trace evidence.

Given the limitations of using the Bayesian network, especially the complexity of the tool, legal practitioners tend to be apprehensive about its broader use. This often stems from lawyers in criminal cases simply not being well acquainted with the basics of Bayesian analysis. Most lawyers are not accustomed to using mathematical formulae. Nevertheless, Prakken and Meester argue[21] that the Bayes rule can be applied in a scientifically reliable and useful way to analyse complex criminal cases as a whole, provided that certain guiding principles are followed:

i) there needs to be a co-operation between subject matter experts and Bayesian experts;
ii) different kinds of findings require different kinds of expertise, so (usually) more than one matter expert is needed;
iii) subjective assumptions and estimations based on common sense need to be explicitly indicated as such;
iv) there needs to be at least two alternative analyses by two different groups of experts.

9.4. Arguments

9.4.1. A Description

A second approach for proving facts is based on argumentation. Argumentation is the practice of justifying (not proving) conclusions under conditions of uncertainty.[22] People argue by constructing and justifying arguments in many contexts, through conversation, speeches, writings, and even nonverbal expressions.[23] The fundamental process of argumentation involves providing reasons for a

[21] Hendrik Prakken and Ronald Meester, "Bayesiaanse analyses van complexe strafzaken door deskundigen: Betrouwbaar en zo ja: nuttig?" [Bayesian Analysis of Complex Criminal Cases by Experts: Reliable and If So: Useful?], in *Expertise en Recht*, 2017, vol. 5, pp. 185–197.

[22] David Zarefsky, *The Practice of Argumentation. Effective Reasoning in Communication*, Cambridge University Press, 2019, p. 3.

[23] Zarefsky, 2019, p. 29, see *supra* note 22.

given state of affairs.[24] It often involves offering what are thought to be good reasons that are related to claims that we are asking others to accept.[25]

Argumentation relies on *inferential justification.* An inference is a logical and reasonable conclusion of a fact, not presented by direct evidence but which, by process of logic and reason, a trier of fact may conclude exists given the established facts.[26] Put differently, an argument consists of the production, in one's mind or in conversation, of a set of statements (the premises) that are meant to support a conclusion.[27]

Making the various inferences in an argument explicit allows one to identify sources of doubt in these arguments.

> Imagine an investigation about allegations of systematic fraud in scientific research projects funded by the European Union ('EU'), where participating organizations submitted very high claims for personal costs, supported by time-sheets indicating up to 10 working hours per day. To prove fraud, the investigator will have to:
>
> - establish the materiality of a misstatement (for example, working time for a researcher reported to have worked 10 hours on one project, was also claimed in another project the same day), *and*
> - demonstrate that these wrong claims were made knowingly and willingly to obtain illegitimate funds and not by error (for example, it was not caused by the company's secretary's inattention when filling in the time sheets).
>
> As regards the latter, the investigators (prosecutor) will have to prove beyond reasonable doubt the suspect's guilty intent to commit fraud. This can require complex argumentation, constructed given the available evidence and the inferences it warrants.

Illustration 9.2.: The need for argumentation via inference.

9.4.2. Deductive Arguments

Deductive arguments allow one to draw conclusions that are definitively true[28] if the argument's premises are true. For example, consider these two premises:

---

24 Other objectives of argumentation is better understanding for the arguer him- or herself (justifying beliefs), persuasion, and the refutation of arguments by others. See Walter Sinnott-Armstrong, *Think Again: How to Reason and Argue*, Oxford University Press, 2018, pp. 173, 249.

25 Zarefsky, 2019, p. 5, see *supra* note 22.

26 Robert J. Girod, *Logical Investigative Methods*, CRC Press, Taylor and Francis Group, Boca Raton, 2015, p. 3.

27 Sinnott-Armstrong, 2018, p. 105, see *supra* note 24; Girod, 2015, pp. 28 and 52, see *supra* note 26.

28 In formal logic, validity designates a test for the quality of an argument that is independent of the truth of the propositions (that is, the evidence or claims made in the argument). Validity is concerned with argument *structure*. In other words, an argument can be valid but the

(1.) 'all humans die', and (2.) 'you are a human'. It follows from this that (3.) 'you will die' is true. In this case, the premises are trivially true, though that need not be the case for the argument to be valid nevertheless.[29] In this way, deduction involves certainty because a valid argument is necessarily true if its premises are true. Another advantage of deduction is that validity is *indefeasible* in the sense that, if an argument is valid, adding an extra premise can never make it invalid.[30]

The main form deductive arguments take is the syllogism, a form of reasoning in which a conclusion is drawn from two or more propositions (premises) that are asserted or assumed to be true. Classic examples of deductive arguments are:[31] (a) 'if X, then Y. X, so Y' (called *modus ponens*, or asserting stance) and (b) 'if X, then Y. Not X, so not Y' (*modus tollens*, or denying stance). Such deductive arguments often come with conclusion markers like 'so', 'therefore' and 'hence' or reason markers, like 'because', 'since' and 'as'.

Premise 1	[because] EU staff should uphold the highest principles of ethics.
Premise 2	[and] You are an EU official.
Conclusion	*[So] You should uphold the highest principles of ethics.*
Premise 1	[If] we can prove that the bidding company received the inside information on 23.04.20 before submitting the offer.
Premise 2	[then] there must have been a 'leak'
Premise 3	[since] we can only prove they had the information on 25.04.20 after the tenderer's offers were opened
Conclusion	*We cannot prove there was a 'leak'*

Illustration 9.3.: Possible use of syllogisms in investigation.

conclusion can be false, if the premises are false. If an argument is valid (structurally) and its premises are true, this argument is considered 'cogent'. See Zarefsky, 2019, p. 104, see *supra* note 22.

29 Michael W. Eysenck and Mark T. Keane, *Cognitive Psychology: A Student's Handbook*, 6th ed., Psychology Press, Hove, 2010, p. 533.

30 Sinnott-Armstrong, 2018, p. 187, see *supra* note 24.

31 *Ibid.*, p. 155.

9.4.3. Inductive Arguments

9.4.3.1. Description

While people tend to prefer making deductions because of the 'certainty' they imply, most ordinary reasoning involves induction. Inductive arguments are those in which a conclusion is based on the available evidence, evidence that is often incomplete or might be subject to diverse interpretations.[32] So, such conclusions are never entirely certain. Unlike deductive arguments, inductive arguments are not indefeasible.[33] Rather, they aim to provide the best support they can for the fact-finder's conclusions.

The strength of such conclusions – conclusions that, in the case of investigators, are often working hypotheses about the crime or its components – depends on their premises, which is to say the evidence presented.[34] Evidence for inductive arguments comes in many forms, including physical, testimonial, graphs and charts.[35] The determination of guilty intent in adjudication can, for instance, rely on inductive reasoning comprised of evidence as diverse as: a number of consistent witness statements; patterns of behaviour (for example, application or different prices only in EU tenders); and indications of concealment of certain commercial transactions (for example, the use of shell companies).

A key feature of inductive arguments is that its conclusions are probable, but not necessarily true. Inferences of this sort do not provide certainty. The logic of probability is thus relevant to any discussion of inductive arguments, and any system of inductive logic involves an assignment of probabilities.[36] To be useful, conclusions based on inductive reasoning and argument must reach a reasonable degree of probability. In law, this is the standard of proof. So, even when it is said that the objective of any investigation is to establish the truth, it is difficult to maintain that any findings should be accepted as establishing the definitive truth. Justice hence has to settle for the best that can be attained. As a bottom line, one could at least expect both solid findings of fact, as well as a firm belief on the part of the fact-finder that the probability of claims he supports is not liable to decrease as a result of the presentation of further (new) evidence.

---

[32] Girod, 2015, p. 31, see *supra* note 26.

[33] Sinnott-Armstrong, 2018, pp. 184, 189, see *supra* note 24.

[34] *Ibid.*, p. 189.

[35] Robert H. Gass and John S. Seiter, *Persuasion, Social Influence and Compliance Gaining*, Routledge, New York, 2018, p. 214; Jay Heinrichs, *Thank You for Arguing*, Penguin Books, London, 2017.

[36] James D. Carney and Richard K. Scheer, *Fundamentals of Logic*, 3rd ed., Macmillan Publishing Co., New York, 1980, p. 436.

9.4.3.2. Evidence, Warrant and Claim

A classic inductive argument consists of: (a) evidence; (b) a warrant (or generality); and (c) a claim (or inference or conclusion).

For an argument to be successful, all parties to a dispute must accept the truth of the *evidence*. They may disagree about why it matters; what it means (interpretation), and if it really functions to support the claim it supports (relevance), but they need to agree the evidence is true. This is why fact-finding is central in investigations and various procedures provide the defence with an opportunity to contest the factual findings before drawing conclusions.

Conclusions from inductive arguments are 'suggested' with varying degrees of certainty. Whether an inductive conclusion is convincing depends on how much (quantity) evidence there is in the premises supporting the conclusion[37] and the strength (quality) of the argument linking the premises to the conclusion. The latter depends not only on the quantity of evidence at hand, but also on its representativeness (sample size/base rate). A conclusion (for example, a 'high fraud risk' assessment) based on the analysis of 5 out of 13 EU-funded research projects submitted over the last year has less persuasive strength than an analysis of 256 projects of 400 submitted over the last six years. This, however, requires the recipient to think a bit and overcome the cognitive ease of sticking with the simple figures to conclude almost half of the projects were impacted.

The link between evidence and the claim it supports is called a *warrant*. It concerns a more generalizable statement, implicitly legitimizing the inference that the evidence gathered counts as evidence for a particular claim.[38] For instance, a witness testimony supports a belief by virtue of the common knowledge that witnesses usually tell the truth. Such generalization is considered acceptable if over time similar judgments have been borne out by subsequent experience to be reasonable and to not lead people astray. That is what the warrant licenses us to assume.[39] Also, for example, when an interviewer notes that an interviewee's company registered a consistent loss of 25 per cent of its annual income (and might thus have been inclined to make illicit price agreements), this claim is based on his analysis of the accounting books of the company. The warrant in this case is that turnover figures are a *sign* of a company's position.[40]

37 Carney and Scheer, 1980, p. 11, see *supra* note 36.

38 Zarefsky, 2019, p. 51, see *supra* note 22.

39 *Ibid*., p. 107.

40 Adapted from *ibid*., pp. 34–35.

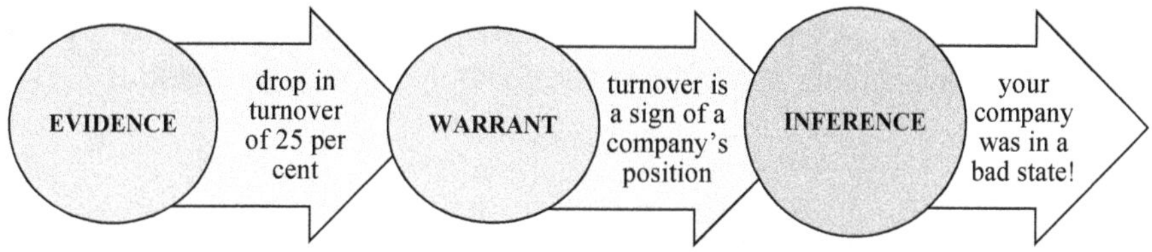

Illustration 9.4.: A simple argument.

9.4.3.3. Inductive Argument Schemes

Just as there are several types of evidence, there are several types of warrants (or inference). These different patterns of inference are called argument schemes and include:[41] (a) arguments from example (based on the warrant of representativeness); (b) arguments from analogy (based on the warrant of similarity); (c) arguments from sign (based on the warrant of predictiveness); (d) arguments from cause (based on the warrant of influence); and (e) arguments from testimony (based on the warrant of credibility).

Recall that inductive arguments do not assert that the claims (conclusions) supported by the premises are necessarily true, but rather that the claims are reasonable when sufficient grounds are provided for sensible people to accept them. This means that the claim is not guaranteed by the evidence (like in deduction), but needs a warrant to license the claim (based on the evidence). Generalizations (from the specific to the general) thus play an important part in argumentation. They are the glue that holds evidential arguments together.[42]

9.4.4. Argument Frameworks

Arguments are structured in frameworks that individuals can use strategically, enabling them to anticipate counter-attacks. These frameworks can be used in all sorts of combinations to support a main claim. It is important to differentiate between: (a) subordinative arguments; (b) co-ordinative arguments and (c) multi-structured arguments.

In *subordinative arguments*, each step in an argument depends on all the steps that have preceded it. All of the previous steps are needed in order to establish the main claim.[43] This is arguably the strongest way of presenting a claim. However, a critic would only have to break one link in the chain for the entire

---

[41] *Ibid.*, p. 107. See also Chapter 10 for a return to these inductive argument schemes to prove intent.

[42] William Twining, "Necessary but Dangerous? Generalisations and Narrative in Argumentation About "Facts" in Criminal Process", in Marijke Malsch and Johannes Fredrikus Nijboer (eds.), *Complex Cases: Perspectives on the Netherlands Criminal Justice System*, Thela Thesis, Amsterdam, 1999, pp. 69–98.

[43] Zarefsky, 2019, p. 43, see *supra* note 22.

chain to be broken. In the example below such refutation could be: 'I did not need this contract, I had obtained an emergency loan from my bank'.

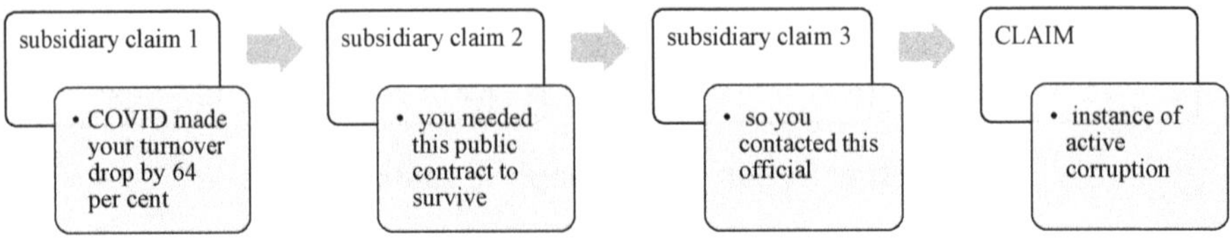

Illustration 9.5.: A subordinative argument in a case of corruption.

Other claims will get their strength from an accumulation of sub-claims. It is the overall pattern, not one specific finding, that establishes the conclusion. The structure of such an argument framework is called *co-ordinative*. Since the power of such arguments comes from their accumulation of claims, some degree of compilation, say, at least three or four of the subsidiary claims will be necessary. Once the cumulative force is established, citing additional subsidiary claims may be piling on more claims than are needed or useful.[44]

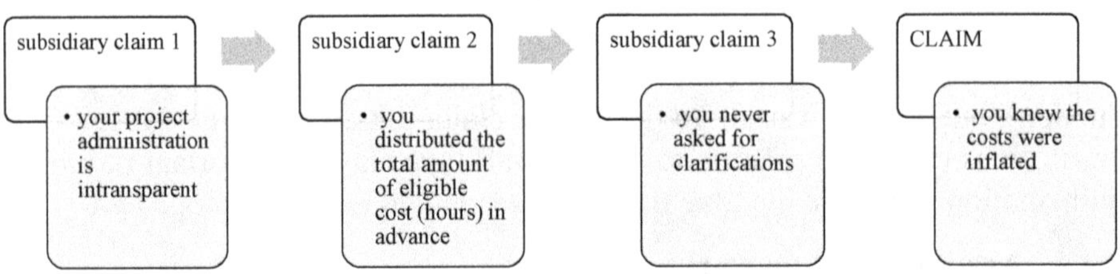

Illustration 9.6.: A co-ordinative argument in a case of false cost claims.

Finally, a *multiple structured argument* consists of different claims that do not depend on one another and each by itself establishes the main claim. In such case, the arguer can fail to make a case for any given sub-claim without necessarily discrediting the main claim.

[44] *Ibid.*, p. 42.

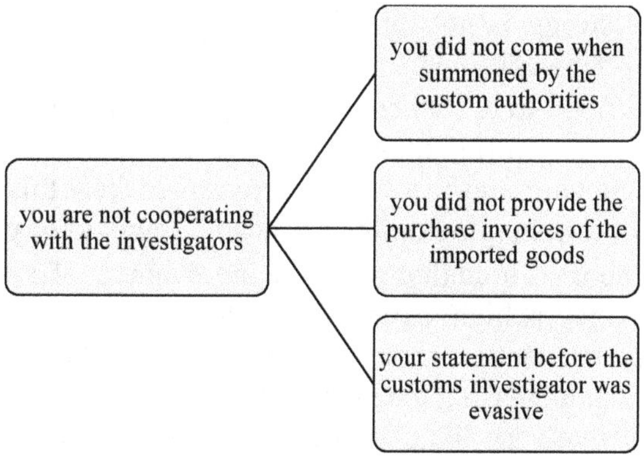

Illustration 9.7.: A multiple-structured argument.

In practice, complex argument contexts will often require a combination of different argument frameworks. This will not necessarily strengthen the conclusion(s). The different argument frameworks are summarized below:

Multiple arguments	Subsidiary claims are *independent* of each other Subsidiary claims *individually* establish the main claim
Coordinative arguments	Subsidiary claims are *independent* of each other Subsidiary claims, *taken together*, establish the main claim
Subordinative arguments	Subsidiary claims are *not independent* of each other Subsidiary claims, *taken together*, establish the main claim

Illustration 9.8.: Panorama of complex argumentation frameworks.

9.4.5. Strength of Inductive Arguments

Conclusions from inductive arguments are 'suggested' with varying degrees of certainty, depending on how much (quantity) evidence there is in the premises leading to the conclusion[45] and the strength (quality) of the argument. What

[45] Carney and Scheer, 1980, p. 11, see *supra* note 36.

makes arguments strong is not only its validity (internal logic), but also its soundness (solid premises).[46]

It is often difficult to tell when a main argument is ultimately persuasive. There is some boundary differentiating credible from unbelievable arguments; however, there is no hard-and-fast way to determine where this line is. It is ultimately a judgment call, hinging on the applicable standard of proof.

Persuasion theorists hold that when the involvement of a person in the outcome of a controversy is high, as is the case for a suspect in an investigation, the quality of evidence matters more than the quantity.[47] Findings in this line of research suggest that increasing the number (quantity) of items of evidence does not necessarily increase the likelihood that a certain proposition is proven (or negated). In fact, the more evidence becomes available, the less certain an adjudicator may become about the facts of a case, as more non-cumulative evidence may generate more plausible explanations. Accordingly, the judge's confidence in a given judgment may diminish as more additional evidence becomes available.[48]

Evidence is called *cumulative* when it proves a proposition that is already proven by another item of evidence. If the available evidence has already given the adjudicator such a strong categorical belief in the proposition that he considers further evidence could not change that belief (that is, he thinks the new evidence cannot defeat the old), adding additional evidence will not advance the fact-finding process. Under such conditions, and if allowed by the applicable legal framework, cumulative evidence may thus be left out of the evidential dataset.[49] However, the above findings on the persuasiveness of the appropriate amount of evidence can never overrule legal obligations of transparency and case file composition, nor should it justify selective and biased evidence gathering and presentation.

9.4.6. Harnessing Arguments

It is good practice to think strategically and anticipate possible defence lines or counterclaims the defence may bring against the arguments put forward by the investigative team. Thus, the investigator should well understand what kind of

[46] Sinnott-Armstrong, 2018, p. 156, see *supra* note 24.

[47] See, for example, Richard E. Petty and John T. Cacioppo, *Communication and Persuasion: Central and Peripheral Routes to Attitude Change*, Springer, New York, 1986; Shelly Chaiken, *The Heuristic Model of Persuasion, Social Influence: The Ontario Symposium*, Erlbaum, Hillsdale, 1987; Shelly Chaiken, Akiva Liberman and Alice H. Eagly, *Heuristic and Systematic Information Processing Within and Beyond the Persuasion Context, Unintended Thought*, Guilford Press, New York, 1989; Gass and Seiter, 2018, p. 214, see *supra* note 35.

[48] De Smet, 2020, p. 109, see *supra* note 2.

[49] *Ibid.*, p. 110.

claims he or she is making in the final report. The latter will typically include four types of claims:[50] (a) claims of fact; (b) claims of definition; (c) claims of value; and (d) claims of policy.

Claims of fact involve a description of reality. They assert that a given factual circumstance is the case and can be verified independently of the arguers. We proposed above that the essence of investigation is fact-finding and that all parties should agree on the facts first.

Claims of definition (or interpretation) concern meaning or interpretation. In investigation, this will mainly concern whether the established facts fall under the legal provisions sanctioning the alleged behaviour; which is to say the legal qualification of the facts.

Claims of value involve judgment, that is, an appraisal or evaluation. An example is when a defence lawyer frames the fraud of her client as an act of goodwill (for example, 'it was wrong, but my client did it for a good reason, to at least avoid more harm for the entire sector').

Claims of policy are about action. They state what should be done or not (for example, a recommendation to an organization to change its rules on consultancy after an investigation brought to light systematic fraud).

In addition to claims of fact and definition, legal disputes typically also involve *claims of procedure*.[51] Defence mechanisms (for lawyers), also called '*stance*', include challenges to:[52]

- the facts, see the advice to 'focus on facts if they work in your favour, if not…';
- the definitions: 'redefine (reframe) the terms('fraud?'), if that doesn't work';
- the quality of the evidence: 'argue your opponent's argument is less important or credible than it seems', or finally;
- the relevance: 'surely, the Prosecutor is not interested in such cases and discussion is irrelevant'.

These defences are often combined and have a regressive nature. For example, referring to a matter of definition implies consenting to the facts, and referring to a justification (value), implies admitting the wrongdoing.[53]

[50] Zarefsky, 2019, p. 64, see *supra* note 22.

[51] *Ibid.*, p. 82.

[52] Heinrich, 2017, p. 131, see *supra* note 35.

[53] Zarefsky, 2019, p. 71, see *supra* note 22.

	Controversy	Central Question
Claim: 'You transferred the advance payment to your own account!' **Counter-Claim:** 'I never received it.'	Facts	Is it the case? Did beneficiary take possession of funding or not?
Claim: 'You took the advance payment!' **Counter-Claim:** 'I just borrowed it for a week.'	Interpretation	How should we call the act? Can this act be legally characterized as misappropriation?
Claim: 'You embezzled the advance payment!' **Counter-Claim:** 'That's only fair, after waiting so long for my previous payment.'	Value	Was it justified?
Claim: 'You should have reported fraud!' **Counter-Claim:** 'I will explain in court.'	Policy	Is this the right forum or paradigm?

Illustration 9.9: Harnessing claims.

Argumentation theory proposes that arguments can be bolstered against counter-arguments by using:[54] (a) guarding terms; (b) assuring terms; (c) evaluative or normative language; and (d) discounting terms.

'Guarding terms' make premises less vulnerable to objections by avoiding absolute statements.[55] Examples include avoiding words like 'in all cases' or 'certainly', but to replace these quantifiers by 'a significant chance', 'many', 'most', 'often' or 'I believe', 'I think', 'I suspect', or omitting quantifiers altogether (for example, 'people in that situation turn to fraud').

'Assuring terms' suggest that there is a reason for a claim, without specifying what that reason is or explaining the searches done and sources used.[56] Common examples include formulations like: 'I assure that we looked for another explanation', 'of course', 'obviously' and 'as a matter of fact'. Abusive

[54] Sinnott-Armstrong, 2018, pp. 120–147, see *supra* note 24.

[55] *Ibid.*, p. 122.

[56] *Ibid.*, p. 127.

assuring includes phrasing like:[57] 'you would have to be blind not to see that …' or 'everybody who knows anything about keeping accounting records knows that you falsified the registered transactions'.

A third way to block counter-arguments is to use evaluative or normative language, for instance when calling something 'good' or 'bad' (also: 'safe', 'best', 'poor', like in performance). This is basically saying it (does not) meet the relevant standards without specifying what those standards are. The claim's vagueness makes it harder for opponents to object it.

Finally, the arguer can anticipate and defuse objections by using 'discounting terms'[58] like the 'but' in 'the company won several procurement contracts, *but* faces financial problems' versus 'the company faces financial problems *but* won several procurement contracts': what comes after 'but' suggests more importance and hence prevails in dictating action. Other discounting terms include 'whereas' and 'though'. Raising the objection and responding to it (discounting) makes critics more reluctant to object to your premises.[59]

9.5. Scenario Approaches

9.5.1. Description

Argumentative reasoning does not explicitly allow the construction and comparison of alternative scenarios in order to maintain an overview of a mass of evidence. This is precisely the strength of the third approach to evidence: the scenario approach (sometimes also called the story-based or narrative approach). It consists of narrating an explanation to create, evaluate and select scenarios, which is to say hypotheses, about an action (or event), developing a chronological and causal description of that action.[60]

The term *script* is used by psychologists to refer to a person's subjective point of view, his or her mental representation of a certain type of event or situation.[61] Scripts are the most common narrative framework used in the scenario approach. They contain general background knowledge, a mixture of implicit assumptions and explicit assertions about the event.

[57] *Ibid.*, p. 128.

[58] *Ibid.*, p. 133.

[59] *Ibid.*, p. 136.

[60] Peter J. van Koppen and Anne Ruth Mackor, "A Scenario-Approach to the Simonshaven Case", in *Topics in Cognitive Science*, 2020, vol. 12, no. 4, pp. 1132–1151.

[61] Roger C. Schank and Robert P. Abelson, *Scripts, Plans Goals and Understanding: An Inquiry Into Human Knowledge Structures*, Psychology Press, Hove, 1977.

When listening to a story about a diner in a restaurant, the listener will, for instance, be tempted to include routine restaurant rituals (for example, waiting for table, receiving the menu, having dinner and paying the check) in his reconstruction of events, even if some of these events were not mentioned in the account.

Illustration 9.10.: The 'going-to-a-restaurant' script.

9.5.2. The Power of Stories

Story-telling is a widely used rhetorical tool aimed at making a case more persuasive in legal contexts.[62] The reconstruction of what happened is central to adjudication, and story construction is believed to be a core cognitive process by which facts in adjudication are determined.[63]

Empirical research suggests that when dealing with a mass of evidence, it is much easier for anybody to construct scenarios that explain the evidence instead of building the arguments based on evidence alone.[64] Reasoning about evidence gathered in investigations automatically comes in terms of causal explanations,[65] and storytelling is arguably the most natural means of making sense of criminal evidence. Thus, the scenario approach is arguably the most cognitively feasible in that it makes use of the very processes people actually use when reasoning through a great deal of evidence.[66]

It can be argued that constructing stories about what might have happened is actually the best way for investigators to structure the information they gather. These stories make sense of the available evidence by explaining what might

---

62 See, for example, Philip J. Mazzocco and Melanie C. Green, "Narrative Persuasion in Legal Settings: What's the Story?", in *The Jury Expert*, 2011, vol. 23, no. 3, pp. 27–38; for a recent survey of Belgian magistrates who all reported trying to find a story that could explain the indictment, see Pieter Tersago, Miet Vanderhallen, Joelle Rozie and Sara-Jane Mclntyre, "From Suspect Statement to Legal Decision Making How Do Judges Weigh the Evidence?", in *Zeitschrift Fur Psychologie* [*Journal of Psychology*], 2020, vol. 228, no. 3, p. 181.

63 Nancy Pennington and Reid Hastie, "A Cognitive Theory of Juror Decision Making: The Story Model", in *Cardozo Law Review*, 1991, vol. 13, pp. 519–557.

64 Nancy Pennington and Reid Hastie, "The Story Model for Juror Decision Making", in Reid Hastie (ed.), *Inside the Juror: The Psychology of Juror Decision Making*, Cambridge University Press, 1993, pp. 192–221.

65 Pennington and Hastie, 1991, see *supra* note 63.

66 Prakken, Bex and Mackor, 2020, p. 1057, see *supra* note 6.

have caused the evidence to be available,[67] by offering a chronological and causal description of the event(s) under investigation.[68]

9.5.3. Combinations

Whereas an argumentation starts with evidence and uses a warrant to come to a conclusion, a scenario builds from a hypothesis to explain the evidence found by means of causal reasoning.

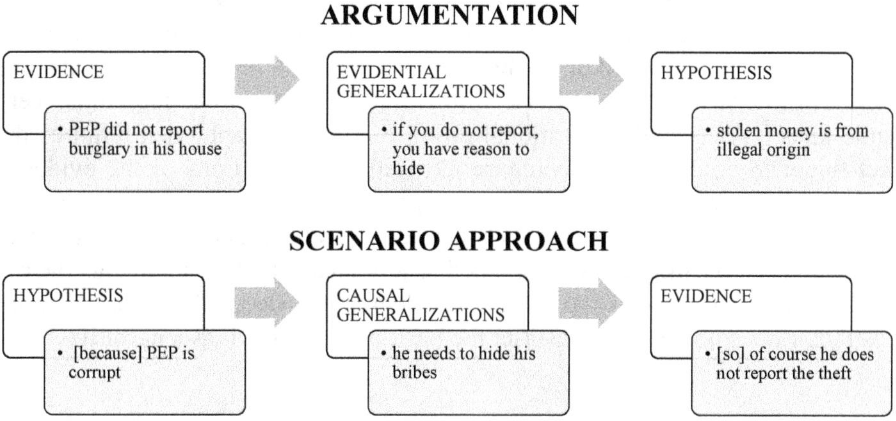

Illustration 9.11.: Argumentation versus scenario building.[69]

An investigator can use a scenario approach in conjunction with standard argumentation by embedding the evidence in a convincing narrative. Not surprisingly, researchers find that stories with strong arguments are more persuasive than stories with weak arguments.[70] Yet, even weak arguments become more persuasive when embedded in stories.[71] However, the strength of the arguments will considerably increase the persuasive impact of a story, particularly if the audience is initially rather sceptical toward an issue. This research counters

[67] Floris Bex, Hendrik Prakken, Chris Reed and Douglas Walton, "Towards a Formal Account of Reasoning About Evidence: Argumentation Schemes and Generalisations", in *Artificial Intelligence and Law*, 2003, vol. 11, no. 2, pp. 125–165.

[68] van Koppen and Mackor, 2020, see *supra* note 60.

[69] See John Eligon, "For South Africa's Leader, Being a Burglary Victim Spells Trouble", *New York Times*, 10 June 2022.

[70] Constanze Schreiner, Markus Appel, Maj-Britt Isberner and Tobias Richter, "Argument Strength and the Persuasiveness of Stories", in *Discourse Processes*, 2018, vol. 55, no. 4, pp. 371–386.

[71] *Ibid.*

the idea that people might be carried away by a story,[72] leaving less cognitive resources and motivation to carefully process the strength of arguments. Thus, argument strength seems to play a similar role in narrative and non-narrative persuasive contexts.[73]

Visual evidence is very persuasive, but remains highly dependent on the narratives that surround the images.[74]

9.5.4. Alternative Stories

Scenario construction can be a risk. Investigators might be tempted to create a scenario of what happened on the basis of one, a few, or all known facts at some stage of the investigation. This scenario is then also used to explain those very same facts.[75] As a model of rational proof, the scenario approach requires the fact-finder to construct and compare alternative explanations of the evidence gathered.[76] The essence of the scenario approach is that fact-finding in criminal procedures should take the form of constructing and comparing alternative scenarios about what might have happened. The scenario that best explains the evidence should, if it does so to a sufficient degree, be accepted as true.[77] The investigator does not only reconstruct the past, but presents it as a narrative.[78]

---

[72] Psychologists call this 'transportation'; that is, the effect of narratives to engage the recipient and transport him or her into the world of the story (see, for example, Melanie C. Green and Timothy C. Brock, "The role of Transportation in the Persuasiveness of Public Narratives", in *Journal of Personality and Social Psychology*, 2000, vol. 79, no. 5, pp. 701–721.

[73] See Schreiner, Appel, Isberner and Richter, 2018, see *supra* note 70, and research quoted there.

[74] Keith Hiatt, "Open Source Evidence on Trial", in *Yale Law Journal Forum*, 2016, vol. 125; Floris Bex *et al.*, "Sense-Making Software for Crime Investigation: How to Combine Stories and Arguments?", in *Law Probability and Risk*, 2007, vol. 6, nos. 1–4, pp. 145–168.

[75] Anne Ruth Mackor, "Novel Facts: The Relevance of Predictions in Criminal Law", in *Strafblad: tijdschrift voor wetenschap en praktijk*, 2017, vol. *15, no.* 2, pp. 145–156.

[76] Prakken, Bex and Mackor, 2020, p. 1056, see *supra* note 6.

[77] Willem A. Wagenaar, Peter J. van Koppen and Henricus F.M. Crombag, *Anchored Narratives: The Psychology of Criminal Evidence*, St. Martin's Press, New York, 1993.

[78] Guillaume Louis, «Enquête policière et techniques d'enquête: un regard scientifique» ["Police Investigation and Investigative Techniques: A Scientific View"], in *Criminologie*, 2021, vol. 53, no. 2, p. 3: "L'enquêteur non seulement reconstruit le passé, mais il en propose une narration".

Research experiments indicate that when the defence presents a written alternative story to the one in the police report (instead of just claiming innocence), even without adding new evidence, this still reduced the perception of guilt and the likelihood of being charged. The alternative story implies that the evidence is not as incriminating as the summary of the preliminary investigation suggests.

Illustration 9.12.: The power of an alternative story.[79]

9.5.5. Scenario Qualities

For a story to 'stick', it should be anchored internally and externally.[80] External anchoring means that the story must be linked to the available evidence by plausible evidential generalizations enabling one to make correct inferences (see above). Internal anchoring means that the story should conform to the background knowledge of the presenter and adjudicator. Thus, stories should at least contain a sequence of events on a timeline. They also become stronger if the connections between the events it contains are not just temporal but also causal (for example, the president of an evaluation committee raising his voice will impact evaluators) or intentional (for example, a member of the evaluation committee offering privileged information on a tender to a bidder will expect the latter to use it).

In addition to coherence with general background knowledge (see the concept of scripts, explained above) and support – or at least no contradiction – by the available evidence, the strength of any scenario also depends on internal coherence.[81] This relates to qualities of consistency (for example, statements within a scenario should not contradict each other), completeness (for example, the story contains initiating events which cause the main actor to have intentions, which give rise to actions, which have consequences)[82] and cognitive ease (a simple and smooth story, covering as much evidence as possible).

[79] Susanne M. Schmittat, Birte Englich, Lyane Sautner and Petra Velten, "Alternative Stories and the Decision to Prosecute: an Applied Approach Against Confirmation Bias in Criminal Prosecution", in *Psychology, Crime & Law*, 2022, vol. 28, no. 6, pp. 608–635.

[80] Bex *et al.*, 2007, p.148, see *supra* note 74.

[81] See, for example, Amalia Amaya, "Inference to the Best Legal Explanation", in Hendrik Kaptein, Henry Prakken and Bart Verheij (eds.), *Legal Evidence and Proof: Statistics, Stories, Logic*, Ashgate, Farnham, 2009, pp. 135–160; Paul Thagard, "Evaluating Explanations in Law, Science and Everyday Life", in *Current Directions in Psychological Science*, 2006, vol. 15, no. 3, pp. 141–145; John R. Josephson, "On the Proof Dynamics of Inference to the Best Explanation", in *Cardozo Law Review*, 2001, vol. 22, p. 1628.

[82] Henry Prakken, presentation at the OLAF conference on "Judgement and Decision-Making in Investigations", 7 December 2022.

9.5.6. Inference to the Best Explanation

The scenario qualities described above can help in assessing which story is the most plausible. A story with high coverage (a strong match between evidence and story) and coherence (a consistent, complete and realistic story) will have great appeal, but other stories might also remain credible.[83] In order to convict a defendant, the evidence should not only better match the guilty scenario than other innocent scenarios (falsification). Ideally, the accepted story should be the sole narrative that best explains all the evidence.[84]

Inference to the Best Explanation ('IBE')[85] is a form of inductive reasoning in which one selects a story that explains the evidence better than other propositions.[86] It is a decision rule proposing that the acceptance of hypotheses and theories should be pegged to the explanatory virtues of the various candidates under consideration. Thus, it involves comparing hypotheses to identify the one that best accounts for the established facts.[87]

In practice, IBE works as follows:[88] (a) the fact-finder is presented with a finite amount of evidence; (b) from this evidence, it is possible to infer a number of hypotheses, scenarios or narratives, which each explain (part of) the available evidence in a different manner; and (c) the hypothesis which, if true, would best explain the available evidence should, according to IBE, be retained as the correct factual finding.

This process is *abductive* in nature,[89] to the extent that plausible explanations must be generated from the evidence. At the same time, it is also a process of elimination, or at least ranking, of explanations until only one remains as the best. Thus, if we can figure out which among the possible hypotheses for explaining the facts in question does the best job of explaining them, then that is the hypothesis to be accepted as true. The result is acknowledged to be fallible

83 Pennington and Hastie, 1991, see *supra* note 63.

84 Peter J. van Koppen, *Overtuigend bewijs: Indammen van rechterlijke dwalingen* [*Convincing Evidence: Reducing the Number of Miscarriages of Justice*], Nieuw Amsterdam, Amsterdam, 2011.

85 Gilbert H. Harman, "The Inference to the Best Explanation", in *The Philosophical Review*, vol. 74, no. 1, p. 88.

86 Moa Lidén, "Confirmation Bias in Investigations of Core International Crimes: Risk Factors and Quality Control Techniques", in Agirre, Bergsmo, De Smet and Stahn (eds.), 2020, p. 489, see *supra* note 2.

87 Sinnott-Armstrong, 2018, p. 202, see *supra* note 24.

88 De Smet, 2020, p. 97, see *supra* note 2.

89 See Section 2. of Chapter 1 for an introduction to abduction, as a principal way of reasoning in investigations.

(IBE does not claim that the best explanation is necessarily a perfect explanation) but held to be generally reliable.

Flaws in IBE reasoning include instances when:[90]

- the observation is not accurate (for example, figures in the company's account are misinterpreted by the investigative team);
- the hypothesis does not really explain the observation (for example, it is not Covid-19 that led to a dramatic drop of turnover but a failed take-over bid in Asia);
- the comparison is biased because a competing hypothesis is better than the arguer thinks or because the arguer overlooked an alternative hypothesis that provides an even better explanation (for example, the company turned to fraudulent practices because of extortion after cyber-hacking).

9.6. The Presentation of Evidence

9.6.1. 'Telling or Selling'

The selection and presentation of evidence at the end of the investigation should be impartial and respectful of the rights of defence. In accordance with the prevailing procedural rules, the suspect will have access to all the pieces of the file and be able to present his or her own arguments or story.

There is debate about how to balance the need for a fair and transparent presentation of evidence with the aim of making investigative reporting efficient. Should the investigative team report everything that has been done and found, or can it make a selection and present a coherent story? The question reveals a difference between the objectives of fact-finding (based on accuracy goals: individuals strive to form an accurate belief or judgment) and persuasion (based on directional goals: individuals seek a particular desired conclusion).[91]

From a 'selling' (persuasion) perspective, the findings of the investigation can be best presented as a story, containing only the consistent components.[92] As set out above, explanations naturally come in a causal story structure[93] and any story can be made more credible, even at the expense of being less likely, if

---

90 Sinnott-Armstrong, 2018, p. 203, see *supra* note 24.

91 Ziva Kunda, "The Case for Motivated Reasoning", in *Psychological Bulletin*, 1990, vol. 108, no. 3, pp. 480–498.

92 Lance Bennett, "Rhetorical Transformation of Evidence in Criminal Trials: Creating Grounds for Legal Judgment", in *Quarterly Journal of Speech*, 1979, vol. 65, pp. 311 and 321: "[a] story is an elegant symbolic framework in which a large amount of information can be organized, compared, tested, and interpreted to yield a clear judgment about disputed versions of an action […]. If the tactics through which evidence is introduced in a case are not aimed at establishing the status of the evidence within the overall story, the evidence simply won't make sense".

93 Bex *et al.*, 2007, p. 147, see *supra* note 74.

filled with internally consistent details. Whereas the detail of an account can be perceived as enhancing its accuracy, it in fact relates more to credibility.[94] Less is sometimes more, when it contributes to a consistent story. Moreover, the representativeness heuristic[95] will make the presentation of (real) findings as a 'typical corruption' case - with for instance fake identities, off-shore constructions and middlemen - very salient in the adjudicator's mind and increase the credibility of the story.

The investigator should however be aware of the risk for, and avoid conscious use of the narrative fallacy. This is a thinking error, occurring when fact-finders attempt to use narratives in order to make sense of insufficient information, but choose the wrong or an over-simplifying narrative and so end up distorting the evidence presented.[96] Stories feel better than randomness but can never compensate for significant, noticeable gaps in the findings of the investigations.

9.6.2. Expressing Uncertainty

The choice between 'telling or selling' the results of the investigation also brings up another question about whether to express uncertainty about the findings of the investigation, and, if so, how this should be expressed. Several smaller scale studies have revealed conflicting information about whether explicitly acknowledging (either numerically or verbally) uncertainty enhances or undermines the extent to which people trust or find the information credible.[97] Communicating uncertainty might have negative consequences, such as signalling incompetence, encouraging critics and decreasing trust. By contrast, transparency might build rather than undermine trust.[98]

In the latter view, fact-finders should resist the natural urge to present unequivocal and categorical findings, but rather:

- strive for greater precision and transparency about the doubts and uncertainties that still remain after the investigation has been closed;
- identify the reasons for those doubts and uncertainties;

---

[94] Erik Rassin, "Heuristieken", in Peter J. van Koppen, Jan W. de Keijser, Robert Horselenberg and Marko Jelicic (eds.), *Routes van het recht: Over de rechtspsychologie*, Den Haag, Boom juridisch, 2017, p. 408.

[95] See Section 6.8.3.4. of Chapter 6.

[96] Doron Menashe and Hamutal E. Shamash, "The Narrative Fallacy", in *International Commentary on Evidence*, 2006, vol. 3, no. 1.

[97] Anne Marthe van der Bles *et al.*, "Communicating Uncertainty About Facts, Numbers and Science", in *Royal Society Open Science*, 2019, vol. 6, no. 5, p. 27. We note that the studies concerned scientific uncertainty, so it is not sure if these findings can be transposed as such to the field of investigation and prosecution.

[98] *Ibid.*, p. 2.

- give details about the limitations of the investigation and how this has affected the weight of its evidential dataset;
- identify gaps in the evidence and acknowledge the potential impact on the findings;
- mention questions that may still remain concerning the trustworthiness of the evidence;
- expose potential inferential weaknesses and problematic generalizations that were relied upon.[99]

By providing such nuanced and transparent description of the strengths and weaknesses of every finding, including the reasoning, method and limitations on which it relies, the receiver of the report is given maximal insight in the justifications for each of the findings and is thereby able to critically evaluate them.[100]

Until more research is conducted, it is however difficult to reach firm conclusions about these mixed findings across domains about the way and extent to which communicating uncertainty affects the perceived credibility of, and trust in, both the message and the communicator.[101] The preliminary conclusion that explicitly acknowledging uncertainty does not always lead to an inherent decrease in trust or credibility, though, is worth noting.[102]

9.6.3. A Combination

The investigative report will often combine argumentation and narrative. There is no clear consensus in the existing research about which presentation format is best. Regardless, a number of studies note that:

- statistical proof is more effective than anecdotal or narrative proof when making generalizations, when there is *a lot of evidence,* or when the receiver involvement is *high*;[103]
- narrative proof works best when narratives are *vivid* or when receiver involvement is *low*;[104]

---

[99] See De Smet, 2020, p. 143, see *supra* note 2, referring to international fact-finders (in International Criminal Court cases).

[100] *Ibid.*, p. 143.

[101] van der Bles *et al.*, 2019, p. 26, see *supra* note 97.

[102] *Ibid.*, p. 27.

[103] Mike Allen and Ray W. Preiss, "Comparing the Persuasiveness of Narrative and Statistical Evidence Using Meta-Analysis", in *Communication Research Reports*, 1997, vol. 14, pp. 131–152; Sang-Yeon Kim *et al.*, "Testing the Additive Model for the Effectiveness of Evidence on the Persuasiveness of a Message", in *Social Influence*, 2012, vol. 7, no. 2, pp. 65–77.

[104] See research cited in Gass and Seiter, 2018, p. 215, see *supra* note 35.

- starting with a *narrative or example and following up with statistics* to show that the example is not atypical, produces maximum effect;[105]
- a repetition of arguments is persuasive up to a certain point (about three repetitions) but decreases afterwards because of perceptions of source credibility;[106]
- the strongest arguments should not be presented in the middle of an argumentation;[107]
- evidence that is relatively non-salient, noncontroversial, uninteresting and unfamiliar can best be presented at the *end* of an argumentation;[108]
- salient, interesting, controversial and familiar material can better be presented at the *start* of an argument, because the audience starts with a high level of interest that decreases over time; [109]
- when the recipient is ambivalent about the issue[110] it can be effective to use two-sided messages (arguments in favour of a proposition and considering opposing arguments) *only* if refutation of these opposing arguments (that is, not just mentioning them!) is possible and when dealing with highly involved, intelligent receivers (as it makes the speaker seem more informed and more trustworthy);[111]

[105] John C. Reinard, "The Empirical Study of the Persuasive Effects of Evidence: The Status After Fifty Years of Research", in *Human Communication Research*, 1988, vol. 15, no. 1, pp. 3–59.

[106] Marc-André Reinhard *et al.*, "Less Is Sometimes More: How Repetition of an Antismoking Advertisement Affects Attitudes Toward Smoking and Source Credibility", in *Social Influence*, 2014, vol. 9, no. 2, pp. 116–132.

[107] See, for example, Donald E. Sikkink, "An Experimental Study of the Effects of the Listener of Anticlimax Order and Authority in an Argumentative Speech", in *Southern Speech Journal*, 1956, vol. 22, no. 2, pp. 73–78.

[108] See research quoted in Eyal Zamir and Doron Teichman, *Behavioral Law and Economics*, Oxford University Press, 2018, p. 534.

[109] Gass and Seiter, 2018, p. 220, see *supra* note 35.

[110] Erlinde Cornelis, Veroline Cauberghe and Patrick De Pelsmacker, "Two-Sided Messages for Health Risk Prevention: The Role of Argument Type, Refutation, and Issue Ambivalence", in *Substance Use & Misuse*, 2013, vol. 48, no. 9, pp. 741–752.

[111] Daniel J. O'Keefe, "How to Handle Opposing Arguments in Persuasive Messages: A Meta-Analytic Review of the Effects of One-Sided and Two-Sided Messages", in *Communication Yearbook*, vol. 22, pp. 209–249; Allen and Preiss, 1997, pp. 14, 131–152, see *supra* note 103; Gass and Seiter, 2018, p. 225, see *supra* note 35.

- forewarning of the topics and position the persuader wants to take, makes people more resistant to persuasion by encouraging counter-arguing[112] and increasing resistance.[113]

9.7. Concluding Remarks

This chapter presented three models of rational proof. Its key messages include that:

- Most proof in the real world happens in contexts of uncertainty. Whatever model of proof is used, the arguments, probabilities and stories presented are always defeasible.
- Methods concerning the presentation and contingent decision on proofs of facts in criminal law must be rational because of what is at stake. Fact-finders should only make factual claims which they themselves believe to be true and they are expected to be able to 'justify' their beliefs.
- 'PIF' investigations (concerning the protection of the financial interests of the EU) do not generally seem to call for an extensive use of probabilistic proof. Sometimes statistics (for example, container traffic) can be useful, but belief-type probabilities (for example, 'our findings strongly suggest') will typically support claims of argumentation or most plausible scenarios.
- Argumentation is the most common form of proof in PIF investigations. These arguments are almost always inductive, in that they are comprised of conclusions which can always be contested, whether in relation to the strength of the evidence used to support them or the generalizations drawn from them.
- Inductive arguments can be structured on the basis of inference schemes and are most potent (yet vulnerable) when they come in the shape of a subordinative argument.
- The creation of a narrative or story is the most important way people make sense of what happened, even in criminal justice contexts. However, the story should not replace or contradict evidence-based fact-finding.
- By presenting a coherent story, including a chronological account and causal explanations ('because') of what seems to have happened, the investigative team can present its best explanation for the alleged offence. Alternative stories should allow the trier of facts to choose the best story and decide whether this story meets the adequate standard of proof.

---

112 Gass and Seiter, 2018, p. 226, see *supra* note 35.

113 *Ibid.*, p. 228.

10

'To Intend or Not to Intend?', That Is the (Difficult) Question

Tom Willems, Anna Sagana and Jennifer Vanderputten*

10.1. Introduction

Other chapters in this volume have highlighted the importance of solid fact-finding and suggested different models for presenting proof in a rational way. This proof, or the evidence gathered supporting it, will need to demonstrate beyond reasonable doubt,[1] the existence of the reprehensible act or omission, and the guilty mindset.

Earlier, the concept of guilty mind ('*mens rea*') was described as a constituent part of any criminal offence. In contrast to the objective component of the crime ('*actus reus*'), it represents the subjective component of the crime, the 'guilty mind'.[2] The importance of the concept of intent in financial-economic misconduct in general, and investigations concerning the protection of the European Union's ('EU') financial interests ('PIF' investigations) in particular, can hardly be overstated:

- corporate investigators distinguish between non-compliance (no reporting duty) and fraud (to be reported) based on the lack of intent;[3]
- the European Court of Auditors distinguishes error and irregularity from fraud (and decides on its contingent reporting duties to EPPO or OLAF) on the basis of the intentionality of the act or omission;[4]

* **Tom Willems** is co-ordinator for inter-institutional relations at the European Anti-Fraud Office ('OLAF'). **Anna Sagana** is an Assistant Professor of Legal Psychology at Maastricht University. **Jennifer Vanderputten** is European delegated prosecutor at the European Public Prosecutor's Office ('EPPO'). This chapter is authored in the contributors' personal capacity and does not necessarily reflect the views of EPPO, OLAF or other institutions mentioned therein.

1 We remain, for the purpose of this chapter, within the realm of criminal investigations. For other standards of proof, see Section 6.6. of Chapter 6.

2 See Section 8.6.2. of Chapter 8.

3 Judith Seddon *et al.* (eds.), *The Practitioner's Guide to Global Investigations*, Global Investigations Review, 2020, p. 375.

4 Nikolaos Kilonis, "The ECA Statement of Assurance – Separating Errors From Alleged Fraud", *ECA Journal*, 3 July 2019, p. 45.

- the assessment of intent informs the reporting duties of other EU or Member State authorities to OLAF and/or EPPO;[5]
- the concept of intent is pivotal in deciding to open an administrative investigation of irregularities by OLAF, or a criminal investigation on PIF offences by the EPPO;[6]
- EPPO only investigates and prosecutes offences committed intentionally.[7]

To successfully prosecute EU fraud,[8] the investigator must prove not only the punishable material act (for example, using an incorrect or incomplete statement, or omitting to disclose mandatory information), but also guilty intent. Understanding, let alone proving, intent is not easy. Legal definitions come in many shapes, may differ by country, and are, in practice, sometimes based on rather arbitrary, intuitive judgments. This is why we now take the time to focus on the concept, to better understand its manifestations, and to explore what possibilities exist to better prove its occurrence.

To begin, we present the concept of intent and explain how it plays out in the legal framework of PIF investigations. We then propose a structured approach to test and possibly demonstrate its occurrence, along with the relevant models of rational proof presented in a previous chapter.[9] Questions we aim to address include: What exactly is intent, how can we prove it, and is this proof a matter of rational deliberation one of intuitive judgment?

---

5 See Chapter 5.

6 Article 24 of the Council Regulation (EU) No. 2017/1939 of 12 October 2017 implementing enhanced cooperation on the establishment of the European Public Prosecutor's Office ('the EPPO') ('EPPO Regulation') (https://www.legal-tools.org/doc/plfszr14/), and Article 12c of the 'OLAF Regulation', Consolidated text of Regulation (EU, EURATOM) No. 883/2013 of the European Parliament and of the Council of 11 September 2013 concerning investigations conducted by the European Anti-Fraud Office (OLAF) and repealing Regulation (EC) No. 1073/1999 of the European Parliament and of the Council and Council Regulation (Euratom) No. 1074/1999 (https://www.legal-tools.org/doc/6f0ede/).

7 The 'PIF Directive' (Directive (EU) No. 2017/1371 of the European Parliament and of the Council of 5 July 2017 on the fight against fraud to the Union's financial interests by means of criminal law (https://www.legal-tools.org/doc/3lsm7y4u/)) explicitly states that "Member States shall take the necessary measures to ensure that fraud affecting the Union's financial interests, corruption and misappropriation constitute a criminal offence when committed intentionally" and that the "notion of intention must apply to all the elements constituting those criminal offences. [...] Criminal offences which do not require intention are not covered by this Directive" (see Recital 11 and Articles 3(1), 4(2) and 4(3) of the PIF Directive).

8 See Articles 3 and 5 of the PIF Directive, *ibid.*

9 See Chapter 9.

10.2. An Understanding of Intent

10.2.1. General Concept

In its everyday sense, 'intent' is the "state of mind of one who aims to bring about a particular consequence".[10] It refers to the causation of actions, the sense of doing something agentively, deliberately, or for some kind of end or purpose, rather than, say, by accident or chance. It comprises an element of knowledge and an element of will: an intended act must be done knowingly and willingly.[11]

In law, terms like intent, guilt, culpability and free will are often understood in a specific legal manner. Though sometimes circular, consistent aspects of guilty intent across legal systems include:[12]

- acting *willingly*: a determination to perform or forbear a particular act in a particular manner, for instance when the general manager of a food processing plant gives the instruction to change the composition of the meat;
- acting *knowingly*: the same manager knows, or should know (in the case of negligence) that the result (a food poisoning) of his conduct (replacing expensive food additives by cheaper ones) is reasonably certain to occur. This does not mean he necessarily had the purpose or desire that it occur;
- acting on *purpose*: a resolution to use certain means to reach a specific end, for example, when the same manager gave instruction to reduce the price of the meat in order to win a tender for an EU-financed contract;
- being fully *aware* of the nature and consequences of the act to be performed: the actor has a clear foresight of the consequences of his actions and desires those consequences to occur). This would be the case when this manager delivers the same batch of bad meat to a competitor, with the aim that the latter be rejected as a candidate supplier and ruin his chances of further contracts with the EU.

The aforementioned manifestations of intent inform the distinction criminal law typically makes between the concepts of 'specific intent' and 'general

---

10 See the definition of 'intent' in *Oxford Learner's Dictionary*: "(*formal*) determined to do something, especially something that will harm other people[:] intent on/upon something – *They were intent on murder*".

11 Derek Edwards, "Intentionality and *Mens Rea* in Police Interrogations: The Production of Actions as Crimes", in *Intercultural Pragmatics*, 2008, vol. 5, no. 2, pp. 177–199.

12 See, for example, the agreed definitions across the United Nations system of fraud ("Any act or omission whereby an individual or entity *knowingly* misrepresents or conceals a fact") and corruption ("any act or omission that misuses official authority or that seeks to influence the misuse of official authority *in order to* obtain an undue benefit for oneself or a third party") (Conclusions of the High-Level Committee on Management at Its Thirty-Third Session, UN Doc. CEB/2017/3, 26 April 2017, para. 98(b) (emphasis added) (https://www.legal-tools.org/doc/x42dxbjg/)).

intent'. General intent refers to the intent to do what the law prohibits. It is not necessary to prove that the perpetrator intended the precise harm or the precise result that occurred (element of knowing). Specific intent refers to a particular state of mind that seeks to accomplish the precise act the law prohibits with a specific purpose (an element of willing, purpose and consequences).

Intent can be related to, but should be distinguished from, *motive*, which is the ultimate drive of the 'willing' component of intent. The manager in the examples above may start tampering with the quality of the meat to try save his company, because he is threatened by his shareholders to raise the profit margins, or simply because he is driven by greed. Although intent is a constituent part of the criminal offence, the motive is not. It cannot be used as a defence against the commission of the offence. At most, an 'acceptable' motive may be addressed in the sentencing part of the trial, when the court considers what punishment, if any, is appropriate. However, elucidating the author's motive can contribute significantly to the suspicion of guilty intent. For example, a gift from a contractor to an EU official will be assessed differently if it is explained by a romantic relation between their children or if it preceded a first invitation to participate in a public tender managed by the official. In the former case, the contractor might successfully argue the gift was done willingly and knowingly, but unrelated (purpose) to the invitation to tender.

10.2.2. The PIF Directive

Although the PIF Directive[13] highlights the importance of establishing guilty intent in the proof of a PIF offence, it is not very explicit about the specifics of what this entails. In line with the general approach in the EPPO setup to delegate much of the legal fine-tuning to the national legislations,[14] it is up to the Member States to fill in the details of the required intent in accordance with their national law. References to intent in the PIF Directive include, for EU fraud:[15]

- the use of "false [...] documents",[16] with the term 'false' already implying intent;

[13] See Article 3 of the PIF Directive, *supra* note 7.

[14] See Luca De Matteis, "The EPPO's Legislative Framework: Navigating Through EU Law, National Law and Soft Law", in *New Journal of European Criminal Law*, 2023, vol. 14, no. 1, pp. 6–17.

[15] Referring to the definition of fraud in Article 3(2) of the PIF Directive, see *supra* note 7, the OLAF web site defines fraud as a "deliberate act of deception intended for personal gain or to cause a loss to another party". Neither 'deliberate', nor 'deception' are mentioned in that Article 3(2). The web site quotation thus seems to be a reductive reading of EU fraud, as submitting an incomplete statement could also be the result of negligence. See OLAF, "Report Fraud" (available on its web site).

[16] Articles 3(2)(a), (b), (c) and (d) of the PIF Directive, see *supra* note 7.

- fraud in procurement-related expenditure committed "to make an unlawful gain",[17] integrating purpose in the intent;[18]
- fraudulently "disguising" the non-payment or wrongful creation of rights to VAT refunds,[19] again implying specific intent in the term used;

for corruption:

- a corrupt official is the person who requests, receives, or offers an advantage of any kind (purpose) "to act or to refrain from acting in accordance with his duty or in the exercise of his functions";[20]

for money laundering:

- the "conversion or transfer of property, *knowing* that such property is derived from criminal activity or from an act of participation in such activity, *for the purpose of concealing or disguising* the illicit origin of the property or of assisting any person who is involved in the commission of such activity to evade the legal consequences of his action".[21]

Regarding the challenge to demonstrate guilty intent of non-human actors, the PIF Directive expressly obliges Member States to take the necessary measures to ensure that legal persons can be held liable for PIF offences committed for their benefit by persons having a leading position within the legal person.[22] Moreover, the same article also expressly obliges Member States to take the necessary measures to ensure that legal persons can be held liable for negligence. This occurs when "the lack of supervision or control by one of their managers has made possible the commission, by a person under its authority, of

---

17 *Ibid.*, Article 3(2)(b).

18 The introductory wording of Article 3(2)(b), *ibid.*, sets a special qualification for intent (in comparison to the other PIF offences) and states that procurement fraud should be criminalized "at least" when committed in order to make an unlawful gain for the perpetrator or another by causing a loss to the Union's financial interest. The margin of interpretation left to Member States regarding the intentional element with the terms 'at least' may lead to issues regarding uneven protection of the Union's interests, as certain fraudulent activities may not be investigated or prosecuted in certain Member States (due to the lack of proven intent), despite being investigated and prosecuted in others (see Second report on the implementation of Directive (EU) 2017/1371 of the European Parliament and of the Council of 5 July 2017 on the fight against fraud to the Union's financial interests by means of criminal law, 19 September 2022, p. 13).

19 PIF Directive, Article 3(2)(d)(iii), see *supra* note 7.

20 *Ibid.*, Article 4(2).

21 Definition of 'money laundering' under EU law, since Council Directive 91/308/EEC of 10 June 1991 on prevention of the use of the financial system for the purpose of money laundering, p. 1 (https://www.legal-tools.org/doc/efaadb/).

22 See *ibid.*, Article 6(1).

any of the criminal offences referred to in the PIF Directive for the benefit of that legal person".[23]

10.3. Proving Intent

10.3.1. The Challenge

In the area of criminal fact-finding, no generally accepted and generally applicable normative framework of proof exists.[24] Factual arguments imply uncertainty, and this uncertainty is typically expressed in belief-type probability ('How likely is it that ...?'). Individual probability assessments about the same event often differ depending on the amount of information available to each person. In most cases, the only person who knows for certain whether the defendant is guilty is the defendant, and investigators, lawyers and judges in any particular case will only ever have partial (that is, incomplete) information about the defendant's guilt or innocence.[25] This inevitable uncertainty is even more pressing when considering intent.

Proving intent is key, but far from easy. Finding proof that the perpetrators acted with the requisite guilty mind is often the most difficult part of the investigation,[26] as it is very difficult to get evidence of what was going on in someone's head. This is unique and complicated in that it requires a retrospective evaluation of a person's mental state at the time of the alleged offense. What the suspect thought, knew, wanted, or could have known at the time of the offense cannot generally be determined using accurate, scientifically validated methods.[27] Moreover, many PIF offences concern breaches of complex and ambiguous regulatory law, open to different interpretations. The question is often not

[23] See *ibid.*, Article 6(2).

[24] Bart Verheij *et al.*, "Arguments, Scenarios and Probabilities: Connections Between Three Normative Frameworks for Evidential Reasoning", in *Law, Probability & Risk*, 2016, vol. 15, no. 1, p. 36.

[25] Norman Fenton, Martin Neil and David A. Lagnado, "A General Structure for Legal Arguments Using Bayesian Networks", in *Cognitive Science*, 2013, vol. 37, no. 1, p. 66.

[26] Tor-Geir Myhrer, "The Importance of Successful Co-operation Between Police Investigators and the Prosecution Service to Secure Efficient and Fair Court Proceedings and Verdicts", in Xabier Agirre, Morten Bergsmo, Simon De Smet and Carsten Stahn (eds), *Quality Control in Criminal Investigation*, Torkel Opsahl Academic EPublisher, Brussels, 2020, p. 1023 (https://www.toaep.org/ps-pdf/38-qcci/).

[27] Jeffrey Waal and Sjors Lighthart, "Over de empirie van gevaar en de normativiteit van should" [On the Empiricism of Danger and the Normativity of Guilt], in *Rechtsgeleerd Magazijn Themis*, 2023, vol. 6, p. 316.

who has committed the crime, but whether, in fact, a crime was committed at all.[28]

In criminology, the term 'neutralizations' refers to mental representations that reduce negative feelings internally before committing an offence, or when justifying them to the external world afterwards.[29] Examples include ignoring culpability by claiming the practices were normal (for example, 'everybody does it!'), or ignoring the seriousness of the acts by denying injury (for example, 'we got the job done. They should thank us.'). In terms of argumentation, a neutralization can be a justification, when it is supposed to show that the act was the right thing to do, or an excuse, when it admits that the act was wrong but tries to show that the agent was not fully responsible for doing it.[30] Neutralizations are often rooted in the professional environment of the person using them,[31] and white-collar crime is reported to be particularly prone to neutralizations.[32] This is because fraud is often intertwined with legitimate activities, allowing white-collar criminals to rationalize their crimes by attaching a moral argument to the offence, pointing to a higher purpose for the fraud (for example, 'normal business practice' or the 'necessity to act') that pre-empts an unsavoury explanation such as greed.[33] Moreover, the abstract and complex nature of white-collar crime is often more detached from clearly immoral acts, like

28 Maxime Reeves-Latour, "Stratagèmes criminels à la jonction des pouvoirs publics et des milieux d'affaires: les élites délinquantes et le processus d'octroi des contrats publics de construction", Ph.D. Thesis, Université de Montréal, 2017, p. 246.

29 Aleksandra Jordanoska, "The Social Ecology of White-Collar Crime: Applying Situational Action Theory to White-Collar Offending", in *Deviant Behavior: An Interdisciplinary Journal*, 2020, vol. 39, no. 11, pp. 1441–1442.

30 Walter Sinnott-Armstrong and Robert Fogelin, *Understanding Arguments: An Introduction to Informal Logic*, 9th ed., Cengage Advantage Books, Wadsworth, 2015, p. 12.

31 Paul M. Klenowski, "Learning the Good with the Bad: Are Occupational White-Collar Offenders Taught How to Neutralize Their Crimes?", in *Criminal Justice Review*, 2012, vol. 37, no. 4, pp. 461–477.

32 Scott M. Kieffer and John J. Sloan III, "Overcoming Moral Hurdles: Using Techniques of Neutralization by White-Collar Suspects as an Interrogation Tool", in *Security Journal*, 2009, vol. 22, no. 4, p. 320; see Van Onna for a different view, arguing that many white-collars are detached from conventional norms and hence do not need a neutralization to avoid cognitive dissonance (Joost Van Onna, *Blurred Lines: A Study of White-Collar Crime Involvement*, Ph. D. Thesis, Vrije Universiteit Amsterdam, 2018).

33 Frank S. Perri, "White-Collar Criminals: the 'Kinder, Gentler' Offender?", in *Journal of Investigative Psychology and Offender Profiling*, 2011, vol. 8, no. 3, p. 223.

harming another person, making the crime amenable to rationalization, within which stealing can be made to seem as though it is not stealing.[34]

In this setting, proving intent is often a very hard thing to do. Many alternative scenarios may go a long way in explaining why something happened, as in the example below.

> Jérôme managed to impress his father. To save the struggling family business, he succeeded in setting up a rum distillery in the French overseas territories, thanks to generous public funding. He did not only receive EUR 1,5 million from an EU programme promoting investment in the local industry, but also EUR 500,000 from an innovative technology fund and a EUR 350,000 national fund for the transition to green energy. The centrepiece for all three successful claims is the production from a new distillery installation, imported under preferential customs and tax regimes, thanks to a Ukrainian declaration of origin.
>
> Local farmers have now raised a complaint for irregularities and fraud. The first verifications of the grant files indicate that public money was spent on the repair of an old installation and that parts of the equipment were fabricated in the Peoples' Republic of China.
>
> Is this fraud or an overzealous son lost in the complexity of EU rules? The investigators are conflicted.

Illustration 10.1.: A smart business plan or fraud?

10.3.2. Evidence of Intent

When determining guilt as a basis for criminal justice intervention, the judge is faced with tremendous uncertainty. Intent generally cannot be directly observed, as it is an internal, mental or psychological condition, unavailable to direct observation.

The best and most direct evidence of criminal intent is the suspect's own account, when he or she truthfully responds to claims made within the investigation. This is why suspect interviews are quite important.[35] An admission or confession, especially those including a plan or detailing motivation for the sanctionable act(s) or omission(s), is a strong account of the interviewee's intentions. A good interviewer should make sure that the interview record contains language indicating the subject knowingly and intentionally committed the act and that the subject knew the act was wrong (for example, 'I would not have done it if the company had not been in such a bad financial state. I did not mean

[34] Max Bazerman and Francesca Gino, "Behavioral Ethics: Toward a Deeper Understanding of Moral Judgment and Dishonesty", in *Annual Review of Law and Social Science*, 2012, vol. 8, pp. 85, 95–96.

[35] For a book addressing the particularities of interviewing suspects in fraud and corruption investigations, see Tom Willems, *Behaviorally Informed Interviewing*, Maklu, Antwerpen, 2020.

to benefit personally.'). Other examples of direct evidence of intent include documents or recordings of the perpetrator, clearly expressing the intentions motivating the material acts.

In practice, direct evidence of intent is rare, and the investigator must look for and interpret surrounding facts and external circumstances to build a case for intent. It is now generally accepted that guilt is a legal-normative concept, which can be reconstructed and determined based on objective or normative standards of intentionality. Guilt is objective in the sense that the subjective components are partly derived from objective circumstances. It is normative in the sense that guilt is necessarily interpreted in terms of social norms, as social behaviour simply has to 'count as' intentional behaviour.[36]

The reconstruction of intent in terms of objective standards is the domain of *inference*, in which conclusions are reached by connecting circumstantial evidence by argument. The PIF Directive holds that the "intentional nature of an act or omission may [only] be inferred from objective, factual circumstances".[37] Such inferential leaps are not without risks and require careful consideration by the arguer and the recipient. To strengthen and improve the quality of the evidence gathered regarding possible criminal liability, it is crucial for any PIF investigation that the investigator attends to, and fully documents, the factual circumstances related to the conclusion of guilty intent.[38] Examples of indirect evidence of intent include (in relation to the example above):

- different versions of a grant application (for example, changing the word 'new installation' to 'modernized installation');
- email correspondence between Jérôme and a consultant inquiring whether he can apply for the local grant without mentioning the EU funding;
- audio-recordings of Jérôme assuring his father everything "will be arranged" regarding the financial figures of the company that would otherwise make them ineligible for grants.

10.3.3. Models and Standards of Proof

Reasoning with evidence is difficult. This is especially pertinent in court, where reasoning correctly about evidence can mean the difference between a rightful

36 Constantijn Kelk and Frank De Jong, *Studieboek materieel strafrecht* [*Manual of Substantive Criminal Law*], Wolters Kluwer, Deventer, 2019, p. 249.

37 Recital 11 of the PIF Directive, see *supra* note 7. See, for a similar wording, Article 28 of the United Nations Convention Against Corruption, 31 October 2003 (https://www.legal-tools.org/doc/hwuihi/): "Knowledge, intent or purpose required as an element of an offence established in accordance with this Convention may be inferred from objective factual circumstances".

38 See recommendation in OLAF Supervisory Committee, "Opinion no. 1/2021: OLAF's Recommendations Not Followed by the Relevant Authorities", 4 February 2021, point 67, p. 26.

conviction and a wrongful imprisonment. Rational models of proof come in three main forms.[39] In (a) scenario-approaches, the emphasis is on providing a globally coherent interpretation of the available evidence, given the most sensible explanatory scenarios; in (b) argumentative approaches, the emphasis is on the adversarial setting of evidential reasoning, focusing on managing conflicting information, and in (c) probabilistic approaches, the emphasis is on the uncertainty of evidential reasoning, and how that uncertainty comes in degrees that can be measured numerically.[40] Scholars explore and have developed hybrid forms of evidential reasoning combining elements of the three main models, without a clear winner.[41]

In the section below, we present a practical and sequential combination of elements of these rational models, which disentangle complex judgments of intent into several sub-questions. We do this with the understanding that the claim of guilt or innocence is always defeasible and the awareness that such a model should not overstretch the judge's cognitive resources. Research shows that even on important matters decision makers do not always get to the bottom of things, and, for instance, often neglect to read formulations of probability (expressing degrees of uncertainty) needed to accurately understand the strength and scope of conclusions.[42] However, the proof of guilt 'beyond reasonable doubt' forces the approach to be very critical, even sceptical, about the completeness and reliability of the evidence, the strength of the warrants, and the quality of the conclusions.[43] Let us see if we manage to find this balance.

10.4. A Modular Approach for Proving Intent

10.4.1. Introduction

The question whether the facts support (beyond reasonable doubt) proof of guilty intent in PIF investigations could be decomposed into: (a) an identification of main competing hypotheses and the attempt to falsify each of these; (b)

---

[39] See Chapter 9.

[40] Verheij *et al.*, 2016, p. 37, see *supra* note 24.

[41] See, for hybrid approaches combining scenarios, arguments and probability assessments to evidential reasoning, for example Verheij *et al.*, *ibid.*; Ludi Van Leeuwen and Bart Verheij, "A Comparison of Two Hybrid Methods for Analyzing Evidential Reasoning", in Michał Araszkiewicz and Víctor Rodríguez-Doncel (eds.), *Legal Knowledge and Information Systems*, IOS Press, Amsterdam, 2019, p. 53.

[42] See Penny Kloprogge, Jeroen P. van der Sluijs and Arjan Wardekker, *Uncertainty Communication: Issues and Good Practice*, Copernicus Institute, University of Utrecht, 2007, and research quoted there.

[43] Anne Marie Borg and Floris Bex, "Explaining Arguments at the Dutch National Police", in Víctor Rodríguez-Doncel *et al.* (eds.), *AI Approaches to the Complexity of Legal Systems XI–XII*, Springer, New York, 2021, p. 186.

an analysis of indications of intent using argumentation schemes; (c) a presentation of the evidence and its tentative strength in a Bayesian network; and, finally (d) an inference to the best explanation.[44]

The basis of this modular approach is inductive reasoning, which does not provide necessary proof, but often justifies suitable conclusions in contexts of uncertainty.[45] This decision model can thus never lead to absolute conclusions on intent. All evidence is, by definition, defeasible, and the parties are committed to attempting to falsify each other's evidence and arguments. This dialectic process should lead to legal proof.

10.4.2. Competing Hypotheses and Falsification

Throughout this book, authors have highlighted the need to consider different hypotheses explaining the investigated events and to gradually eliminate some of these hypotheses by falsification.[46] As a reminder: falsification involves looking for evidence that can disprove an idea or theory.[47] Instead of proving that you are right (in the example: 'Jérôme knew he was not entitled to claim the national grant!'), the focus here is trying to show that you are wrong (for example, 'What could have made Jérôme legitimately think he was entitled to claim funding from the three different sources?'). It is an invaluable process when trying to determine what most likely happened, as failed attempts at disproving a theory can indirectly act as support for the theory.[48]

In a judicial context, the competing hypotheses and contrastive explanations that support them are usually provided by the parties. They naturally formulate different, and usually conflicting, hypotheses and offer different explanations of the evidence. When, however, the investigators are not presented with competing claims, it is good practice to formulate alternative hypotheses *proprio motu*. This not only makes the case of the prosecution more solid, but also helps anticipate the defence's arguments, which might be presented last minute during the trial.

Competing hypotheses in PIF investigations typically take a standard form: one side suggests that misstatements are either the result of an error or a mistake,

---

44 See other chapters of this volume for these approaches, in particular Chapters 1 (falsification and hypotheses) and 9 (argumentation schemes, Bayesian networks and IBE).

45 David Zarefsky, *The Practice of Argumentation: Effective Reasoning in Communication*, Cambridge University Press, 2019, p. 3.

46 See, for example, Sections 1.4.3. of Chapter 1 and 8.2. of Chapter 8.

47 Karl Popper, *The Logic of Scientific Discovery*, Routledge, New York, 1959.

48 Henricus F.M. Crombag, Peter J. van Koppen and Willem A. Wagenaar, *Dubieuze zaken: De psychologie van strafrechtelijk bewijs* [*Dubious Cases: The Psychology of Evidence in Criminal Law*], Olympus, Amsterdam, 2006.

while the other side rather suggests they represent a conscious violation of the rules. In the first case, we are talking about a possible irregularity,[49] while the latter is a case of fraud. Errors are unconscious and may be accidental (clerical) or the result of insufficient care in the functioning of the supervisory and control systems. They may occur individually or alongside other mistakes and outright fraud. Mistakes are conscious and can be based on ignorance or misinterpreting rules (in the example: Jérôme honestly understood from his reading of the complex rules that the grant for innovation could be approved for the modernization of an existing installation, and was not limited to the purchase of new equipment).

A first step in the advocated approach here thus consists of validating or falsifying the competing hypotheses that remain at the end of the investigation, where the facts are systematically checked (and subsequently argued) against the following questions:

(a) 'Why fraud?', including:
   i. validation, like in 'What would it take for the answer to be yes?'; and
   ii. falsification, like in 'What would it take for the answer to be 'no'?';
(b) 'why irregularity?', including validation and falsification;
(c) 'why not fraud?', based on an assortment of subsidiary deductive questions in the format 'if a fraud, then [you would expect to find] elements of … deception (see hereafter)';
(d) 'why not irregularity' plus subsidiary deductive questions in the format 'if a mistake, then [you would expect to find] also other mistakes in similar cases'.

	IRREGULARITY	**FRAUD**
What Would It Take to Be an Error? (Not Knowing)		
Was there a process of verification of the grant application before signature and submission?		
Did the claim contain other clerical errors?		
What Would It Take to Be a Mistake? (Willing, but Misunderstanding)		
Was the company		

49 See Section 5.3.1. of Chapter 5, where, referring to Article 1(2) of Regulation 2988/95 of 18 December 1995 on the protection of the European Communities financial interests (https://www.legal-tools.org/doc/95p8lazw/), irregularities are defined as "any infringement of a provision of EU law by an economic operator prejudicing the EU budget".

involved in previous projects (without similar 'mistakes')?		
Did the company solicit further explanations?		
Are there any language issues, preventing a full understanding?		
Were the grant conditions ambiguous (new versus modernized installation)?		
If It Was a Mistake, Then...		
The application records should be transparent.		
The company did not claim other grants it might have been entitled to.		

Illustration 10.2.: Validation and falsification of competing hypotheses (with random results).

Asking investigators to invest time and capacity in proving that a misstatement or other material wrongdoing is the result of an error or a mistake might be a significant request. Some might argue this is the exclusive job of the defence, and something already expected, and generally well executed, by them. Our perspective is that the investigators strengthen their claim that a PIF offence has been committed by demonstrating and communicating that the investigation followed a procedure of progressive elimination of explanations consistent with mere irregularity.

10.4.3. Argumentation Schemes

10.4.3.1. Evidence, Warrants and Conclusions

Having one hypothesis (for example, guilty intent, hence fraud) stand out as the better one does not, of course, mean that it is factually correct. It only means that it is better than the alternative(s) under consideration. Hypotheses are tools and not findings, and they are always in need of further inductive and deductive verification. This is where argumentation steps in, the practice of justifying (*not* proving) conclusions (guilty intent) under conditions of uncertainty.

It was explained earlier that most argumentation in a legal setting is inductive, meaning that it is always defeasible and that the strength (probability) of a conclusion depends on its premises, that is the evidence presented.[50] This evidence comes in many forms, and it enables the formulation of conclusions by means of *warrants*. The latter are generalizable statements, implicitly legitimizing the inference that the evidence gathered counts as evidence for a particular claim.[51] A claim there was guilty intent can, for instance, rely on inductive reasoning comprising evidence and warrants as diverse as:

- a number of consistent witness statements (warrant that, in general, witness testimonies are credible);
- patterns of behaviour (warrant of analogy: this is a typical fraud scheme in that sector);
- indications of concealment (warrant that honest persons do not have to hide anything).

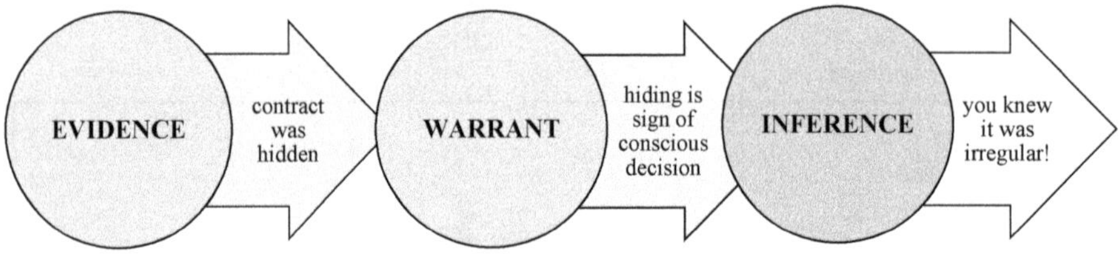

Illustration 10.3.: An inductive argument based on sign.

In the following sections, we present some argumentation schemes[52] that allow one to unify the findings of the investigation and claim there was guilty intent. Argumentation schemes can be thought of as semi-formal generalizations of the formal rules of logic, covering reasoning patterns in a specific, concrete setting.[53] They allow one to better understand and structure the relevant elements of the investigation file while identifying possible gaps. An additional advantage is that the use of such schemes requires careful ('System 2')[54] reasoning, going beyond the 'quick and dirty' decisions our intuition may readily offer.[55]

---

[50] See Chapter 9 for more detail on the different kinds of evidence.

[51] Zarefsky, 2019, p. 51, see *supra* note 45.

[52] Douglas Walton, Chris Reed and Fabrizio Macagno, *Argumentation Schemes*, Cambridge University Press, Cambridge, 2008.

[53] Floris Bex and Bart Verheij, "Stories About Evidence", in Robert Horselenberg, Vere van Koppen and Jan de Keijser (eds.), *Bakens in de rechtspsychologie: Liber amicorum voor Peter van Koppen* [*Beacons in Legal Psychology. Liber amicorum for Peter van Koppen*], Boom Criminologie, The Hague, 2020, p. 314.

[54] See Chapter 4.

[55] Zarefsky, 2019, p. 11, see *supra* note 45.

Argumentation schemes include: (a) arguments from sign; (b) arguments from cause; (c) arguments from example; (d) arguments from testimony; and (e) arguments from analogy. To some extent, these different categories overlap.

10.4.3.2. Arguments Based on Sign

Arguments from sign often make the strongest claims. They are based on the warrant of predictiveness, meaning that the presence of the sign enables the presence of the signified to be inferred. The key relationship is the coexistence of the two. If two events or things habitually occur together, and we notice one of them, it is a reasonable inference that the other is present as well.[56]

The strongest sign of guilty intent is any form of *deception*. Deception can be described as the deliberate attempt to create in another a belief which the communicator considers to be untrue.[57] It is sometimes considered to be an upgraded form of dishonesty, where lying is only deliberately stating false information, while deceiving additionally includes the urge to convince the other person of the truth of the lie. It incorporates the aim to mislead.

	Knowledge	Statement	Reality
Truth	+	+	+
Error-mistake	+	+	-
Deception	+	-	+

Illustration 10.4.: Truth, lie and error.

Indications of *deception* include (referring to the fictitious case example in Illustration 10.2.):

- concealment (for example, emails with the consultant are kept in an encoded folder or the declaration of origin of the equipment is missing);
- the (sudden) use of code-names in e-
- mail correspondence;
- the existence of false documents (for example, double versions of invoices or contracts);
- deviations from standard operating procedures (for example, EU project management is archived differently compared to other projects, or a consultancy contract is booked under a wrong section of the accounts);
- deviations from base line behaviour (for example, when a businessman is found to be very organized in his general management of the company, this

[56] *Ibid.*, p. 115.

[57] Aldert Vrij, *Detecting Lies and Deceit: Pitfalls and Opportunities*, 2nd ed., John Wiley and Sons, Chichester, 2008, p. 15.

warrants the inference that the erroneous claim is also the result of organized action and hence indicates intent);

- collusion to stick to the same story by persons invited for interview (for example, Jérôme and his father tell exactly the same story, even though the latter was not really involved in the project).

Other possible, but weaker, signs of guilty intent include:

- any form of destruction of evidence (for example, the 'typical' computer crash or IT replacement explaining the absence of evidence for the relevant period);
- indications of planning of the material act of the offence (for example, Internet history indicates searches on how to import Chinese equipment under favourable EU import regimes);
- disrespect of reporting or authorization rules or practices within the organization (for example, Jérôme did not consult his father on this project, even though the latter was known to be adamant of knowing everything what happened in the company);
- the presence of seemingly causeless complexity (for example, setting up a financial construction with offshore companies);
- the discovery of contingency plans in case of audit or investigation (for example, instructions to move evidence, or implement changes in bank accounts or corporate structure);
- the finding that other persons feel betrayed by Jérôme;[58]
- a lack of co-operation or even obstruction to the investigation.

10.4.3.3. Arguments Based on Cause

Many explanations we come up with for what happened depend on causal generalizations. When our car goes dead in the middle of the road after a recent check-up, our first reaction might be that it ran out of fuel because we believe all cars stop running when they run out of fuel and trust the car is in good shape following the check-up. In arguments from cause, the inference is thus about influence of one factor on another, referring mainly to causal explanations ('because …'). It relates to the mechanisms of story-building, the attempt to answer the question 'why did X happen?' by providing explanations for given effects.[59]

---

[58] In psychology, acts of betrayal are considered to be so strongly felt, that they are assumed to always be intentional. See Emma Barrett, "The Science of Betrayal", *CREST Security Review*, 4 August 2022.

[59] See Chapter 9 for the power of scenario- or story-building.

In relation to the assessment of guilty intent, inferences based on the warrant of cause speak to elements of opportunity, incentives and rationalizations. We can refer here to the 'fraud triangle',[60] where guilty intent is derived from:

- a motivational explanation (incentive): for example, Jérôme had to engage in fraudulent activities [because] to save the company of his father;
- an opportunity: for example, Jérôme decided to engage in fraudulent activities [because] his consultant had informed him of the generous national and international support schemes;
- a rationalization (neutralization): for example, Jérôme took the risk because it was clear that the French government wanted to save the island's economy and was hence happy to support any investment, without asking too many questions.

Causal reasoning relies on background assumptions of 'common knowledge' and an expectation of normality. It can be tested against (a) necessary and (b) sufficient conditions.[61] A necessary condition is a condition that must be present for an event to occur. Being a public official is, for instance, a *necessary* condition for being a passive corruptor, but it is not a *sufficient* condition for being corrupt. *Illusory correlation*[62] consists of pinpointing relationships between concepts, events, and other occurrences that are not in fact associated with each other. The arrival of Jérôme at the helm of the company can concur with a dramatic increase of turnover (correlation, suggesting engagement in fraudulent practices), but this can be due to circumstances outside of his will and management. An inaccurate perception of correlation leads to a false perception of cause and effect.

---

[60] Donald Cressey, *Other People's Money: A Study in the Social Psychology of Embezzlement*, The Free Press, New York, 1953. We remark that the fraud triangle has been criticized as an explanatory model for fraud, on the one hand because it does not take into account the perpetrator's abilities and capacity (better captured in the 'fraud diamond', see David T. Wolfe and Dana R. Hermanson, "The Fraud Diamond: Considering the Four Elements of Fraud", in *CPA Journal*, 2004, vol. 74, no. 12, pp. 38–42), and on the other hand because its underlying assumption of people as rational decision makers (see Gary S. Becker, "Crime and Punishment: An Economic Approach", in Nigel G. Fielding, Alan Clarke and Robert Witt (eds.), in *The Economic Dimensions of Crime*, Palgrave Macmillan, London, 1968) has been superseded by the heuristics- and cognitive bias-programme (see Daniel Kahneman, *Thinking, Fast and Slow*, Farrar, Straus and Giroux, New York, 2011, and Chapter 3 for many others).

[61] Sinnott-Armstrong and Fogelin, 2015, p. 217, see *supra* note 30.

[62] See, for example, Klaus Fiedler, "Illusory Correlation", in Rüdiger F. Pohl (ed.), *Cognitive Illusions: Intriguing Phenomena in Judgement, Thinking and Memory*, Routledge, London, 2016, pp. 115–133.

10.4.3.4. Arguments Based on Example

Arguments based on example are those that use specific instances to make a broader point or draw a general conclusion. In relation to PIF investigations, arguments from example beg the question: How many examples would be required to make for a case of error, mistake or fraud? The answer speaks to findings of:

- repetition (for example, number of occurrences of alleged 'errors'?);
- sample size (for example, did investigators check a representative number of significant containers to allege systematic under-evaluation fraud?);
- base rates: (for example, what would be an average or acceptable rate of errors in the company's accountancy?).

In a case of suspected inflation of personnel costs presented for reimbursement, the argument of fraud will gain traction if the high number of inflated claims discredits an explanation of clerical error. Likewise, an audit reporting that four out of ten verified cost claims show discrepancies raises stronger suspicions of fraud than a single finding.

10.4.3.5. Arguments Based on Testimony

Arguments from testimony rely on the reliability of the source making the statement and the credibility of the information provided. An assertion that "the accounts of a company have been cooked", has more weight (reliability) when based on the statement of an expert accountant than on a layperson's, and it is more credible when the accountant worked for the organization involved.

Interestingly, even when statistical evidence (for example, international trade figures show that only 0.3 per cent of Ukrainian export relates to distillery equipment) is equally capable of making a same proposition probable (here: the equipment could not originate from Ukraine), triers of fact privilege testimonial over statistical evidence.[63]

10.4.3.6. Arguments Based on Analogy

Arguments from analogy are about similarity (for example, 'we have seen this in other cases: son wanting to impress his father and ends up in trouble'). The model analogical warrant is that things that are alike in most respects are probably alike in the respect at hand.[64] They are considered to be the weakest kind of inference,[65] and potentially misleading.

---

[63] See Martin Smith, "When Does Evidence Suffice for Conviction?", in *Mind*, 2018, vol. 127, no. 508, p. 1198.

[64] Zarefsky, 2019, p. 111, see *supra* note 45.

[65] *Ibid.*, p. 113.

Compendia of 'red flags' in procurement procedures[66] are based on analogies. Such red flags do not mean that fraud exists, but they can reinforce a suspicion of fraud, based on the literature or extracted from the caseload of an investigative or audit body. Red flags for guilty intent include findings of the occurrence of fraud patterns (for example, creation of new companies with every new multi-annual financial framework, or the dissolving of a company soon after receiving public funding), and the identification of tendering conditions allowing favouritism (for example, short notice periods for participation, derogations from principle of open competition, *et cetera*).

Analogies in behaviour of the suspect can also serve to argue guilty intent. When, for instance, Jérôme never submitted any individual tax declarations, it would be more difficult to accept his explanation that he *forgot* to send in mandatory grant forms by oversight. Rather, his continuous neglect of reporting duties indicates a conscious and systematic behaviour which could warrant the suspicion of intent.[67]

10.4.3.7. An Argumentation Map

After the identification and testing of competing hypotheses, argumentation schemes as presented above can make for a second step of the intent assessment. The state of play at this stage can be presented in an argumentation map, containing the two competing scenarios (irregularity and fraud) and their main (counter-) arguments.

Below is a case example where Jérôme is required to explain how part of his grant administration went missing, whether because of a mistake (scenario A: Jérôme's explanation) or to obscure fraud (scenario B).

66 See, for example, the compendium of "Red Flags Suggesting a Fraud" of the European Court of Auditors, under "Procurement" (available on its web site).

67 Adapted from Myhrer, 2020, p. 1026, see *supra* note 26.

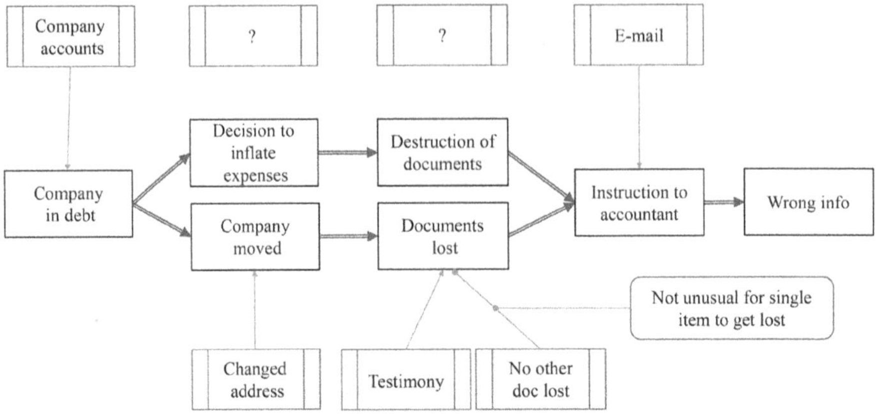

Illustration 10.5.: An argumentation map comparing two scenarios.

10.4.4. Expressing Probability

10.4.4.1. The Challenge

The great insight of argumentation theory is that it explains how all inferential reasoning depends on generalizations and that generalizations come in many different forms, some of which provide a strong warrant (for example, signs of deception), whereas others offer no warrant to speak of (for example, analogy with similar fraud). Argumentation schemes are thus useful for thinking methodically and analytically about inferences, but they do not explain how one is to assess the actual strength of the warrant of a particular argument. The justification for believing a proposition (here: the strength of an argument claiming there was intent) is a matter of ensuring that it is *sufficiently probable*, given one's evidence.[68] Probabilistic approaches to proof[69] analyse how hypothetical events are probabilistically related to the evidence and make the uncertainty of evidential reasoning more explicit. Its tools are premised on the idea that uncertainty comes in degrees that can be expressed (numerically)[70] and updated as a function of the evidence that is gathered.

10.4.4.2. Visual Presentations

The appropriate use of graphical visualizations may aid in ensuring a better understanding of the uncertainty of a given case.[71] Various researchers have

---

[68] Smith, 2018, p. 1198, see *supra* note 63, and research quoted there.

[69] See Chapter 9.

[70] Verheij *et al.*, 2016, p. 37, see *supra* note 24.

[71] Anne Marthe van der Bles *et al.*, "Communicating uncertainty about facts, numbers and science", in *Royal Society Open Science*, 2019, vol. 6, no. 5, p. 27.

proposed methods and models to analyse (parts of) legal cases in terms of probabilities and present these graphically.[72] Bayesian 'networks' are arguably the best known model.[73] They combine a graphical structure with *conditional probability tables*. Each node in the graph represents a probabilistic variable and has an associated table of the probabilities of the node's values, conditioned on the values of the node's parents in the graph. It thus provides for a visualization enabling one to process large volumes of complex information and to determine how a vast collection of evidence relates to one or more hypotheses.[74]

The probabilistic reasoning about legal evidence often boils down to a causal scenario, where:

a) the analysis includes some hypothesis H (normally the ultimate hypothesis that the defendant is or is not guilty); and
b) observe some evidence E (such as the whistle-blower's testimony);
c) the initial prior assumption of guilt (presumption of innocence) is 'attacked' by the (reliability and credibility of the) initial allegation and presented in a probability table, which is gradually updated taking into account the likelihood of the (new) evidence, which is the chance of seeing the evidence if H is true.

In practice, it is often not straightforward to perform a numerical, probabilistic analysis of the evidence, especially when attempting to model all the evidence and all the relevant interpretations.[75] Scholars have therefore developed some general guidelines, structuring the Bayesian networks on the basics of some generic patterns in legal decision-making. This includes distinctions between evidence corroborating or conflicting with the hypothesis (of the prosecution or the defence); the notion of dependency between different pieces of evidence, and the distinction between direct versus circumstantial evidence.[76]

---

[72] See, for example, John H. Wigmore, *The Principles of Judicial Proof or the Process of Proof*, 2nd ed., Little, Brown and Company, Boston, 1931; Terence Anderson, David Schum and William Twining, *Analysis of Evidence*, 2nd ed., Cambridge University Press, 2005, pp. 134–135; Fenton, Neil and Lagnado, 2013, see *supra* note 25. See also Charlotte S. Vlek, Henry Prakken, Silja Renooij and Bart Verheij, "A Method for Explaining Bayesian Networks for Legal Evidence with Scenarios", in *Artificial Intelligence and Law*, 2016, vol. 24, no. 3, pp. 285–324.

[73] See Section 9.3.4. of Chapter 9.

[74] Norman Fenton, Marin Neil and Daniel Berger, "Bayes and the law", in *Annual Review of Statistics and Its Application*, 2016, vol. 3, pp. 51–77.

[75] Bex and Verheij, 2020, p. 321, see *supra* note 53.

[76] These generic BN structures are called 'idioms'. See Amanda B. Hepler, Philip Dawid and Valentina Leucari, "Object-Oriented Graphical Representations of Complex Patterns of Evidence", in *Law, Probability & Risk*, 2007, vol. 6, nos. 1–4, pp. 275–293; Martin Neil, Norman Fenton and Lars Nielsen, "Building Large-Scale Bayesian Networks", in *Knowledge*

All or part of the findings of the investigation can thus be presented in a structured graphical representation of probabilistic relationships between two types of variables: evidence and hypotheses. As the graphical structure contains information about dependencies between variables, a Bayesian network is particularly suitable for modelling complex relations, for instance causal relationships between different hypotheses and pieces of evidence in a complex legal argument.[77] In addition to its powerful visual appeal, Bayesian networks have an underlying calculus (based on Bayes' theorem)[78] that determines the updated probability beliefs about all uncertain variables when any piece of new evidence is presented.[79]

In a case of assessing (the hypothesis of) guilty intent, the investigators might 'score' the different pieces of evidence as a function of their probative weight for guilty intent, starting with the initial allegation and adapting the conditional probability table as evidence is gathered during the investigation. Importantly, when sketching the Bayesian network, the evaluator can usefully run over the intent argumentation schemes presented above to identify and map all present and absent evidence of *mens rea*.

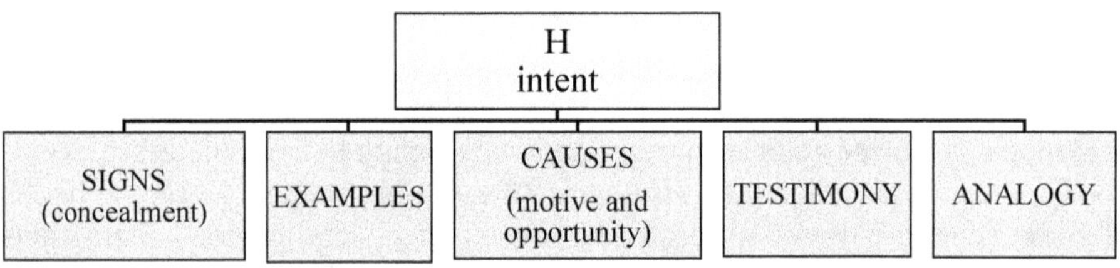

H guilty	**False**	**True**
SIGNS	**0.37**	**0.63**
Concealment	0.40	0.60
Obstruction	0.82	0.18
CAUSE	**0.65**	**0.35**
Motive	0.65	0.35
EXAMPLES	**0.38**	**0.62**
Correct administration in the past	**0.38**	**0.62**
TESTIMONY	**0.30**	**0.70**
Statement consultant	0.22	0.78
Statement father	1	0

Engineering Review, 2000, vol. 15, pp. 257–284; Fenton, Neil and Lagnado, 2013, p. 69, see *supra* note 25.

77 Fenton and Berger, 2016, see *supra* note 74.

78 See Section 9.3.4. of Chapter 9.

79 Fenton, Neil and Lagnado, 2013, p. 62, see *supra* note 25.

ANALOGY	**0.40**	**0.60**
Typical problem in that region/sector	0.40	0.60
OVERALL	**0.08**	**0.92**

Illustration 10.6.: A Bayesian network about intent.

These visualizations of evidence and the claims they support can be made with specialized software that can link components of the visualizations and pieces of text within source documents.[80]

When lay people are first introduced to Bayesian networks there is a tendency to recoil in horror at the thought of having to understand and complete a probability table. In general, fact-finders and lawyers are more trained in the use of non-probabilistic information and argumentation, rather than in estimating, calculating or updating probabilities.[81] Hence, it can be hard for investigators, prosecutors and judges to score and interpret evidence of a probabilistic nature and to combine this evidence with other, often non-numeric, kinds of evidence. Therefore, efforts have been made to developing verbal reporting techniques for probabilistic information suitable for the forensic domain.[82] However, this is still a relatively new and challenging field, and earlier contributors have highlighted the finding that there is substantial individual variability (or 'noise') in how people numerically represent probabilities and uncertainties in verbal statements (for example, 'it is very likely that …').[83]

Nevertheless, the great benefit of the Bayesian network and its probability tables is to make the investigator's assumptions explicit rather than hidden.[84] In practice, the very same assumptions that are required for such a table are normally made implicitly anyway! As much as this seems arbitrary and counter-intuitive, 'scoring' the different pieces of evidence as a function of their probative weight for guilty intent renders explicit a process that investigators otherwise do mentally and implicitly, thus making the process transparent and open for debate.

10.4.5. From Best Explanation to Beyond Reasonable Doubt

10.4.5.1. The Standard of Proof

Finally, what the legal puzzle requires for its resolution is typically a standard that demands more than probability, though less than certainty: 'beyond

[80] Floris Bex, Susan van den Braak, Herre van Oostendorp and Henry Prakken, "Sense-Making Software for Crime Investigation: How to Combine Stories and Arguments?", in *Law, Probability & Risk*, 2007, vol. 6, nos. 1–4, pp. 145–168.

[81] Verheij *et al.* 2016, p. 57, see *supra* note 24.

[82] *Ibid.*, p. 37.

[83] See Section 3.3.1 of Chapter 3.

[84] Fenton, Neil and Lagnado, 2013, p. 69, see *supra* note 25.

reasonable doubt'.[85] Testing and falsifying alternative explanations is a good start for proving beyond a reasonable doubt what a particular person knew or intended when they (c)omitted a certain act. Relatedly, identifying argument schemes based on the available evidence and plotting them out in probability charts is an efficient and transparent way of weighing the evidence. Yet, eventually the investigator will still have to demonstrate that the guilty hypothesis is the most reasonable one. The identification of the best explanation does not, however, automatically equal a sufficient explanation to meet the standard of proof. In the following sections, we explore how practitioners can further improve their analysis and presentation of the argument of guilty intent.

10.4.5.2. The 'Stopping' Problem

The 'stopping problem' refers to the challenge of finding a rational principle to decide when to stop acquiring evidence before making a decision. In other words, when does the judge have sufficient evidence when forming a probability judgment of intent? In this respect, scholars refer to the Keynesian weight of evidence. Keynes[86] pointed out that such decisions should rely on a combined assessment of probability (the balance of evidence in favour of a particular proposition) and weight of evidence (the quantity of evidence supporting that balance). As regards the latter, he advised the decision maker to consider the degree of completeness of the available information ('relevant knowledge'), but also of his 'relevant ignorance'[87] or the 'known unknowns'. The latter refer to factors that affect our probability relation and about which one is ignorant (for example, the ultimate beneficiaries of a bank transfer, suspected to be the return to a corrupt official). Different from the term 'known unknowns' (relevant ignorance), 'unknown unknowns' refers to unknown factors that might explain the turn of events (for example, Jérôme has gambling debts).[88]

The investigator (or prosecutor leading the investigation) can usefully consider these different parameters in order to decide when there is sufficient evidence to indict, bring to court, or dismiss. Often time and resource constraints will play an important role in such assessments.

---

85 See also Chapters 5 and 9.

86 John Maynard Keynes, "A Treatise on Probability", in Elizabeth Johnson and Donald Moggridge (eds.) *The Collected Writings of John Maynard Keynes: Volume VIII*, Macmillan, London, 1973.

87 Jochen Runde, "Keynesian Uncertainty and the Weight of Arguments", in *Economics and Philosophy*, 1990, vol. 6, no. 2, pp. 275–292.

88 Alberto Feduzi, "On Keynes's Conception of the Weight of Evidence", in *Journal of Economic Behavior and Organization*, 2010, vol. 76, no. 2, pp. 338–351.

10.4.5.3. Inference to the Best Explanation

The reasoning schemes above, and the checklist and visualization they inform, can lead to a set of arguments enabling judges to make the inferential leap from circumstantial evidence to a determination of guilty intent. Inference to the Best Explanation ('IBE') is a form of inductive reasoning in which one chooses a story that explains the evidence better than other propositions.[89] Such inferential leaps are however not without risks and require careful consideration by the arguer. Vulnerabilities include inferential fallacies, 'noise', and cognitive biases,[90] leading to either deficient reasoning or attributing disproportionate weight to particular aspects of the information at hand. Moreover, the assessment of the best explanation is not a straightforward and linear exercise,[91] and there is no clear set of criteria on offer to decide what makes for the 'best' explanation. These judgements are often of a holistic nature, based on global impressions and informed by heuristic processes of 'System 1'.[92]

When, however, the investigative team can demonstrate that (a) all reasonable hypotheses have been tested; (b) other reasonable explanations have been disproved; (c) the available evidence argues in favour of a specific explanation; and (d) that the relevant ignorance is limited, a single story may emerge of guilty intent that might meet the relevant standard of proof. In criminal cases, this will often be 'proof beyond reasonable doubt', meaning that guilty intent should not just be the best explanation, but the *only* reasonable one.[93] It will be for the trier of facts, in the adjudication phase, to finally judge whether this 'best explanation' (here: guilty intent rather than an irregularity or error) satisfies this high burden of proof.

[89] See Section 8.6.6.3. of Chapter 8.

[90] See Chapters 3 and 4.

[91] Simon De Smet, "Justified Belief in the Unbelievable", in Agirre, Bergsmo, De Smet and Stahn (eds.), 2020, p.143, see *supra* note 26.

[92] See, for instance, Xavier Agirre Aranburu, "The Contribution of Analysis to the Quality Control in Criminal Investigation", in *ibid.*, p. 236; Catherine Esnard, Rafaele Dumas and Stephanie Bordel, "Incidences de l'induction d'intime conviction sur le traitement de l'information judiciaire", in *Revue Européenne de Psychologie Appliquée*, 2013, vol. 63, pp. 121–128; Paul Thagard, "Evaluating Explanations in Law, Science and Everyday Life", in *Current Directions in Psychological Science*, 2006, vol. 15, no. 3, pp. 141–145; Larry Laudan, "Strange Bedfellows: Inference to the Best Explanation and the Criminal Standard of Proof", in *The International Journal of Evidence and Proof*, 2007, vol. 11, no. 4, p. 307.

[93] Critics of the theory of IBE hold that it is impossible to unambiguously determine which explanation is the 'best' and that IBE is simply not good enough for the purposes of the criminal law. See, for example, Laudan, 2007, *supra* note 92.

10.4.5.4. Presentation of the Best or Only Explanation of Intent

A final challenge for the investigative team is to present its claim of intent as best it can. No matter how good the investigation was conducted and how much evidence was gathered, the final product of the investigative process, its concluding report, must be presented in a manner that is acceptable and most effective for the decision maker. We refer to a previous contribution in this book for a concise overview of research on the matter.[94] The debate on whether to 'tell' or to 'sell' the findings of the investigation is still open, and particularly relevant on the topic of intent.

By providing a nuanced and transparent description of the strengths and weaknesses of the findings on intent, including the reasoning method and limitations on which it relies, the receiver of the report is given maximal insight into the justifications for each of the findings and is thereby able to critically evaluate them.[95] Instead of being too affirmative, it is arguably better to strive for greater precision and transparency about the doubts and uncertainties that are left after the investigation has been closed. Communicating uncertainty does not necessarily affect the credibility of, and trust in, both the message and the communicator.[96] Such transparency might rather build than undermine trust.[97]

On the other hand, a more narrative approach, focussing on a consistent story that accounts for the findings has great appeal and persuasive power. Such an approach could be seen to advocate against a too nuanced, double-sided presentation, as a story can be made more believable, even at the expense of being less likely, by adding or leaving out details enhancing its internal coherence. Presenting Jérôme as 'an ambitious but naïve son wanting to impress his father', or rather as a 'scrupulous businessman instrumentalized by his father to save the company by fraud' are two very different but strong competing narrative frames, which may impact the decision maker beyond the actual weight of the evidence gathered. It is clear that such framing and story-telling should not lead to an arbitrary, biased presentation of the investigative findings and its conclusions. Rather, the defence should always have access to all evidence to present its own version of what happened, and it should be able to contradict the investigative findings.

In any case, some level of uncertainty will always remain. Good practice would seem to offer decision makers various formats of presentation, while

[94] See Section 9.6. of Chapter 9.

[95] De Smet, 2020, p. 143, see *supra* note 91.

[96] Van der Bles *et al.*, 2019, p. 26, see *supra* note 71.

[97] *Ibid.*, p. 2.

making sure the (implied) messages are consistent.[98] 'Muscular uncertainty'[99] refers to an approach in which the fact-finder can present a 'best' and 'only' explanation in the shape of a narrative, but should give details about the limitations of the investigation and explain how these have affected the weight of the evidential dataset. The report should be transparent about its potential inferential weaknesses and clearly expose potentially problematic generalizations that were relied upon.[100] The investigators might also contrast the lead story with an adequate overview of the evidence-based findings, including the demonstration that alternative explanations have been explored, and an indication of doubts and evidence gaps.[101]

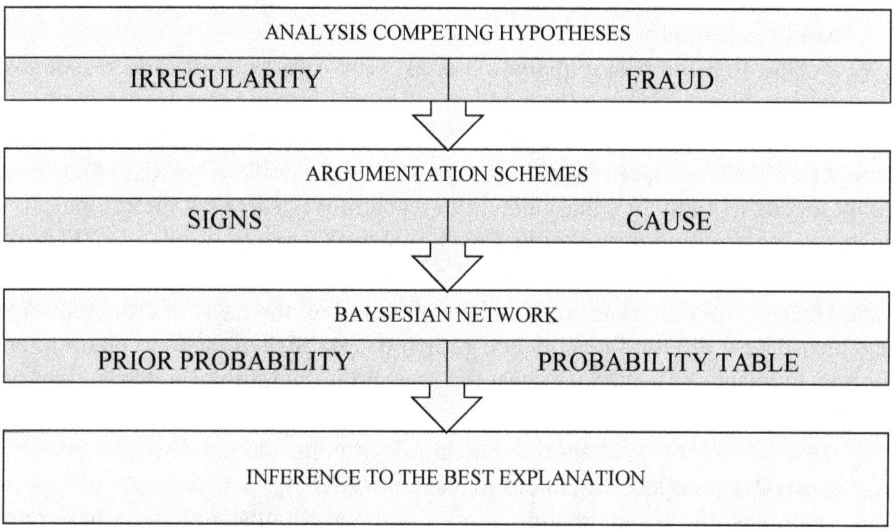

Illustration 10.7.: The intent evaluation matrix.

10.5. Concluding Remarks

To successfully prosecute PIF crimes, the investigator must prove the punishable material act ('*actus reus*') *and* guilty intent ('*mens rea*') of the criminal offence. Most legal conceptualizations of intent comprise an element of knowing (conscious act or omission) and an element of willing (foreseeable consequences of the act or omission).

[98] Kloprogge, van der Sluijs and Wardekker, 2007, p. 49, see *supra* note 42.

[99] Van der Bles *et al.*, 2019, p. 36, see *supra* note 71.

[100] De Smet, 2020, p. 143, see *supra* note 91.

[101] Sagana, 2022, during the OLAF conference on "Judgement and Decision Making in Investigations", Brussels, 7–8 December 2022.

What the suspect thought, knew, wanted, or could have known at the time of the offense cannot generally be determined using accurate, scientifically validated methods. Except for a confession by the perpetrator, the investigator must look for and interpret surrounding facts and external circumstances to build a case for intent.

Instead of relying on an intuitive judgment, the challenge to (dis)prove intent can be decomposed into a series of practical and sequential sub-questions, including:

- an identification of main competing hypotheses and falsification;
- an analysis of indications of intent using argumentation schemes;
- a presentation of the evidence and its tentative strength in a Bayesian network; and, finally
- a claim that the best explanation is also the only possible and reasonable explanation, satisfying the standard of proof (beyond reasonable doubt).

In a first step, the investigator should revisit all reasonable hypotheses brought forward or identified as regards intent, and falsify or validate their merits by means of inductive and deductive reasoning ('if it were intentional, or a mistake, or a wrong interpretation, then you would expect to find …'). Disproving one theory gives credit to a competing one.

The remaining hypotheses can be elaborated on the basis of argumentation schemes. These rely on the evidence gathered (established facts) to claim intent (or not) by means of generally accepted reasoning, including (in descending order of strength):

- signs of intent (for example, indications of concealment or deception);
- motivations supporting intent (causal narratives);
- examples, figures and patterns (taking into account sample size, base rates and representativeness);
- testimony;
- analogies (red flags).

Bayesian networks not only allow one to visualize the different findings underpinning a claim there was intent, but to also 'score' them, making for an overall probability calculus. Such exercise might be counterintuitive for fact-finders and judges, but corresponds to what happens in reality (one piece of evidence will be perceived as much more convincing in claiming there was intent than another one).

The best explanation remaining after competition with the alternatives, the explanation supported by sound arguments, does not necessarily satisfy the standard of proof (beyond reasonable doubt). By making explicit and transparent the process of coming to such best and only reasonable explanation, the investigator will however allow the trier of facts to make informed decisions, assured of the quality and rationality of the reasoning.

Index

A

B

C

F

G

K

L

M

N

O

P

Q

R

S

T

U

V

W

TOAEP TEAM

VOLUMES IN TOAEP'S *PUBLICATION SERIES*

Morten Bergsmo, Mads Harlem and Nobuo Hayashi (editors):
Importing Core International Crimes into National Law
Torkel Opsahl Academic EPublisher
Oslo, 2010
FICHL Publication Series No. 1 (Second Edition, 2010)
ISBN: 978-82-93081-00-5

Nobuo Hayashi (editor):
National Military Manuals on the Law of Armed Conflict
Torkel Opsahl Academic EPublisher
Brussels, 2023
Publication Series No. 2 (Third Edition, 2023)
ISBN print: 978-82-8348-226-3
ISBN e-book: 978-82-8348-225-6

林 伸生 (主编):
国家武装冲突法军事手册研究
Torkel Opsahl Academic EPublisher
Brussels, 2023
Publication Series No. 2 (Chinese Edition, 2023)
ISBN print: 978-82-8348-119-8
ISBN e-book: 978-82-8348-120-4

Morten Bergsmo, Kjetil Helvig, Ilia Utmelidze and Gorana Žagovec:
The Backlog of Core International Crimes Case Files in Bosnia and Herzegovina
Torkel Opsahl Academic EPublisher
Oslo, 2010
FICHL Publication Series No. 3 (Second Edition, 2010)
ISBN: 978-82-93081-04-3

Morten Bergsmo (editor):
Criteria for Prioritizing and Selecting Core International Crimes Cases
Torkel Opsahl Academic EPublisher
Brussels, 2024
Publication Series No. 4 (Third Edition, 2024)
ISBN print: 978-82-8348-238-6
ISBN e-book: 978-82-8348-239-3

Morten Bergsmo and Pablo Kalmanovitz (editors):
Law in Peace Negotiations
Torkel Opsahl Academic EPublisher
Oslo, 2010
FICHL Publication Series No. 5 (Second Edition, 2010)
ISBN: 978-82-93081-08-1

Morten Bergsmo, César Rodríguez Garavito, Pablo Kalmanovitz and María Paula Saffon (editors):
Distributive Justice in Transitions
Torkel Opsahl Academic EPublisher
Oslo, 2010
FICHL Publication Series No. 6 (2010)
ISBN: 978-82-93081-12-8

Morten Bergsmo, César Rodriguez-Garavito, Pablo Kalmanovitz and María Paula Saffon (editors):
Justicia Distributiva en Sociedades en Transición
Torkel Opsahl Academic EPublisher
Oslo, 2012
FICHL Publication Series No. 6 (2012)
ISBN: 978-82-93081-10-4

Morten Bergsmo (editor):
Complementarity and the Exercise of Universal Jurisdiction for Core International Crimes
Torkel Opsahl Academic EPublisher
Oslo, 2010
FICHL Publication Series No. 7 (2010)
ISBN: 978-82-93081-14-2

Morten Bergsmo (editor):
Active Complementarity: Legal Information Transfer
Torkel Opsahl Academic EPublisher
Oslo, 2011
FICHL Publication Series No. 8 (2011)
ISBN print: 978-82-93081-56-2
ISBN e-book: 978-82-93081-55-5

Morten Bergsmo (editor):
Abbreviated Criminal Procedures for Core International Crimes
Torkel Opsahl Academic EPublisher
Brussels, 2017
FICHL Publication Series No. 9 (2017)
ISBN print: 978-82-93081-20-3
ISBN e-book: 978-82-8348-104-4

Sam Muller, Stavros Zouridis, Morly Frishman and Laura Kistemaker (editors):
The Law of the Future and the Future of Law
Torkel Opsahl Academic EPublisher
Oslo, 2010
FICHL Publication Series No. 11 (2011)
ISBN: 978-82-93081-27-2

Morten Bergsmo, Alf Butenschøn Skre and Elisabeth J. Wood (editors):
Understanding and Proving International Sex Crimes
Torkel Opsahl Academic EPublisher
Beijing, 2012
FICHL Publication Series No. 12 (2012)
ISBN: 978-82-93081-29-6

Morten Bergsmo (editor):
Thematic Prosecution of International Sex Crimes
Torkel Opsahl Academic EPublisher
Brussels, 2018
Publication Series No. 13 (Second Edition, 2018)
ISBN print: 978-82-8348-025-2
ISBN e-book: 978-82-8348-024-5

Terje Einarsen:
The Concept of Universal Crimes in International Law
Torkel Opsahl Academic EPublisher
Oslo, 2012
FICHL Publication Series No. 14 (2012)
ISBN: 978-82-93081-33-3

ترجِ آینارسن
مفهوم جرایم جهانی در حقوقِ بین الملل
ترجمه دکتر فریدون جعفری
Torkel Opsahl Academic EPublisher
Brussels, 2023
Publication Series No. 14 (Persian Edition, 2023)
ISBN print: 978-82-8348-202-7
ISBN e-book: 978-82-8348-203-4

莫滕·伯格斯默 凌岩(主编):
国家主权与国际刑法
Torkel Opsahl Academic EPublisher
Beijing, 2012
FICHL Publication Series No. 15 (2012)
ISBN: 978-82-93081-58-6

Morten Bergsmo and Ling Yan (editors):
State Sovereignty and International Criminal Law
Torkel Opsahl Academic EPublisher
Beijing, 2012
FICHL Publication Series No. 15 (2012)
ISBN: 978-82-93081-35-7

Morten Bergsmo, Cheah Wui Ling and Antonio Angotti (editors):
Old Evidence and Core International Crimes
Torkel Opsahl Academic EPublisher
Brussels, 2024
Publication Series No. 16 (Second Edition, 2024)
ISBN print: 978-82-8348-228-7
ISBN e-book: 978-82-8348-229-4

Yi Ping:
戦争と平和の間——発足期日本国際法学における「正しい戦争」の観念とその帰結
Torkel Opsahl Academic EPublisher
Beijing, 2013
FICHL Publication Series No. 17 (2013)
ISBN: 978-82-93081-66-1

Morten Bergsmo and Song Tianying (editors):
On the Proposed Crimes Against Humanity Convention
Torkel Opsahl Academic EPublisher
Brussels, 2014
FICHL Publication Series No. 18 (2014)
ISBN: 978-82-93081-96-8

Morten Bergsmo and Carsten Stahn (editors):
Quality Control in Fact-Finding
Torkel Opsahl Academic EPublisher
Brussels, 2020
Publication Series No. 19 (Second Edition, 2020)
ISBN print: 978-82-8348-135-8
ISBN e-book: 978-82-8348-136-5

Morten Bergsmo, Cheah Wui Ling and Yi Ping (editors):
Historical Origins of International Criminal Law: Volume 1
Torkel Opsahl Academic EPublisher
Brussels, 2014
FICHL Publication Series No. 20 (2014)
ISBN: 978-82-93081-11-1

Morten Bergsmo, Cheah Wui Ling and Yi Ping (editors):
Historical Origins of International Criminal Law: Volume 2
Torkel Opsahl Academic EPublisher
Brussels, 2014
FICHL Publication Series No. 21 (2014)
ISBN: 978-82-93081-13-5

Morten Bergsmo, Cheah Wui Ling, Song Tianying and Yi Ping (editors):
Historical Origins of International Criminal Law: Volume 3
Torkel Opsahl Academic EPublisher
Brussels, 2015
FICHL Publication Series No. 22 (2015)
ISBN print: 978-82-8348-015-3
ISBN e-book: 978-82-8348-014-6

Morten Bergsmo, Cheah Wui Ling, Song Tianying and Yi Ping (editors):
Historical Origins of International Criminal Law: Volume 4
Torkel Opsahl Academic EPublisher
Brussels, 2015
FICHL Publication Series No. 23 (2015)
ISBN print: 978-82-8348-017-7
ISBN e-book: 978-82-8348-016-0

Morten Bergsmo, Klaus Rackwitz and Song Tianying (editors):
Historical Origins of International Criminal Law: Volume 5
Torkel Opsahl Academic EPublisher
Brussels, 2017
FICHL Publication Series No. 24 (2017)
ISBN print: 978-82-8348-106-8
ISBN e-book: 978-82-8348-107-5

Morten Bergsmo and Song Tianying (editors):
Military Self-Interest in Accountability for Core International Crimes
Torkel Opsahl Academic EPublisher
Brussels, 2015
FICHL Publication Series No. 25 (2015)
ISBN print: 978-82-93081-61-6
ISBN e-book: 978-82-93081-81-4

Wolfgang Kaleck:
Double Standards: International Criminal Law and the West
Torkel Opsahl Academic EPublisher
Brussels, 2015
FICHL Publication Series No. 26 (2015)
ISBN print: 978-82-93081-67-8
ISBN e-book: 978-82-93081-83-8

ولفگانگ کالک
معیارهای دوگانه:
حقوق کیفری بین‌المللی و غرب
Torkel Opsahl Academic EPublisher
Brussels, 2025
Publication Series No. 26 (Persian Edition, 2025)
ISBN print: 978-82-8348-259-1
ISBN e-book: 978-82-8348-260-7

Liu Daqun and Zhang Binxin (editors):
Historical War Crimes Trials in Asia
Torkel Opsahl Academic EPublisher
Brussels, 2016
FICHL Publication Series No. 27 (2015)
ISBN print: 978-82-8348-055-9
ISBN e-book: 978-82-8348-056-6

Morten Bergsmo, Mark Klamberg, Kjersti Lohne and Christopher B. Mahony (editors):
Power in International Criminal Justice
Torkel Opsahl Academic EPublisher
Brussels, 2020
Publication Series No. 28 (2020)
ISBN print: 978-82-8348-113-6
ISBN e-book: 978-82-8348-114-3

Stian Nordengen Christensen:
Counterfactual History and Bosnia-Herzegovina
Torkel Opsahl Academic EPublisher
Brussels, 2018
Publication Series No. 30 (2018)
ISBN print: 978-82-8348-102-0
ISBN e-book: 978-82-8348-103-7

Stian Nordengen Christensen:
Possibilities and Impossibilities in a Contradictory Global Order
Torkel Opsahl Academic EPublisher
Brussels, 2018
Publication Series No. 31 (2018)
ISBN print: 978-82-8348-104-4
ISBN e-book: 978-82-8348-105-1

Morten Bergsmo and Carsten Stahn (editors):
Quality Control in Preliminary Examination: Volume 1
Torkel Opsahl Academic EPublisher
Brussels, 2018
Publication Series No. 32 (2018)
ISBN print: 978-82-8348-123-5
ISBN e-book: 978-82-8348-124-2

Morten Bergsmo and Carsten Stahn (editors):
Quality Control in Preliminary Examination: Volume 2
Torkel Opsahl Academic EPublisher
Brussels, 2018
Publication Series No. 33 (2018)
ISBN print: 978-82-8348-111-2
ISBN e-book: 978-82-8348-112-9

Morten Bergsmo and Emiliano J. Buis (editors):
Philosophical Foundations of International Criminal Law: Correlating Thinkers
Torkel Opsahl Academic EPublisher
Brussels, 2018
Publication Series No. 34 (2018)
ISBN print: 978-82-8348-117-4
ISBN e-book: 978-82-8348-118-1

Morten Bergsmo and Emiliano J. Buis (editors):
Philosophical Foundations of International Criminal Law: Foundational Concepts
Torkel Opsahl Academic EPublisher
Brussels, 2019
Publication Series No. 35 (2019)
ISBN print: 978-82-8348-119-8
ISBN e-book: 978-82-8348-120-4

Morten Bergsmo, Emiliano J. Buis and Song Tianying (editors):
Philosophical Foundations of International Criminal Law: Legally-Protected Interests
Torkel Opsahl Academic EPublisher
Brussels, 2022
Publication Series No. 36 (2022)
ISBN print: 978-82-8348-121-1
ISBN e-book: 978-82-8348-122-8

Terje Einarsen and Joseph Rikhof:
A Theory of Punishable Participation in Universal Crimes
Torkel Opsahl Academic EPublisher
Brussels, 2018
Publication Series No. 37 (2018)
ISBN print: 978-82-8348-127-3
ISBN e-book: 978-82-8348-128-0

Xabier Agirre Aranburu, Morten Bergsmo, Simon De Smet and Carsten Stahn (editors):
Quality Control in Criminal Investigation
Torkel Opsahl Academic EPublisher
Brussels, 2020
Publication Series No. 38 (2020)
ISBN print: 978-82-8348-129-7
ISBN e-book: 978-82-8348-130-3

Tom Willems, Carsten Stahn, Darren Frey and Antonio Angotti (editors):
Quality Control in Fraud and Corruption Investigations
Torkel Opsahl Academic EPublisher
Brussels, 2025
Publication Series No. 39 (2025)
ISBN print: 978-82-8348-281-2
ISBN e-book: 978-82-8348-282-9

Morten Bergsmo, Wolfgang Kaleck and Kyaw Yin Hlaing (editors):
Colonial Wrongs and Access to International Law
Torkel Opsahl Academic EPublisher
Brussels, 2020
Publication Series No. 40 (2020)
ISBN print: 978-82-8348-133-4
ISBN e-book: 978-82-8348-134-1

Morten Bergsmo and Kishan Manocha (editors):
Religion, Hateful Expression and Violence
Torkel Opsahl Academic EPublisher
Brussels, 2023
Publication Series No. 41 (2023)
ISBN print: 978-82-8348-141-9
ISBN e-book: 978-82-8348-142-6

Gavin E. Oxburgh, Trond Myklebust, Mark Fallon and Maria Hartwig (editors):
Interviewing and Interrogation: A Review of Research and Practice Since World War II
Torkel Opsahl Academic EPublisher
Brussels, 2023
Publication Series No. 42 (2023)
ISBN print: 978-82-8348-200-3
ISBN e-book: 978-82-8348-201-0

Mark Klamberg, Jonas Nilsson and Antonio Angotti (editors):
Commentary on the Law of the International Criminal Court: The Statute
Volume 1
Torkel Opsahl Academic EPublisher
Brussels, 2023
Publication Series No. 43 (Second Edition, 2023)
ISBN print: 978-82-8348-204-1
ISBN e-book: 978-82-8348-205-8

Mark Klamberg, Jonas Nilsson and Antonio Angotti (editors):
Commentary on the Law of the International Criminal Court: The Statute
Volume 2
Torkel Opsahl Academic EPublisher
Brussels, 2023
Publication Series No. 44 (Second Edition, 2023)
ISBN print: 978-82-8348-206-5
ISBN e-book: 978-82-8348-207-2

Mark Klamberg, Jonas Nilsson and Antonio Angotti (editors):
Commentary on the Law of the International Criminal Court:
The Rules of Procedure and Evidence
Torkel Opsahl Academic EPublisher
Brussels, 2023
Publication Series No. 45 (2023)
ISBN print: 978-82-8348-208-9
ISBN e-book: 978-82-8348-209-6

Song Tianying:
Legal Construction of Common Humanity: Human Agency in a Cosmopolitan War Crimes Law
Torkel Opsahl Academic EPublisher
Brussels, 2025
Publication Series No. 46 (2025)
ISBN print: 978-82-8348-255-3
ISBN e-book: 978-82-8348-275-1

All volumes are freely available online at http://www.toaep.org/ps/. For printed copies, see http://www.toaep.org/about/distribution/. For reviews of earlier books in this Series in academic journals and yearbooks, see http://www.toaep.org/reviews/.

www.ingramcontent.com/pod-product-compliance
Lightning Source LLC
Chambersburg PA
CBHW071337230926
51849CB00006B/508/J
* 9 7 8 8 2 8 3 4 8 2 8 1 2 *